WORTH SAVING

Manchester University Press

Series editors
Dr Julie Anderson, Professor Walton Schalick, III

This new series published by Manchester University Press responds to the growing interest in disability as a discipline worthy of historical research. The series has a broad international historical remit, encompassing issues that include class, race, gender, age, war, medical treatment, professionalisation, environments, work, institutions and cultural and social aspects of disablement including representations of disabled people in literature, film, art and the media.

Already published
Deafness, community and culture in Britain: leisure and cohesion, 1945–1995
Martin Atherton

WORTH SAVING

DISABLED CHILDREN DURING THE SECOND WORLD WAR

Sue Wheatcroft

Manchester University Press

Manchester and New York

distributed in the United States exclusively by Palgrave Macmillan

Published by Manchester University Press
Oxford Road, Manchester M13 9NR, UK
and Room 400, 175 Fifth Avenue, New York, NY 10010, USA
www.manchesteruniversitypress.co.uk

Distributed in the United States exclusively by
Palgrave Macmillan, 175 Fifth Avenue, New York,
NY 10010, USA

Distributed in Canada exclusively by
UBC Press, University of British Columbia, 2029 West Mall,
Vancouver, BC, Canada V6T 1Z2

British Library Cataloguing-in-Publication Data
A catalogue record for this book is available from the British Library

Library of Congress Cataloging-in-Publication Data applied for

ISBN   978 0 7190 8800 1   hardback

First published 2013

Typeset in 10/12pt Arno Pro
by Servis Filmsetting Ltd, Stockport, Cheshire
Printed in Great Britain
by The MPG Books Group, Bodmin

For
Vicky Eller

Contents

List of figures

List of tables

Series editors' foreword

You know a subject has achieved maturity when a book series is dedicated to it. In the case of disability, while it has co-existed with human beings for centuries the study of disability's history is still quite young.

In setting up this series, we chose to encourage multi-methodologic history rather than a purely traditional historical approach, as researchers in disability history come from a wide variety of disciplinary backgrounds. Equally 'disability' history is a diverse topic which benefits from a variety of approaches in order to appreciate its multidimensional characteristics.

A test for the team of authors and editors who bring you this series is typical of most series, but disability also brings other consequential challenges. At this time disability is highly contested as a social category in both developing and developed contexts. Inclusion, philosophy, money, education, visibility, sexuality, identity and exclusion are but a handful of the social categories in play. With this degree of politicization, language is necessarily a cardinal focus.

In an effort to support the plurality of historical voices, the editors have elected to give fair rein to language. Language is historically contingent, and can appear offensive to our contemporary sensitivities. The authors and editors believe that the use of terminology that accurately reflects the historical period of any book in the series will assist readers in their understanding of the history of disability in time and place.

Finally, disability offers the cultural, social and intellectual historian a new 'take' on the world we know. We see disability history as one of a few nascent fields with the potential to reposition our understanding of the flow of cultures, society, institutions, ideas and lived experience. Conceptualizations of 'society' since the early modern period have heavily stressed principles of autonomy, rationality and the subjectivity of the individual agent. Consequently we are frequently oblivious to the historical contingency of the present with respect to those elements. Disability disturbs those foundational features of 'the modern.' Studying disability history helps us resituate our policies, our beliefs and our experiences.

Julie Anderson
Walton O. Schalick, III

Preface

When I began writing about disabled children during the Second World War the general reaction of both friends and colleagues was that, whilst interesting, it must be a disheartening, or even depressing, subject. To some extent I was guilty of this misconception myself; surely disabled people led a tragic life in the late 1930s and early 1940s and the war must have made the situation must worse? Whilst it is true that circumstances were difficult, writing about these children was far from a depressing experience. As is so often the case when faced with extreme situations, many adults rose to the occasion and went the extra mile to ensure that the children were kept safe and well. As for the children themselves, they faced the added problems with fortitude and, like their able-bodied counterparts, made the best of their situation. As is perhaps inevitable in times of social upheaval and financial hardship, there were those who questioned the extent to which certain groups of people should be provided for, and in researching this subject I found evidence of prominent individuals who would have preferred disabled people, including children, to have been overlooked when organising 'safe' accommodation. Fortunately, reason prevailed and, as will become clear, the majority of children (but not all) were provided with places of safety.

My interest in this subject stems from my Master's dissertation which focused on residential special schools housing disabled children from English cities during the same period. The wealth of untapped material encouraged me to explore all areas of disabled children's lives during the war and this book is, in fact, an adaptation of my PhD thesis. However, the subject of the evacuation is immense and, in line with earlier projects, I have concentrated on children within England rather than Britain as a whole, although areas within Wales are touched upon where they accommodated schools from within England. Certain cities within Wales, Scotland and Northern Ireland were evacuated on a similar basis to those in England, albeit on a much smaller scale, and have been dealt with by other historians.

I have enjoyed the process of researching the children's experiences very much. This is mainly due to the work of the premier inspector of special schools, whose reports I found to be informative, sometimes blunt, often funny and, I believe, always honest. I examined over a hundred of his reports and was pleasantly surprised at the content. Another misconception, that all government documents are dry and uninteresting!

Another source, of equal importance but more limited in number, is the personal testimony of several former evacuees. The individuals I interviewed either in person or by letter or email have been most kind in sharing their stories with me and I enjoyed the experience both on a personal and on an academic level. I know that, for some, it brought back painful memories but was also cathartic. It is my hope that this book will be read by other former evacuees so that they will know that, at last, their story is recognised as an important part of the Second World War. Equally, I hope that it will be read by members of the general public so that they also will be aware of this previously unrecorded part of our history. Finally, I hope that the book will be used by scholars as a basis for further research into the subject.

Acknowledgements

This book would not have been possible without the advice and support of my former PhD supervisor Dr. Sally Horrocks. I owe a debt of gratitude both to her and to the University of Leicester. I would also like to acknowledge the Open University and, in particular, the Crowther Fund. The fact that such a small charity continued its support over so many years has given me great encouragement and I appreciate the faith placed in me. Thanks also, to Emma Brennan and Manchester University Press for giving me this opportunity.

Certain individuals and associations have given me invaluable practical support. I would like to thank 'I CAN' (formerly the Invalid Children's Aid Association) for allowing me access to their wartime records; the Evacuation Reunion Association for placing an advertisement in their newsletter, and Anne Rattue, Jessica Axford and Ken Giles (and his wife Maureen) for responding and providing me with an insight into their wartime experiences. Sheila Meredith and Ernie Jones have supplied much valued information on the Lancasterian Special School. I have also used the personal testimony of Dennis Ford, R. Balister and G. R. Bevan, whose stories appeared on the Imperial War Museum and BBC People's History websites. Despite my best efforts, I have been unable to locate these individuals to ask permission to include them in this book. I hope they understand why I decided to go ahead and include them; although only brief, their contribution is valuable and much appreciated.

On a more personal level, I would like to thank Glenice Hill, and Kath and Mike Smith, for their unending generosity and support. Their friendship over the years has made my work both easier and worthwhile. A special mention should also be made of the late Ron Hill. Finally, to the most important person in my life, Vicky Eller, this book is for you.

List of abbreviations

ARP	Air Raid Precautions
CAMW	Central Association for Mental Welfare
CGC	Child Guidance Clinic
COS	Charity Organisation Society
EHS	Emergency Hospital Service
EMS	Emergency Medical Services
ESN	Educationally Subnormal
HMI	His Majesty's Inspector
ICAA	Invalid Children's Aid Association
LCC	London County Council
LEA	Local Education Authority
LMA	London Metropolitan Archive
MD	Mentally Defective
MHEC	Mental Health Emergency Committee
MO	Medical Officer
NCC	National Camps Corporation
NCMH	National Council for Mental Hygiene
NCSS	National Council of Social Services
NHS	National Health Service
OA	Open-Air (School)
PD	Physically Defective
PH	Physically Handicapped
PS	Partially Sighted
PSW	Psychiatric Social Worker
SEN	Special Educational Needs
SMS	School Medical Service
TB	Tuberculosis
TES	*Times Educational Supplement*
TNA	The National Archive
WVS	Women's Voluntary Service

INTRODUCTION

Harry Hendrick wrote, 'Unlike women, black people, and the working class, children are not in a position either to write their own history or to ask awkward questions of those who exercise power over them'.[1] Perhaps 'disabled' should be listed alongside 'children'. Tom Compton maintains that disabled people have lacked the health, education and leisure to record their own plights.[2] Certainly there are few personal accounts written by disabled people, and published testimony of disabled people who were children at the time of the Second World War is extremely limited. Similarly, although there are copious amounts of scholarly literature on able-bodied evacuees, very little has been published on the subject of disabled children during this time, and their personal experiences have not been examined in any great detail.[3] This means that a significant part, not only of children's experiences of the Second World War but also of the history of disability, is missing.

The primary aim of this book then, is to bring attention to this group of children and to highlight their experiences during the war, thereby correcting the current imbalance in the historical record. In doing this, the book discusses the policies and procedures that shaped the children's wartime experiences, and the personnel and institutions that were responsible for their welfare. It examines how the children coped on a day-to-day basis: the conditions in which the disabled evacuees lived, and how those who were not evacuated, for whatever reason, were cared for and educated. In short, the book presents a broad overview of the development of policy towards disabled children during the war and the way they were dealt with in practice. Looking primarily at the accommodation, safety and educational aspects of the children's wartime experiences, the book addresses the following questions: to what extent were the 'decision-makers' aware of the problems faced by disabled children during the war; how did they attempt to deal with the problems; and to what extent were they successful?

Despite the lack of an existing analysis of how and where disabled children lived during the war, certain important details can be found in the works of those historians writing on behalf of, or in some other way connected to, the government's education and/or health departments. The evacuation provided a unique opportunity to study children, including disabled children. During the war the State became more involved in their welfare than ever before and so they became more visible in the historical record. In 1950 the social scientist Richard Titmuss, having been commissioned by the government, published *History of the Second World War: Problems of Social Policy*.[4] The book contains an extensive step-by-step account of the effect that the war had on British civilians, with a particular emphasis on the evacuation. According to the Board of Education's Accountant General and official war diarist, Titmuss should not have discussed the evacuation because he wrote mainly from the Ministry of Health's point of view and schoolchildren should have been dealt with by the Board of Education.[5] However, perhaps because of this association with the Ministry of Health, the author makes a relatively large number of references to disabled children, certainly more than any other historian dealing with such a wide range of issues. By putting his references to disabled children in the context of a wider discussion on social policy, Titmuss shows that they were a legitimate concern.

The only other major piece of research that includes detailed information on disabled children during the war was done by Dr Sophia Weitzman, a lecturer in History Teaching who in 1945 was appointed by the government to write the official history of education. A number of chapters were written, including a significant amount on disabled children during the Second World War, but the volume remained unpublished at the time of her death in 1965. In 1976 a colleague of Dr Weitzman, Nigel Middleton, incorporated some of her work in his book *A Place for Everyone*.[6] Disappointingly, the book makes only brief mention of disabled children. Clearly this was a missed opportunity but perhaps illustrates the lack of interest in the subject in the 1970s and, indeed, in subsequent decades.[7]

Whilst disabled children have been largely omitted from studies of the Second World War, the effects of the war on children in general continue to be discussed. The long-term psychological effects on those who were children during the war have long been the subject of debate.[8] However, recent studies of children who suffered psychological problems during the war are few, and tend to focus on the general history of child guidance.[9] More specific studies, such as those by Deborah Thom or John Stewart, have concentrated on the interwar period and/or the perception of child guidance from within.[10] Again children suffering any form of mental or physical difficulty during the war received more interest from scholars in the decade after the war than in the years since.[11]

The ways in which the evacuation highlighted the level of poverty in which many children were living continue to be of particular interest to scholars. The evacuation, it is argued, drew attention to many aspects of English life that had previously gone undetected, or were ignored. According to Titmuss, large numbers of evacuated children suffered from lice infestation. Accompanying problems of bad behaviour, and poor clothing and eating habits, led to public opinion being in a type of shock which 'rivalled the outcry after the Boer War with its disclosure of sickness and low physical standards'.[12] Titmuss believed that the new awareness of how children in towns and cities lived led to a consensus of opinion that radical social reform was needed and in 1998, in his reassessment of the relationship between the evacuation and social policy, John Welshman concluded that Titmuss was 'undoubtedly correct in arguing that the evacuation profoundly altered attitudes to State welfare and led to significant policy changes'.[13] However, this view has been challenged by the revisionist John Macnicol[14] and by Rodney Lowe, who found that although some upper- and middle-class people were sympathetic to the invasion of their homes by evacuees, others found that the children's (and sometimes their mothers') behaviour and condition confirmed their negative preconceptions of the working classes.[15] The concept of the 'problem family' in particular continues to be discussed.[16]

Such debates are vital for an understanding of the extent to which the war changed the lives of children, including disabled children. This book examines wartime debates and postwar legislation including the Education Act, 1944, the Disability (Employment) Act, 1944, the National Health Service Act, 1946 and the Children Act, 1948. Julie Anderson has examined the development of rehabilitation techniques which occurred largely as a result of the war and which benefited all disabled people.[17] This book complements Anderson's work by adding the experiences of those children who would benefit from these new techniques as well as those who contributed to the war effort whilst in hospital training colleges, or in factories as school-leavers.

The new education legislation was particularly important for disabled children and will be examined in depth, although it could be said that the act was a turning point in the education of all children. In 1944 H. C. Dent wrote 'It is broadly true to say that up to the outbreak of the present war, the average English man or woman was not interested in education. Today, the reverse is the case; there is throughout the country, the keenest interest.'[18] The degree of interest assumed by Dent may have been overstated. In a survey carried out six months after the enactment of the 1944 Education Bill, only 45 per cent of those polled had heard of it.[19] However, it is true to say that the circumstances of war highlighted deficiencies in education. When speaking of the government's change in attitude towards spending on education, P. H. J. H. Gosden stated that 'The predominant pre-war attitude had been one of containment of, or an actual reduction in, expenditure. This change was no doubt a reflection of changed social and political values as a consequence of the war.'[20] This book shows that to all intents and purposes the changes in educational provision for disabled children after the war were largely the result of a 'knock-on' effect of changes in the educational system as a whole. It supports D. G. Pritchard's contention that 'Any consideration of the history of the disabled must take into account the development of educational provision for ordinary children': 'educational and social trends are followed, not created, by provision for the disabled'.[21]

The details of the 1944 Education Act as it applied to disabled children have been discussed, albeit briefly, in various books on the history of special education and in books on the act itself.[22] On the whole, though, historians have tended to concentrate on the professionals, philanthropists and policy-makers involved with disability issues rather than on disabled people themselves. Apart from a few notable exceptions, Helen Keller for example, blind, deaf and other disabled individuals have been virtually invisible in historical accounts. Tom Compton says that 'while cripples have subsisted on the fringe of all societies, evidence of their lives is generally absent' because 'negative stigmas and stereotypes attached to cripples rendered them unlikely subjects for the busy scribes and chronicles of earlier eras'.[23] Robert Davidoff believes that this negativity is what differentiates disability studies from those of race, gender, sexuality, class and other commonly addressed forms of human difference. Anyone can become disabled, and a longer life expectancy extends the risk and increases the odds, perhaps making it a more frightening subject.[24] Joyce Goodman highlighted the problems she faced, and that many of us face when dealing with such emotive subjects, when she researched the archive of the Sandlebridge Boarding School and Colony for the Feeble-Minded, 1902–35:

> Research methodology warns against emotional involvement that risks skewing research findings. But I came to realise that to deny, negate and neutralise my emotion in the face of this archive was to remain trapped within the rational ordering of an archive that denies emotion and that denying my emotion repeated the condition of the young women when viewed by certifying doctors who posited emotion as unreason and unreasonableness. Rather than researcherly unreason, here, to be angry was to disrupt the archive's rationalist frame on its own terms. Nonetheless, as researcher I needed to work with and beyond this anger.[25]

Since the 1980s historians have started to reassess how the disabled have been studied, resulting in the emergence of what Paul Longmore has termed the 'new disability history'.[26] Historians now tend to be more aware of the personal issues surrounding their subject and many use personal accounts to enrich their argument. In *Disability and Social Policy in Britain since 1750*, Anne Borsay illustrates the history of disability and social policy with numerous personal accounts, focusing on the various environmental hurdles encountered by disabled people: economic, political and cultural.[27] *Out of Sight: The Experience of Disability 1900–1950* was one of the first texts to allow disabled people to explain, in their own words, how they lived in the first half of the twentieth century.[28] The authors provide an insight into the somewhat harsh and patronising attitudes towards disabled people in the first half of the twentieth century, covering experiences in the home, at school and at work, and in hospitals and institutions. Fifty interviewees were included in the book, aged between fifty and eighty but, as the text covers such a wide time-frame, there is very little on a personal level during the war. Where it helps most is in its discussion of the general social and political climate during the Second World War, providing valuable information on attitudes towards disabled children.[29]

Unfortunately, the increase in personal testimony used in disability studies has not led to a surge of biographies on those who were disabled children at the time of the Second World War.[30] In contrast, accounts of the able-bodied who were children during the war continue to be published, as do scholarly works on the evacuation. The early years of the twenty-first century have seen publications by Roy C. Boud,[31] Mike Brown,[32] Juliet Gardiner,[33] Jessica Mann,[34] Ross Stewart,[35] Jill Wallis[36] and John Welshman.[37]

It is evident, then, that a separate study on the experiences of disabled children during the war is needed. Without this the story of the evacuation and of children and the Second World War is incomplete. This book seeks to fill that void. It has been made possible largely as a result of the reports of His Majesty's Inspectors (HMIs); the reports and correspondence of government officials and members of the voluntary sector; hospital records and school logbooks; and a selection of newspapers and periodicals. *The Special Schools Journal* in particular has been a vital resource for this project. As a result of an advertisement placed in a newsletter for former evacuees[38] this book has also been able to include the personal testimony of a small number of individuals who were classed as physically disabled during the war. In addition the staff and former pupils of the Lancasterian special school in Manchester have provided the information for a relatively extensive case study, to be found in Chapter 2.

The book is divided into five distinct chapters, with Chapter 1 one serving as an introduction to the lives of disabled children at the outbreak of war. One of the aims of the book is to assess the extent to which the children's wartime experiences helped bring about change in respect to their health and educational provision and to future employment opportunities. In order to do this it is necessary to look at the level of prewar activity in special education and, in particular Chapter 1 examines the five official categories of disability as defined in the 1921 Education Act. It also examines the arrangements made for the evacuation of disabled children, beginning with the 'Munich Crisis' of September 1938 and including the 'main' evacuation one year later. For evacuation purposes the children were split into groups depending on their specific disability, with the majority being accommodated in residential special schools in areas deemed safe. The actions and views of those responsible for the Government Evacuation Scheme are examined in some detail.

Chapter 2 examines the experiences of those disabled children who spent their war years in a residential special school, some of which were specially set up for evacuees, others having been established prior to the outbreak of war. Case studies of two residential special schools allow a comparison to be made between those established and maintained by the evacuation authorities and those run privately. A further insight into the former is provided by the testimony of two contributors who also discuss how they were treated by the local population. As will become evident, the experiences and concerns highlighted by these children, whilst not necessarily conflicting with the evidence of government documents, were certainly more personal. A number of residential special schools are examined in Chapter 2, highlighting conditions within the schools and the level of disruption to the children's education, as well as safety measures such as air raid precautions. Also discussed are the teaching staff, most of whom were ordinary teachers who found themselves in extraordinary circumstances and who, in effect, became the children's primary carers. The memoirs of the teacher Jessie Thomas, and the testimony of those who knew her, provide an additional perspective on the running of the schools.

Chapter 3 discusses those children who were deemed too seriously disabled to be evacuated and remained at home or in hospital, as well as those who either remained in, or returned early to, vulnerable areas and attended special day schools where available. Again a small selection of personal testimony is included as well as a case study of a hospital specially selected in order to illustrate vocational training during wartime. The experiences of the more seriously physically disabled, arguably the most 'neglected' group of children with regard to evacuation, are examined in some detail. The importance of the work of certain charitable organisations in all disabled children's safety and welfare, but especially in respect to those with serious physical disabilities, is also discussed.

Chapter 4 focuses on two groups of children who were excluded from the 1921 Education Act, and therefore not included in the government's 'special parties' when it came to evacuation arrangements. The first group is those who were deemed 'ineducable'. Officially, these children were to be accommodated either at home or in a mental institution. However, as is made clear here as well as in Chapter 2, some children were either misdiagnosed or their condition 'ignored' with the result that they spent varying lengths of time in residential special schools. The second group of children is the emotionally disturbed who were usually sent to hostels for 'difficult' children. Studies of emotional disturbance, or 'maladjustment' as it came to be called, was in its relative infancy at the time but it is perhaps the condition about which most was learned during the war.

The final Chapter begins with the return of the evacuees at the end of the war and a look at some of the problems of accommodating those whose parents or peacetime residential schools were unable to accept them back. It then extends the discussion by examining the provisions introduced by postwar legislation in relation to the children's education, health, and employment opportunities and addresses the question, 'To what extent did prewar ideas, wartime debates, the evacuation and the children's own experiences, inform these changes?' The postwar expansion of special schools and the position of teachers within special education are discussed, as is the changing role of the voluntary sector in caring for disabled children. Of equal if not more importance is the way in which disabled children and adolescents were viewed by the general public and potential employers. As is evident throughout the book, partly as a result of the conditions of war and, in particular, the new 'visibility' of disabled people and their contribution to the war effort, perceptions of them began to change.

It is important here to explain some of the language used in this book. Legislation prior to 1944 distinguished between different types of disability and assigned specific terms to particular conditions that were used to classify children and that appeared in official documents. Terms such as 'defective', 'cripple', 'idiot' and 'imbecile' were all commonplace. Usage of these labels in this book in no way reflects the present-day position but is in keeping with the historical period. This book includes many direct quotations from official documents, and to use both present-day and contemporary terminology would have been confusing to the reader. An explanation of the language used to describe the five official 'categories' of disability prior to 1944 is given in Chapter 1.

Notes

1   H. Hendrick, 'Children and Childhood', *ReFresh*, 15 (Autumn 1992), 4.

2   T. Compton, *The Brief History of Disability (or, The World Has Always Had Cripples)* (privately published, 1992), p. 1.

3   An exception is: S. Wheatcroft, 'Children's Experiences of War: Handicapped Children in England during the Second World War', *Twentieth Century British History*, 19:4 (2008), 480–501.

4   R. Titmuss, *History of the Second World War: Problems of Social Policy* (London: Longman, Green & Co., HMSO, 1950).

5   The National Archives (hereafter TNA), ED138/58, letter from Davidson to Bosworth-Smith, 12 February 1944.

6   N. Middleton and S. Weitzman, *A Place for Everyone: A History of State Education from the Eighteenth Century to the 1970s* (London: Gollancz, 1976).

7   Fortunately, Dr Weitzman's original papers are available for researchers at The National Archives: TNA, ED138 series.

8   These are too numerous to mention here, but a number of studies on the long-term effects can be found in the academic journal *Aging & Mental Health*.

9   For a general history of the child guidance service in Britain see O. C. Sampson, *Child Guidance: Its History, Provenance and Future* (London: British Psychological Society, 1980).

10   D. Thom, 'Wishes, Anxieties, Play and Gestures: Child Guidance in Inter-war England', in R. Cooter (ed.), *In the Name of the Child: Health and Welfare 1880– 1940* (London: Routledge, 1992), pp. 200–19; J. Stewart, 'Psychiatric Social Work in Inter-war Britain: Child Guidance, American Ideas, American Philanthropy', *Michael*, 3 (2006), 78–91; J. Stewart, 'I Thought You Would Want to Come and See His Home: Child Guidance and Psychiatric Social Work in Inter-war Britain' in M. Jackson (ed.), *Health and the Modern Home* (London: Routledge, 2007); J. Stewart, 'The Scientific Claims of British Child Guidance, 1918–45', *British Society for the History of Science*, 42:3 (2009), 407–32.

11   See: S. Leff and V. Leff, 'The Maladjusted Child', in *The School Health Service* (London: Lewis, 1959).

12   Titmuss, *Problems of Social Policy*, p. 133.

13   J. Welshman, 'Evacuation and Social Policy during the Second World War: Myth and Reality', *Twentieth Century British History*, 9:1 (1998), 28–53.

14   J. Macnicol, 'The Evacuation of Schoolchildren', in H. L. Smith (ed.), *War and Social Change: British Society in the Second World War* (Manchester: Manchester University Press, 1996), pp. 3–31.

15   R. Lowe, 'The Second World War, Consensus, and the Foundation of the Welfare State', *Twentieth Century British History*, 1:2 (1990), 152–82.

16   See P. Starkey, 'The Medical Officer of Health, the Social Worker, and the Problem Family, 1943 to 1968: The Case of Family Service Units', *Social History of Medicine*, 11:3 (1998), 421–41; J. Welshman, 'In Search of the "Problem Family":

Public Health and Social Work in England and Wales 1940–70', *Social History of Medicine*, 9:3 (1996), 447–65.

17 J. Anderson, 'Turned into Taxpayers: Paraplegia, Rehabilitation and Sport at Stoke Mandeville, 1944–56', *Journal of Contemporary History*, 38:3 (2003), 461–75.

18 H. C. Dent, *Education in Transition: A Sociological Study of the Impact of War on English Education 1939–1943* (London: Kegan Paul, 1944), p. vii.

19 Lowe, 'The Second World War, Consensus, and the Foundation of the Welfare State', p. 175.

20 P. H. J. H. Gosden, *Education in the Second World War: A Study in Policy and Administration* (London: Methuen, 1976), p. 433.

21 D. G. Pritchard, *Education and the Handicapped, 1760–1960* (London and New York: Routledge and Kegan Paul, 1963), p. 1.

22 See J. S. Hurt, *Outside the Mainstream: A History of Special Education* (London: Batsford, 1988); R. Stakes and G. Hornby, *Change in Special Education: What Brings It About?* (London: Cassell, 1997); Pritchard, *Education and the Handicapped*; G. McCulloch, *Educational Reconstruction: The 1944 Education Act and the Twenty-first Century* (Ilford and Portland: Woburn, 1994); M. Barber, *The Making of the 1944 Education Act* ((London and New York: Cassell, 1994).

23 Compton, *The Brief History of Disability*, pp. 1–2.

24 R. Davidoff, Foreword to Paul Longmore, *Why I Burned My Book, and Other Essays on Disability* (Philadelphia: Temple University Press, 2003), p. viii.

25 J. Goodman, 'Reflections on researching an archive of disability: Sandlebridge, 1902–1935', *Educational Review*, 55:1 (2003), 47–54.

26 See P. K. Longmore and L. Umansky (eds), *The New Disability History: American Perspectives* (New York: New York University Press, 2001).

27 A. Borsay, *Disability and Social Policy in Britain since 1750: A History of Exclusion* (Basingstoke and New York: Palgrave, 2005).

28 S. Humphries and P. Gordon, *Out of Sight: The Experience of Disability 1900–1950* (Plymouth: Northcote, 1992).

29 See also D. Atkinson, M. Jackson and J. Walmsley (eds), *Forgotten Lives: Exploring the History of Learning Disability* (Kidderminster: British Institute of Learning Disability, 1997); M. Potts and R. Fido, *A Fit Person to Be Removed: Personal Accounts of Life in a Mental Deficiency Institution* (Plymouth: Northcote, 1991).

30 However, there is testimony from two teachers involved in special education during the war years: S. Smith, *Still Unique after All These Years: A History of Blanche Nevile School, Formerly Tottenham School for the Deaf 1895–1995* (London: The School, 1995); J. E. Thomas, *Hope for the Handicapped: A Teacher's Testament* (London: Bodley Head, 1967).

31 R. C. Boud, *The Great Exodus: The Evacuation of Leeds Schoolchildren 1939–45* (Leeds: Thoresby Society, 2000).

32 M. Brown, *Evacuees: Evacuation in Wartime Britain, 1939–1945* (Stroud: Sutton, 2000).

33 J. Gardiner, *The Children's War through the Eyes of the Children of Britain* (London: Portrait, 2005).

34 J. Mann, *Out of Harm's Way: The Wartime Evacuation of Children from Britain* (London: Headline, 2005).

35 R. Stewart, *Evacuation* (London: Evans, 2002).

36 J. Wallis, *A Welcome in the Hillsides? – The Merseyside and North Wales Experience of Evacuation 1939–45* (Holywell: Avid, 2000).

37 J. Welshman, *Churchill's Children: The Evacuee Experience in Wartime Britain* (Oxford: Oxford University Press, 2010).

38 *The Evacuee: The Newsletter of the Evacuation Reunion Association*, www.evacuees. org.co.uk.

PREWAR DEVELOPMENTS

Special education

By 1939 disabled children had, for the purpose of determining their educational requirements, been divided into five official categories which were used by the evacuation authorities when arranging suitable accommodation in 'safe' areas. Before we discuss these evacuation arrangements, a clarification of each group of children should be made, along with a brief history of each category.[1] The five groups were:

- Blind
- Deaf
- Physically Defective (PD)
- Epileptic
- Mentally Defective (MD)

The blind and the deaf

Out of these strictly defined groups, it is the blind and the deaf whose history, as far as specific provision is concerned, goes back the furthest. Sources suggest that the first school in Britain to accept a disabled pupil was Thomas Braidwood's school in Edinburgh, which admitted a deaf boy in 1760.[2] In England the first school for deaf children opened in London in 1783, with Braidwood's nephew as headmaster. The first blind school was established in Liverpool in 1791.[3] Like other early institutions for disabled people, these schools were at first merely custodial in nature; they gradually incorporated vocational training, and eventually academic education. Vocational training included crafts such as brush-making, basket-making and chair-caning and, as such provisions were made for blind and deaf children before other disabled children, these occupations have become associated with them.[4]

In 1885, after extreme pressure from those working primarily with blind and deaf and dumb children, the Egerton Committee was set up.[5] This was the first formal attempt by national government to investigate the best way of educating disabled children, and was influential in the passing, in 1893, of the Elementary Education (Blind and Deaf Children) Act. The act made it the duty of school boards (established under the Elementary Education Act, 1870) to provide education for blind and deaf children between the ages of seven and sixteen. They were to be accommodated in schools certified as suitable by the education department and, as a result, day schools and institutions were established and existing ones improved.

Early education, as with health, was provided primarily by a mixture of private and charity organisations, including religious institutions. In 1921 the National Institute for the Blind (NIB) opened a college for private fee-paying blind girls. Although initially intended as an institution of higher education, the Chorleywood College accepted a wide range of ages; in 1923 there were eighteen girls between the ages of six and twenty. The NIB had also been supporting a college for blind boys, Worcester College, since 1917. However, neither college was provided for by the State; higher education was not available for most disabled children until after the Second World War. Before then most voluntary organisations, and the State, were concerned only with elementary-level education.

One aspect of education that was continually debated, for both blind and deaf children, was whether those who were not totally blind or deaf should be segregated from those who were. In 1907 the first separate provision was made for partially sighted (PS) children in London, and the next year saw the first special class for partially deaf children, which opened in Bristol.[6] The majority of such children, however, were still being educated either in special schools for blind or deaf children or in ordinary elementary schools. It was not until the 1930s that the government set up two separate committees to investigate the problem.[7] The subsequent reports of both committees recommended that partially blind or deaf children should be educated separately, and separate schools were eventually set up. At the outbreak of the Second World War several schools for PS children had been established, but the partially deaf children had to wait until after the war.

By the end of March 1939 there were 45 certified schools for deaf children in England and Wales, accommodating 4,517 pupils; 26 of the schools were day schools (1,848 pupils) and the rest were residential (2,669 pupils).[8] With regard to blind and PS children, there were 28 schools in January 1939, including 20 residential (although seven of these admitted both residential and day school children) and eight for day only. All schools combined contained places for 2,250 children.[9] The exact number of children requiring such places is unknown, but there was a waiting list in each category.

Physically defective (PD) children

In comparison to children with sensory difficulties, provision for physically disabled children came relatively late. Again, voluntary organisations had been providing for some types of physical disability long before the State. The first school to be opened for orthopaedically disabled children was at Marylebone in 1851.[10] The Cripples Home and Industrial School for Girls began as an industrial school and opened with just three girls, one of whom was a cripple. The committee of ladies who had founded the school decided to extend it in order to incorporate more crippled girls and by 1870, the institution catered for 100 girls, 75 of whom were cripples. In 1865 the same committee opened the National Industrial Home for Crippled Boys, in Kensington. The first school to be officially recognised by the Board of Education was a day school for cripples at the Passmore Edwards Settlement in London, which opened in 1899.[11] In the same year the first statutory provision for physically disabled children was made, under the Elementary Education (Defective and Epileptic Children) Act. Under the act LEAs were empowered (but not required) to provide training for PD children.

The term 'physically defective' covered a wide range of disabilities. In 1899 children attending schools for cripples suffered primarily from TB of the joints and bones, heart disease, congenital physical defects, rickets, severe anaemia and malnutrition.[12] Owing to the severe nature of some physical disabilities, however, it was often impossible for a child to attend any kind of school, or even to attend hospital for treatment. In 1888 the Invalid Children's Aid Association (ICAA) was founded, whose primary aim was to provide visitors to help and advise the seriously disabled children who were confined to the home. At first this help came in the form of voluntary home visitors who took food, bedding and medicine to children and their families, and helped to arrange admission into hospitals and convalescence homes. They also organised holidays, apprenticeships and the loan of spinal carriages and wheelchairs. Eventually, the volunteers were replaced by professional social workers, and 'homes of recovery' were set up for the treatment of children with TB and rheumatic heart disease. During the Second World War the association played a vital part in the welfare of disabled children.

In 1919 members of the ICAA and the British Red Cross Society, along with a few notable philanthropists, formed the Central Council for the Care of Cripples, whose aim was to promote a national scheme for the complete provision of treatment and education for PD children throughout the country.[13]

One of the Council members, the surgeon Sir Robert Jones, had previously been influential in the establishment of the first hospital school for PD children. This was in the West Kirby Convalescent Home for Children and was subsequently certified as a special school in 1901. By 1935 it was acknowledged by the Council that provision for cripples was still seriously inadequate and, with the serious lack of funds, the Council's future looked uncertain. Then, in December of the same year, the philanthropist Lord Nuffield donated the sum of £125,000.[14] The money was held in trust and was used to help disabled children for years to come, including the war years.

Another organisation that was prominent in the early schooling and welfare of disabled children was the Ragged Schools Union (RSU). Primarily set up to help destitute children, the RSU opened special schools for physically disabled children as early as 1917. It pioneered treatment for spina bifida and muscular dystrophy and was influential in the schooling of the more seriously disabled children, taking them out of hospital and into its own residential schools. Throughout the war the organisation, by now called the Shaftesbury Society, after the seventh Earl of Shaftesbury who was so influential in the RSU's formation, kept open a number of residential special schools.

In 1907 the School Health Service (initially called the School Medical Service) began, and the medical inspection of all children became compulsory. By now rickets, severe anaemia and malnutrition had abated somewhat, although paralysis from poliomyelitis was of major concern. The new health inspectors soon came to realise that some children were suffering through neglect, anxiety, lack of proper nourishment, defective teeth or eyesight or other less apparent disabilities. Sometimes these children would be sent to an 'open-air' school for a few weeks until they had recovered or, if they were unable to attend ordinary elementary school regularly, they might become long-term residents.

Originally known as 'bandstand schools', the early versions of open-air schools were operated, literally, in the open air. The idea was that these 'delicate' children would be less troubled if a certain temperature was maintained, and that the spread of disease was less likely in the open air. These classes also differed from others in that they accommodated a smaller number of pupils, they remained open during ordinary school holidays, they had a midday rest period, up to three meals per day, and regular medical and nursing supervision.[15] The first was opened in 1907 at Bostall Wood, Plumstead, and by 1939 there were more than 150 open-air schools in Britain, catering for almost twenty thousand childrens.[16]

After the First World War, with many soldiers returning with disabilities, there was a renewed interest in disabled people, which had a knock-on effect to disabled children. Despite the weak national economy between the wars, there was an expansion in the scale of school medical provision, and in the development and refinements of new medical techniques. In his annual report for 1930, the Chief Medical Officer, George Newman, reported that between 67 and 90 per cent of crippled children in Leeds, Bath, Staffordshire and Shropshire had been able to return to school or work as a result of orthopaedic treatment provided by the education authorities. Between 1925 and 1938 the number of LEAs providing orthopaedic treatment for crippled children rose from 85 to 270, and the number of school clinics offering specialist orthopaedic services rose from 70 to 382.[17] By the end of the 1930s all but one of the LEAs provided school clinics and the average number of clinics in each area had risen to 7.38.

By the time the Second World War began, practically every LEA provided treatment for minor ailments, dental defects and defective vision. Most of the physically disabled children were now being provided with some kind of education, the exception being the more severely disabled who were bedridden or incontinent.[18] Home teaching, although provided sporadically before and during the Second World War, would not become widespread until after the war. Another area where services improved during the interwar years was speech therapy. Manchester LEA had started classes for stammerers as early as 1906 but this duty was not imposed upon LEAs until 1944. As a result of the pressure to add this to the list of statutory responsibilities during the 1930s, many LEAs appointed speech therapists and, by 1939, 90 LEAs offered this service.

The category of 'physically defective' is undoubtedly one of the broadest. Unlike those with sensory difficulties, PD children included several 'types'. It was recognised at this time that physically disabled and delicate children, and those with speech defects, should be educated separately from each other and, to some extent, such provision was already in place. Legal requirement, however, had to wait until after the war.

Children with epilepsy

Arguably one of the most misunderstood disabilities of the nineteenth century was epilepsy. Although not always mentally ill, epileptic children were often confined in asylums where, with recurring attacks and a lack of education, many experienced serious mental decline. In 1888 the first epileptic colony in England opened, at Maghull near Liverpool. Some class teaching was undertaken there but it was not until 1903 that the Board of Education approved a school especially for epileptic children: the St Elizabeth's Roman Catholic Epileptic Colony at Much Hadham, Hertfordshire.

The belief that the mental health of epileptic children would inevitably deteriorate as they grew older ensured that the establishment of more residential schools solely for epileptics remained low priority. Thus, the six residential schools which had been certified by the Board of Education by 1910 were not augmented until the LCC opened a seventh in 1935.[19] The lack of adequate accommodation for epileptic children had been raised at the Conference of Representatives of Schools for Epileptic Children on 28 October 1932, where recommendations were made that more special schools solely for epileptics should be provided.[20] With improving techniques making it easier to distinguish epilepsy from other neurological disorders, along with better treatment, their long-term prognosis improved and in a survey taken shortly before the outbreak of the Second World War, which included 585 cases in 26 LEAs, 261 were eligible for special schools, 26 were assessed as MD (it had been agreed at the conference not to admit MDs into schools for epileptics), and the rest were considered suitable for elementary schools.

Mentally defective (MD) children

Until the mid-nineteenth century children with varying degrees of mental disability were often confined to 'the madhouse' without any constructive training and no hope for the future. Reform began with the Lunatics Act, 1845, which improved standards in the asylums, and two years later the first asylum, for idiots opened (Park House Asylum, Highgate) bringing the first attempt at making separate provision for differing degrees of mental disability. At this stage, however, mentally disabled people were still officially categorised into just two groups: those who suffered from mental incapacity at birth and those who had once been sane. By 1870 there were five such asylums in England, admitting both children and adults, although only three had (limited) arrangements for education.[21]

By this stage the health and education of all disabled children were being seriously debated by voluntary groups, prominent individuals and politicians. The Charity Organisation Society, founded in 1869 in order to raise the standard of administering charity relief, established a special sub-committee to examine the best way of providing education and care for mentally disabled children.[22] The Secretary of the sub-committee, Sir Charles Trevelyan, is credited with being the first to record the term 'feeble-minded'. After visiting the main asylums he noted that there were many patients whose incapacity was not serious enough to warrant incarceration with 'lunatics'.[23] Although the committee failed to bring swift change, the committee members (which included two earls and several medical specialists) managed to bring the plight of mentally disabled children to the fore.

The Elementary Education Act, 1870, which brought 'education for all' (the disabled were neither specifically included nor excluded; the true meaning of education for all would not become reality for another hundred years), resulted in many children of low intelligence attending ordinary elementary schools. Not thought severe enough to be incarcerated as lunatics, these children were deemed feeble-minded and were thought to require special provision outside mainstream education. In 1892 an inspector employed by the Leicester school board opened a special class for them within an elementary school, and later the same year the first school for 'feeble-minded' children, a special day school, opened in London.[24] These were the first special day schools to be opened in England, by the State, for mentally disabled children.

For some, however, day schools were not the answer. There was much confusion in the public mind with regard to the mentally ill, and many prejudices. For example, popular opinion was that the women in particular were immoral; that they were carriers of venereal disease; and that their children would be twice as defective.[25] Many believed that all mentally ill adults, and their children, should be incarcerated. This belief was often reflected in the actions of those who were actively involved in the establishment of schools after the Elementary Education (Defective and Epileptic) Act, 1899, which had empowered local authorities to provide for their education. One such person was Mary Dendy, a member of the Manchester school board. In 1902 Dendy set up the first residential school for feeble-minded children: the Sandlebridge School for Manchester children in Cheshire.

Another major landmark for mentally disabled children, although not necessarily a positive one, was the Mental Deficiency Act, 1913, which defined the categories of 'mental defectives' as follows:

Idiots – persons so deeply defective in mind from birth or from an early age as to be unable to guard themselves against common physical dangers.

Imbeciles – persons in whose care there exists from birth or from an early age mental defectiveness not amounting to idiocy, yet so pronounced that they are incapable of managing themselves or their affairs, or, in the case of children, of being taught to do so.

Feeble-Minded – persons in whose case there exists from birth or from an early age mental defectiveness not amounting to imbecility, yet so pronounced that they require care, supervision, and control for their protection or for the protection of others, or, in the case of children, that they by reason of such defectiveness appear to be permanently incapable of receiving proper benefit from the instruction in ordinary schools.

Moral Imbeciles – persons who from an early age display some permanent mental defect coupled with strong vicious or criminal propensities on which punishment has had little or no deterrent effect.[26]

The wording of 'from birth or from an early age' presented a problem as it did not cater for those who might become defective as a result of illness or accident, or who might be only temporarily affected. In 1925–26 a serious outbreak of encephalitis lethargica left many children brain-damaged.[27] In order to bring those children, and any others who had suffered similar damage through other illnesses or accident, within the mental health framework the Mental Deficiency (Amendment) Act, 1927, reworded the definition of mental defect as a 'condition of arrested or incomplete development of mind existing before the age of eighteen years, whether arising from inherent causes or induced by disease or injury'.[28]

The moral imbecile, renamed moral defective under the 1927 act, was regarded more as a social menace and was not necessarily thought to be ineducable, but was deemed not wholly responsible owing to weakness of mind. Replacing 'from an early age' with 'before the age of eighteen' was particularly significant in the cases regarding morality as, previously, someone (usually the parent) would have to testify as to the child's early behaviour. This new definition allowed for the possible abuse of children who could be taken away for the slightest infringement. Dorothy Atkinson and others have examples of such cases in *Forgotten Lives*.

Another outcome of the 1913 act was the establishment of large specialist 'colonies', where patients could be trained and cared for away from the influence of the other inmates. The first colony to be sanctioned was the Park Colony, which was delayed by the First World War and eventually opened in 1920. Structured into six 'villas' and a school, the colony was designed to prevent the children (and adults) from losing their identity and to give a community spirit; it also served to segregate the sexes. Colonies, as opposed to the more austere workhouses, were seen as 'homely and simple in character and free from unnecessary repressive and restraining methods'.[29] However, despite the rhetoric, incarceration of their children in any kind of mental institution was abhorrent to many parents and those who could fought to keep them in a special school.

As a result of the Mental Deficiency Act 1913, those deemed imbeciles or idiots, and therefore seen as ineducable, became the responsibility of the health authorities, including the Board of Control, whilst the feeble-minded and moral imbeciles (later defectives) remained within the scope of the education authorities. When the Board of Education was given the duty to provide special education for MDs the following year, only the latter two groups were included.[30] The biggest problem here, however, was how to ascertain which group a child should belong to: how the child should be assessed or 'tested'.

In 1913 the London education authorities appointed the first educational psychologist, Sir Cyril Burt, to advise on the selection of children for special schools and classes. Burt was influenced by the work of Alfred Binet, a French schools inspector who had devised a scale of ability against which all school children should be measured.[31] Burt adapted Binet's testing methods, and his own way of testing continued to be used until the Education Act, 1944. The following is an example of how a ten-year-old child would be tested for intelligence at the time of the Second World War:

1. IQ of 85 and above = mental age of 8.5 = normal
2. IQ of 70–85 = mental age of 7–8.5 = dull or backward
3. IQ of 50–70 = mental age of 5–7 = feeble-minded, or educable mentally retarded
4. IQ of below 50 = mental age of below 5 = ineducable[32]

The Education Act, 1921, reiterated that the bottom rung of the intelligence ladder, the idiots and imbeciles, should remain outside the school service.[33] The dull and backwards were generally regarded as being educable in the mainstream school. The defectives, however, (those with an IQ between 50 and 70) were to be educated in a special school, or in a special class in a mainstream school. In order to be given a place, they would need to be certified by the school's medical officer.

The certification of the mentally ill, introduced by the Mental Deficiency Act, 1913, was extremely unpopular with both pupils and parents, who resented the social and educational implications. For example, to be certified as idiot or imbecile, whilst no longer necessarily meaning incarceration (the act allowed for them to be provided for in the community), certainly brought an end to any State education. In 1929 the Wood Report[34] attempted to address this and other concerns regarding disabled children, but in the prevailing economic climate extra funding for special education was low on the list of government priorities. Therefore there would be no major changes for mentally ill children until 1944.

Teachers
The importance of the professional development of teachers in special schools was recognised in 1893, when the Charity Organisation Society advocated the need to improve teachers' skills.[35] In order to attract qualified teachers into London's special schools, extra money was offered. In return, the teachers

were expected to possess 'temperamental and personal qualities which pre-
dispose the staff to undertake this work in what may be called a missionary
spirit'.[36]

Practical skills in the teaching of disabled children were acquired by attending a programme of lectures and classes organised by the LCC. In addition,
relevant examinations had to have been passed. In schools for blind and deaf
children, for example, both the head teachers and the assistant teachers had
to have held the Board of Education certificate for elementary school teaching as well as passing a separate examination, approved by the Board, in the
methods of teaching such children. These examinations could have been
arranged by the Board or by the National College of Teaching of the Deaf and
the corresponding College for the Teaching of the Blind, both of which had
established their own diplomas which were accepted by the Board. In contrast
to teachers of blind and deaf children, teachers of PD and MD children were
not required to pass an examination in the methods of teaching such children;
the certificate for elementary school teaching was deemed sufficient. However,
for prospective teachers of MD children, in addition to the courses arranged
by the LCC, short training courses were organised by the Central Association
for Mental Welfare[37] (CAMW) in centres where the teachers could visit such
schools as observers, as part of the course.

The probationary period for newly qualified teachers of disabled children
was three months, or twelve months if moving from another school outside
the London area, and their ongoing development was aided by the continuing
information received from the National Special Schools Union, which held
conferences every two years as well as other meetings. Teachers of trade
subjects such as tailoring, boot-making or dress-making were not required to
hold the elementary school teachers' certificate. However, they did need the
appropriate technical qualifications and, in most cases, were required to have
some practical experience in their trade.[38]

Despite the extra pay given to teachers of disabled children, recruiting
enough teachers into special schools was an ongoing problem. In the early
years of the twentieth century it was common to employ blind teachers in
schools for the blind, and in some cases this was successful. However, many
teachers were too seriously disabled, and the work fell unfairly on the sighted
teachers. In 1906 it was decided that, although there was always to be at least
one blind teacher in each school, they could no longer work as head teachers,
and there were to be more sighted than blind teachers. Also, the 'experiment'
of teaching blind people to become elementary school teachers (of non-blind
children) was brought to an end.[39]

By 1930 the lack of teachers of blind children was still a problem; only five students undertook the two-year course at the Royal Normal College for the Blind. However, it was no longer seen as quite as urgent as there had been a decrease in the number of blind children being born, and so employment opportunities for future teachers of blind children were not good.[40] The problem of filling teaching vacancies in special schools was even worse outside London, and getting London elementary school teachers to fill these vacancies proved difficult. In 1935 Colonel Eton of the LCC's Education Officers' Department blamed it partly on 'the ignorance on the part of a very large proportion of London teachers in the work and conditions within these schools'.[41] Lower pay outside London; a reluctance to leave the metropolis; the 'institutional atmosphere' of residential schools; and the special qualifications needed in blind and deaf schools were also blamed.

The shortage of teachers for disabled children meant that in elementary schools, where they were formed into special classes, common practice was to put them in charge of young teachers fresh from (elementary school) training college. Without the special skills needed, this was detrimental to both teacher and child. In 1936 Goldsmith's College of Teaching at the University of London proposed a special third-year course of training on the problems and methods of teaching backward, dull and difficult children. The course would be deferred so that the teacher could gain some experience of elementary school teaching first. It would be open to both male and female teachers, and applications would be made by nomination from their LEA. The course was due to commence in September 1936, but by May, after nearly three thousand, copies of the prospectus has been sent out, to LEAs and individual enquiries, only two teachers had been nominated. The course was subsequently scrapped.[42]

As we have seen, in the years leading up to the outbreak of war 'feebleminded' and 'moral defective' children continued to be the subject of debate with regards to their segregation from the rest of society. At this time there was a high degree of stigma attached to mental illness and, to some extent, to those with physical disabilities, which also proved to be a contributing factor in the difficulties experienced when attempting to attract teachers into special education. However, the 1920s and 1930s were, on the whole, a period of relative growth in health and special educational provision. In particular there had been an expansion in school medical services and of school clinics offering specialist orthopaedic services. The number of LEAs providing services for speech defects had also increased. One of the most significant changes in the years leading to the outbreak of war, however, was in regard to epileptics. Owing to advances in diagnostic techniques and treatment, their mental health was no longer assumed to be in decline and many children were found to be capable of ordinary elementary school education. Another educational milestone that occurred in the 1930s was the separation of blind from partially sighted children. However, although it had also been decided to separate deaf from partially deaf children, this had still not been put into practice by the outbreak of war.

One particular group of children who did not benefit from an increase in provision during the prewar years was the seriously physically disabled. These children, more than any other, relied heavily on charitable organisations, some of which were able to accommodate the children in their own convalescent hospitals. Many, though, were forced to remain at home where again the activities of the voluntary sector were paramount in the children's education and general welfare.

It is evident that disabled children were very much the 'poor relation' when it came to education in the years leading up to the Second World War. In order to understand more about how the children were perceived by the government, and the general public, it is necessary to discuss some aspects of the political and social climate. In the 1930s the belief that certain disabilities were hereditary prevailed among many members of the government. The following section discusses some of the ways in which those responsible for disabled children addressed this belief.

The political and social climate

Perhaps the greatest challenge to disabled children (and adults) in the first half of the twentieth century came from the eugenics movement, which came to prominence in 1907. The word 'eugenics' was coined by an English scientist, Francis Galton, who defined it as 'the study of agencies under social control that may improve or impair the racial qualities of future generations, whether physically or mentally'.[43] It was not, he believed, sufficient for it to remain merely a study, however; in 1905 he had written that it must eventually be introduced into the national consciousness as a new religion.

The object of eugenics can be summed up in a statement by W. R. Thomson, FRS, who said that it is 'to ensure that the right people are born'.[44] In 1869[45] Galton had concluded that there was a hereditary base for intelligence and for criminal tendencies, and later scientific research appeared to reinforce this belief. One such study was Henry Herbert Goddard's *The Kallikak Family* (a real family but a fictitious name).[46] The object of the study was a family in the United States (of English middle-class origin). Goddard's research into the family began with a 'normal' man who had children with two women, one normal and the other feeble-minded. With the latter there were defects in every generation, whereas the normal woman had normal descendants with almost no exceptions. Goddard concluded that sterilisation would be only a makeshift and temporary solution and that segregation through colonisation was the ideal and satisfactory method of preventing further hereditary defectives, until more was known on the subject.[47] The less radical eugenicists agreed, believing that it would be sufficient to house the relevant groups in institutions where they could be controlled in order to prevent regeneration.[48] This was more in line with the idea of 'negative eugenics', which sought to ensure that the weak and unfit have fewer children (and often ran alongside the concept of 'positive eugenics', in which the strong and fit have more children). However, many more believed that a policy of sterilisation was the only way forward.

The sterilisation of certain disabled groups was prevalent in many countries in the 1920s and 1930s. The United States, had sanctioned compulsory sterilisation of the inmates of mental institutions, and by the mid-1930s twenty thousand operations had been legally performed. By 1934 there were ten western nations which either had or were in the process of introducing sterilisation laws, including the countries of Scandinavia.[49] Swedish welfare reform in particular was widely admired, and its sterilisation laws were viewed as an integral and widely proclaimed part of the welfare programme. In Germany racial hygienicists studied American policies, and in 1933 established their own programme of eugenics. In 1934 alone twenty thousand women were sterilised.[50]

The consequences of German racist ideology do not need to be elaborated on here – the results are well known – but in the 1930s German genetic studies were renowned. Dr Fischer, the founder director of the Kaiser Wilhelm Institute of Anthropology in Berlin, was admired throughout many countries and his racial doctrine was respected worldwide.[51] From 1933, after Hitler came to power, the medical profession was at the forefront in implementing Nazi racial policies, and forced sterilisation of mentally ill people began almost immediately, with two hundred 'hereditary health courts' being established in order to identify mentally disabled people.[52]

Although eugenic sterilisation laws were never introduced in England, there were many prominent individuals who were in favour of preventing mentally ill people reproducing, either through sterilisation or the less radical method of segregation. Indeed, many politicians in positions of power in the years leading up to the Second World War were members of the Eugenics Society (ES). For example, Lord Beveridge, whose report played such an important part in the creation of the welfare state and had such an impact on all social service departments after the war, was a member. Beveridge was director of the London School of Economics and Political Science until 1937, and so was in a position of influence over future economists, politicians and others. Another notable ES member was John Maynard Keynes, arguably the most influential economist of the twentieth century. Richard Titmuss was also a member. A full list of members would be too large to reproduce here but it is worth noting that several influential journals of the time, including the *British Journal of Psychology* and the *British Journal of Psychiatry*, were edited by ES members.[53]

Despite the growth of the eugenics movement in England there were many who spoke against it. One of the most prominent was the Chief Medical Officer of Health, Sir Arthur Newsholme, who, in giving evidence to the Royal Commission in 1908, argued that many of the children so maligned by the eugenicists were educable, and that the craze for scientific officialdom and social experimentation was acting as a trap for them.[54] Indeed, as with all experiments, the conclusion is a matter of interpretation, and governments are able to manipulate the findings in order to achieve their own ends. For example, in Germany's hereditary health courts, questions such as 'When is the Führer's birthday?' meant that there was no distinction between lack of knowledge and genuine mental illness.[55] Another example comes from Sweden, and is evidence that the criteria for determining mental incapacity were sometimes only a minor physical or social disability. In 1997 a seventy-two-year-old woman brought the subject of Sweden's history of sterilisation policy to world attention when she told her story of being forcibly sterilised as a girl for being 'short-sighted and slow at school'.[56]

In England perhaps the most vehement opposition to sterilisation came from the Catholic Church. In 1933 Monsignor Newsome, Superintendent of an institution for mentally defective boys, declared that no Catholic member of an institution's staff could continue in office if sterilisation was to become compulsory because 'Catholics regard sterilisation as a crime'.[57] Many doctors also disagreed with policies of sterilisation, although there is evidence of illegal sterilisation taking place at Gateshead Poor Law Institution, which also accommodated MD children and adults. In 1930 three males aged twenty-two, fifteen and nine, all of who had been sent there for 'sexual misbehaviour', were castrated by the institutions medical officer, after a request had been made by the boys' parents. The two younger boys had not been certified MD and so, according to a Ministry of Health official, the doctor was guilty of unlawful wounding.[58] No further action was taken, however, as the Chief Medical Officer George Newman agreed to let the matter rest after the doctor agreed not to carry out any more operations.[59]

The extent to which doctors continued to sterilise children in England is difficult to assess. In 1937 there was sufficient concern about the matter for the

Ministry of Health to issue a clarification of the law, stating that only for thera-peutic reasons (performed in the interests of the patient's health) would it be legal, and that eugenic sterilisation (performed for racial and social reasons) was illegal. The authorities were confident that doubt as to the legality of the operation would be almost as effective in deterring doctors from performing the operation as any legal prohibition would be.[60] However, Charles Webster, the official historian of the National Health Service, believes that some medical practitioners were 'willing to defy the law and carry out sterilisation in the interests of what they perceived as the public good'.[61] It is certainly a topic which requires further research.

Eugenic sterilisation may have been impossible to enforce in England, but the supporters of segregation and permanent care for mentally disabled children faced much less opposition. In theory, children who were capable of benefiting from some type of education should not have been sent to a mental institution; the Education Act, 1921, had stated that those with an IQ between 50 and 70 should be educated in special schools or classes. In reality, all classes of mentally disabled, and especially feeble-minded and moral defective children, were blamed for the ills of society, such as crime and immorality, and the prevailing attitude was generally unsympathetic (in contrast to attitudes towards physically disabled children which was, on the whole, compassionate). As such, all four classes of defectives were at risk of being incarcerated.

To some extent, the negative attitudes towards disabled children that existed among certain members of the government and the medical pro-fession were echoed by members of the general public, including the chil-dren's able-bodied counterparts. In the streets, where many working-class children played, anyone with a disability tended to be excluded or, even worse, became the target of physical abuse, because they were 'differ-ent'. Consequently, they became isolated and lonely. Sometimes, though, siblings would protect them and they would be included in street games, perhaps being carried or getting around by using home-made go-carts.[62] Disabled children of the middle classes, on the other hand, tended to be kept away from the streets and played in the home. Again they became isolated and lonely.

The extent to which perceptions of disabled children changed during and after the war will be discussed in Chapter 5, as will developments in their health and education provisions. Despite the immense upheaval caused by the conditions of war, and especially the evacuation, these provisions did not remain static. Although not all children were evacuated during the war, the majority were, and the event played a major part in their lives.

Evacuation policies and personnel

Plans for the evacuation of perceived areas of danger within England began several years before the outbreak of the Second World War. The damage caused by air raids at the end of the First World War suggested that, in any future war, civilian society would be particularly vulnerable to attacks from the air. In 1924 the Air Raid Precautions Committee was set up, and 1931 saw the appointment of the first evacuation committee, the Evacuation Sub-Committee of the Committee of Imperial Defence, which reported in 1934. At this stage, it was thought that the police should be responsible for the evacuation in order to prevent the 'inevitable' panic and, also, that only London would need to be evacuated. However, by 1937, after various reports on all matters of civil defence, it became clear that other areas of high population density might also be vulnerable, and that the task might be too large for the police. The matter was addressed in a Home Office circular in March 1938.[63] Owing to the complexity of such a massive undertaking, it was recognised that no single or comprehensive plan for an evacuation was practicable and, if such an event did become necessary, it would be carried out in co-operation between the government and the local authorities.

On 10 May 1938 the LCC passed a resolution approving the principle of evacuating children and, subsequently, the government appointed a committee, led by Sir John Anderson, to examine the relevant aspects of a large-scale evacuation. The recommendations of the committee would provide the basis for the Government Evacuation Scheme, should it become necessary, and in May 1939 an administrative memorandum, prepared on the recommendations of the Anderson Report and outlining the main aspects of the scheme, was published by the Ministry of Health.[64] For the purpose of the evacuation, there would be three types of geographical area: evacuating, receiving and neutral, the latter neither sending out nor receiving evacuees. It was estimated that evacuation areas contained a total population of around 11 million; neutral areas 13 million; and receiving areas 16 million.[65] After taking into account size, density and vulnerability, evacuation areas totalled 81 and reception areas, which were mainly small towns or rural areas, 1,100. Some major cities such as London, were wholly evacuable, whilst others, such as Manchester, were 'zoned' into evacuating and neutral areas.[66]

Two separate events of the 1930s, in which several thousand children had been moved by public transport under the control of their teachers, served as useful 'rehearsals' for assessing the practicalities of gathering together children *en masse*. In 1935 70,000 schoolchildren had assembled on Constitution Hill and in The Mall, to greet the King and Queen on one of their Jubilee drives.

Then in 1937 37,000 schoolchildren had gathered at the Embankment to cele-
brate Coronation Day.[67] The mass movement of children for both these events
had been organised by Mr G. A. N. Lowndes, who was also heavily involved
in planning for the mass evacuation of London's schoolchildren during the
Munich crisis. After the signing of the Munich Pact, Lowndes was transferred,
on loan, from the LCC where he had been assistant Education Officer to the
Ministry of Health. There he played a prominent role in national planning for
the evacuation of schools and, throughout the war, continued to be a major
decision-maker with regards to both special and elementary schools.[68]

Another prominent individual who affected the lives of children in special
schools during the war, although this time more directly, was His Majesty's
Inspector (HMI) James Lumsden. It had been compulsory since 1920 for all
special schools to be inspected and reported on by the Board of Education's
medical officers. Having the schools inspected by the medical branch was
not universally popular, because teachers within these schools were ordinary
non-medical teachers, and some resented being inspected by those of a different profession. After continual protests the Board made a compromise
by appointing, in 1931, the first non-medical inspector to be responsible for
all special schools. James Lumsden was an educational psychologist whose
reports, and to a lesser extent those of his colleagues, have been the source of
much information for this book. Although most of these reports, along with
the other official documents used in this book, relate directly to the period of
the Second World War, some of them also refer to the immediate prewar and
postwar periods, allowing us to assess both the changes that occurred at the
end of the war and the events leading up to the outbreak of war in 1939.

The 'practice run'

The evacuation of disabled children in the first few days of September 1939 was,
on the whole, a smooth, efficient and successful operation. One reason for its
success was the lessons learnt from a similar, although smaller, evacuation a year
earlier during the Munich crisis. On 16 September 1938, shortly after the Prime
Minister Neville Chamberlain's visit to meet Hitler at Berchtesgaden, the LCC
approached the Board of Education regarding plans to transfer London's most
vulnerable children to a safer destination outside the city, and by the 23rd the
council had negotiated accommodation for 2,100 PD children at St Mary's Bay
Holiday Camp, Dymchurch, Kent. On the 27th administration, inspectorial
and organising staff travelled to the camp and the next day the children were
evacuated, along with their teachers and as much equipment as they could
manage. Further medical and domestic staff arrived in the following two days.[69]

Accommodation at Dymchurch was basic, with children sleeping on camp beds in barrack-style huts (the camp was an old army barracks), some of which had holes in the roof where the rain would leak through.[70] Another problem was the lack of adequate staff. None of the schools' nurses had gone to Dymchurch; instead there was a team of Red Cross nurses. One of the teachers, Jessie Thomas, who accompanied the children, remembered in her autobiography the problems of having to cope with inexperienced nurses, none of whom had any knowledge of dealing with disabled children at night, 'who when the child's leg irons were removed could not stand alone'.[71]

The problems at Dymchurch were mainly due to the fact that the event was unprecedented and, to some extent, an experiment. Despite the efforts of the authorities, the camp was unsuitable for the purpose of housing PD children long-term. Children who suffered other disabilities fared better, certainly in respect to accommodation. As well as making arrangements for the PD children, the London authorities arranged for deaf children in special day and residential schools, along with the blind and the mentally defective (MD) children in residential schools (approximately one thousand in total), to be evacuated outside London, in similar establishments to their regular schools, and this took place on 29 September.[72] In most schools, a number of supplementary places were found to house the extra children, but a number of short-stay residential open-air (OA) schools (at Bushey Park, Margate, and St Leonards-on-Sea) were completely taken over, the resident children returning to their homes and elementary schools in London. Not all disabled children were eligible for evacuation under the government's 'special parties' scheme in 1938 (which, incidentally, included around 1,200 nursery schoolchildren evacuated to ordinary billets along with their mothers and certain other adults). The MD and partially sighted (PS) children attending special day schools, and those in OA day schools, were deemed fit enough to be evacuated in ordinary billets along with elementary schoolchildren.[73]

Plans had also been made for the evacuation of the able-bodied. The LCC estimated that approximately five hundred thousand adults and children (other than those in special parties) would need to be evacuated from London if and when a state of emergency was announced, and exhaustive preparations were made. The arrangements were announced as complete on 27 September.[74] The LCC reported that the parents of 83 per cent of the school population had registered their children for evacuation. Panic buying of groceries and provisions in the West End of London, and the premature panic migration of people to Wales, lay testimony to people's fears at that time.[75] However, after Chamberlain's meeting with Hitler in Berchesgaden on 30 September, and the signing of the Munich Pact, further evacuation plans were put on hold and, by 6 October, the evacuated disabled children had been returned home to London. Although some children were thought not to have profited from their camp life, the overall operation was seen as a success.[76]

Although able-bodied children were not evacuated under the government scheme in 1938, some children attending private schools were evacuated, and in a similar way to the disabled children. The girls of Channing School, Highgate, London, were sent to hotels in Ross-on-Wye.[77] Similarly, the junior boys of the nearby Highgate School were evacuated to Brixham, and the seniors to Ilfracombe and Westward Ho!.[78] As with the special schools and nursery schools, the private schools also preferred large-scale premises and, whilst the lack of such accommodation was not an issue in 1938, it was a sign of the competition that special schools would face the following year.

Despite the optimism surrounding the Munich Pact, the government continued to develop large-scale evacuation plans, this time including vulnerable areas outside London. The scheme devised by the LCC for September 1938, for a possible evacuation of five hundred thousand, was judged satisfactory enough that it was to be adopted in other cities.[79] In November 1938 responsibility for the Government Evacuation Scheme was transferred to the Ministry of Health.[80] In June 1939 a rehearsal of evacuation was held in the London borough of Chelsea, when five thousand (able-bodied) children walked or were taken by buses to railway stations where, if it had been the real thing, they would have boarded the trains taking them to their reception areas. The whole operation, which was to be given one and a half days when the evacuation took place the following September, was condensed into three hours.[81] Although a relatively small-scale event, the rehearsal was useful for assessing the practicalities of gathering together several thousand children.

Evacuation itself was voluntary and it was hoped that, should it be necessary, householders in reception areas would volunteer to provide accommodation for the evacuees.[82] If householders without a legitimate reason were to refuse, and if there was a shortage of accommodation, the Billeting Officer had the power to insist. However, it was recognised that disabled children would need to be treated separately:

> Amongst the children to be evacuated will be a number who are blind or deaf or disabled in some other particular, and yet others who are mentally defective. It would not be proper to attempt to arrange accommodation of the ordinary kind for any of these groups, as the disabled children could not be suitably accommodated in small households and also because the householders would find such children an undue burden.[83]

For those physically disabled children who could not be evacuated in regular billets, seaside or country camps were to be used, along with the large private houses belonging to individuals who were willing to place them, wholly or partly, at the disposal of the authorities.[84]

After the disabled children had returned home in October 1938 a small committee of head teachers from the different schools that had been at Dymchurch was formed to discuss what lessons could be learnt from the experience. It was decided that in any future evacuation each school must be under its own head, with an overall leader acting as 'commandant'. Also, the school nurses should replace the ones from the Red Cross who were unfamiliar with the requirements of vulnerable children. Jessie Thomas provided a graphic example of why this latter provision was important in her autobiography:

> Among my girls was one diabetic child for whom it was imperative to have her special injection before breakfast. I sent her in good time to the medical hut with a note to the nurse there containing written instructions. The nurse put the note in her pocket and told her to run along, she would see her later, the letter unopened. The first I heard of this was when the child was in a near coma, and was sent by ambulance to hospital. She remained there slowly recovering, but was still there when we returned to London a week later.[85]

Lessons learned from the September/October 1938 evacuation were useful for planning subsequent evacuations: to make the process even more efficient and to improve the conditions under which the disabled children would have to live. Firstly, the Special Services Branch of the Education Officer's Department, which had co-ordinated the first evacuation, was given help from the Ministry of Health, and a new Evacuation Division was set up. Secondly, it was decided that the LCC should be the authority responsible for maintaining the accommodation to which London's disabled children would be sent in any future evacuations. This included all finances, although the government undertook to keep the Council in funds for this purpose.[86]

Accommodation for disabled children was decided in advance so that the proper adjustments could be made to cater for their specific needs. Panels of visitors, including heads of various schools, inspectors and administration staff, combed the reception areas to find suitable accommodation.[87] In February 1939 the Education Officer for London had listed a number of considerations that had to be in adequate order before the premises could be regarded as ready. The immediate concern in most premises was with regard to heating. The holiday camps, especially, were designed only for summer use and needed to be made adequate for the oncoming winter. Other issues requiring attention included blacking-out materials; water services; sanitation, including night conveniences near the children's sleeping quarters; air raid precautions, such as shelters and sandbags; fire protection; and a sick-bay.[88]

The officer reported that camps such as Dymchurch were not practicable for PDs. He favoured requisitioning already established residential establishments, such as the Hutton Residential School in Essex, which was 'comfortable and had large grounds with infirmaries within the estates for the seriously handicapped'. He finished his report by saying that these children (along with nursery schoolchildren) were 'the least fitted to withstand the sort of emergency conditions we have to fear if war should come. I think it is due to them that they should have the best accommodation.'[89] This view was in line with that of the LCC; when discussing bedridden and incontinent children in their report on the Government Evacuation Scheme the following month, it was stated that there was 'a great deal of sentiment for these classes and everyone will want to do their best for them'.[90]

However, at a conference of school medical officers two weeks later, an assistant education officer questioned whether seriously disabled children should be included in the official evacuation scheme at all. He referred to the evacuation of the previous September, telling the delegates, 'The teachers had been told beforehand not to take such cases, cases that would prove a real embarrassment'.[91] Apparently the School Medical Service had pressed the teachers into taking the children but, once there, the teachers had complained because the children had to be washed and dressed, and carried to the lavatories. The officer went on: 'It may seem a hard thing to say, but it would be a better thing for the great number of children if really difficult cases were left in London, than if they were taken away.'[92] The evacuation authorities agreed, and a statement was issued regarding seriously disabled children. It had been decided that they would be too great an encumbrance: 'The children concerned cannot therefore be included in the Council's evacuation arrangement and no scheme has hitherto been suggested for the reception in country districts or hospitals of such children.'[93] With no official scheme in place for their safety, the most vulnerable group of disabled children relied on the help of the voluntary sector. The ways in which the various charities helped these, and other disabled children, will be discussed in Chapter 3.

For those who were to be included in the Government Evacuation Scheme, once the accommodation had been determined, the evacuating authorities were to provide the receiving authorities with details of the children who would be arriving, such as the number of children, the nature of their disability, the equipment that would be brought along, and how many adults would be accompanying them. The evacuating authorities would also be responsible for supplying nurses and any managerial staff, including one person who would be responsible for the whole party. These people would normally already be attached to the school. The receiving authorities were to be responsible for

recruiting domestic workers and cooks, and for supplying items that the evacuating day special schools did not have already, such as bedding and kitchen
equipment.[94]

In August 1939 a detailed document was published, focusing solely on
the special parties.[95] This was circulated to all concerned, including party
leaders, clerks of local authorities, directors of LEAs, owners of large houses
and managers of camps, the Board of Transport, Ministry of Health and the
Police Department. Topics covered included finance, detailing the amounts
allowed for the board of each child; transport, with precise times of evacuation according to distance covered; equipment and heating; and catering, with
advice on diets and menus. The owners or managers could choose whether to
arrange the catering themselves and accept the government billeting allowance, or to put the responsibility on the leader of the party. There was also a
section on voluntary help, with information given on the Women's Voluntary
Service (WVS), who were based in many reception areas and had expressed a
particular willingness to help with the special parties. The authors of the document had been thorough in supplying as much advice as possible at that stage.

It is evident then, that the evacuation authorities went to a great deal of
trouble to ensure that the evacuation of disabled children would run smoothly.
Their specific requirements had been noted, and adaptations made to make
their new premises as accessible as possible. Plans had also been made for
able-bodied children. As most were accommodated in individual households,
the level of planning was not as great, but the Ministry of Health had made
extensive enquiries as to the number of places required, and at the beginning of
1939 an 'accommodation census' had been carried out in order to assess how
many billets would be available.[96] However, the scale and nature of the evacuation was unprecedented and it was, perhaps, inevitable that problems, for both
disabled and able-bodied, would come to light after the children had arrived.

Evacuation!

In the first three days of September 1939 nearly one and a half million official
evacuees (those included in the government scheme) and approximately
two million private evacuees (arranged by friends or families) were moved.[97]
Unlike the evacuation of the previous September, priority was not limited to
the disabled and nursery children. The official priority classes were as follows:

(1)   school children in organised units in charge of their teachers;[98]
(2)   children of pre-school age accompanied by their mothers or other persons
      responsible for looking after them;
(3)   expectant mothers;
(4)   the adult blind and cripple population so far as removal may be feasible.[99]

The majority of official evacuees were able-bodied schoolchildren who, accompanied by their teachers, were transported to reception areas by train. The evacuation 'rehearsal' of June 1939 had been useful for the entrainment of the evacuees, but arrival in the reception areas did not always run as smoothly. In some areas fewer evacuees than were expected arrived, and in other areas there were more than had been expected. In Berkshire, for example, billets had been provided for 23,915 evacuees but 46,722 arrived.[100] Consequently, as in many other areas, billeting officers were forced to take those children not 'chosen' from house to house in search of extra beds. An extract from Margaret Stephens's *Evacuation* highlights the feelings of one such child: 'The first children chosen by foster-parents were often the good-looking ones or the quiet one. We felt like cattle at an auction.'[101] Some children were so unhappy they even tried to walk home to London. The story of children bearing luggage labels and (many, but not all) going through the distressing 'selection' process in order to find a billet is well documented.[102]

The method of arranging accommodation for able-bodied children has long been criticised by historians, not only for its selection procedure but also for the lack of co-operation between central and local government. These problems were highlighted as early as 1940, when Richard Padley and Margaret Cole published their findings in the *Evacuation Survey*. It was found, for example, that, when the evacuation system was first set up, the authorities in Sheffield planned to send their children to Derbyshire, to places that were relatively close and familiar. The Derbyshire authorities agreed and educational arrangements were made. However, when the government mapped out reception areas, it did not consult with the local authorities and the children were sent to Lincolnshire.[103]

The official evacuation of disabled children took place in the first two days of September 1939. Not all disabled children were registered to be evacuated; some were too seriously disabled to go with the special parties and remained at home or in hospital. Others remained at home because their parents refused to let them go. In London, of the eight thousand disabled children attending special day schools and eligible for evacuation in the special parties, only 3,200 registered. A further 2,200 attending OA schools were deemed healthy enough to be billeted in the same way as elementary schoolchildren. The remaining 2,600 were either evacuated privately or stayed at home and (initially at least) were unable to attend school.[104] For those who were registered, hundreds of buses and ambulances were made available to transport the children to camps, mansions, hotels and any other type of premises deemed suitable.

Two particular incidents show that not everything ran smoothly for the disabled children. Firstly, when 34 boys, four girls and three teachers arrived in their designated reception area, seemingly as part of the general elementary school evacuation, a local couple agreed to take the four girls, only to learn that one needed massaging, one couldn't walk up the stairs, another needed specialist treatment and the other was full of aches and pains. The couple, who had been unaware that the girls needed treatment, kept them for the night and told the headmaster the next morning. Later that day the matron came looking for her lost 'patients'.[105] Secondly, 18 children left the Maud Maxfield School for the Deaf in Sheffield, along with two mothers, two babies and five staff, on 1 September and boarded the bus for Southwell. Owing to an administrative error the party was not expected, and accommodation was eventually found in an empty school still in the process of being built. They were there for ten days in dirty and primitive conditions, with no blackout provisions and without any outside help. The children found the experience a novelty for the first few days, but then homesickness set in. By the time alternative accommodation was found, all but six of the children had been taken home by their parents.[106] It would seem, though, that such confusion was rare and, on the whole, evacuation day proved to be a more successful operation for disabled children than for their able-bodied counterparts.

In many ways the disabled children were spared the distresses suffered by other children. They were kept together with their friends and teachers, rather than having to settle with a new family, and their accommodation and other essentials had been dealt with before their arrival. For example, parents were not told where their child would be going and so the children often arrived with unsuitable clothing. Extra blankets and gumboots had been ordered for the disabled children by the authorities, and were awaiting the children in their new homes.[107] For the able-bodied children, whose accommodation was to be arranged on arrival, and who were often waiting around for long periods, such items were only requested and were often missing. However, it was recognised that reception areas for the able-bodied would need an influx of helpers in order to cope with the large number of extra children, and to areas which accepted London children the LCC sent extra matrons, cooks and domestic staff (for those able-bodied children who were housed in camps and hostels), wardens for communal billets for mothers and children, canteen workers, staff with nursing experience, health visitors, billeting officers, clerical workers and needlewomen.[108] Similar programmes were in operation throughout the country and, as the war progressed, other schemes such as those for the provision of extra clothing and footwear were introduced.

As we have seen, partly as a result of the bomb damage experienced in the First World War, plans for an evacuation of civilians from cities deemed vulnerable to air attack in any future conflict, began early. By the time a second conflict seemed imminent, provisions were in place to move the most vulnerable groups from areas deemed susceptible to enemy bombing. However, despite the extensive preparations and the various 'rehearsals', evacuation day for some able-bodied children was confusing and emotionally disturbing. For the disabled children evacuated into residential special schools, the day was less chaotic. This was largely due to the 'practice run' twelve months earlier but also because, unlike the able-bodied, the disabled were accommodated *en masse*. This made the whole evacuation process, and the arrival in particular, much easier for both staff and children.

Once ensconced in their new premises, the smooth running of the schools, including matters of health, education, management and the availability of clothing and equipment, was subject to inspection by members of the Board of Education and, where necessary, the Ministry of Health. The issues raised in these inspections, and how they were addressed, will become clear in the following chapter, which deals specifically with those children who spent their wartime years in residential accommodation.

Notes

1 This brief summary is for the sole purpose of introducing the reader to special educational provision at the outbreak of war. Arguably the best and most concise history of special education can be found in Pritchard, *Education and the Handicapped*.
2 Department of Education and Science, *The School Health Service 1908–74* (London: HMSO, 1975), p. 5.
3 J. Solity, *Special Education* (London: Cassell, 1992), p. 2. The schools were the Old Kent Road Asylum for the Deaf and Dumb and the School of Instruction for the Indigent Blind.
4 W. W. Taylor and I. W. Taylor, *Special Education of Physically Handicapped in Western Europe* (New York: International Society for the Welfare of Cripples, 1960), p. 55.
5 Board of Education, *Report of the Royal Commission on the Blind, the Deaf and Dumb and Others of the United Kingdom* (London: HMSO, 1889).
6 Pritchard, *Education and the Handicapped*, pp. 202–3.
7 Board of Education, *Report of the Committee of Inquiry into Problems Relating to Partially Sighted Children* (London: HMSO, 1934), and Board of Education, *Report of the Committee of Inquiry into Problems relating to Children with Defective Hearing* (London: HMSO, 1938).
8 TNA, ED50/284, Report of the North Regional Association for the Deaf, January 1943.
9 TNA, ED50/262, National Institute for the Blind to Board of Education, 2 January 1939.

10   Taylor and Taylor, *Special Education of Physical Handicapped in Western Europe*, p. 40.

11   Department of Education and Science, *The School Health Service*, p. 21.

12   *Ibid.*

13   Pritchard, *Education and the Handicapped*, p. 159.

14   London Metropolitan Archives (hereafter LMA), AST 7/283, Documents relating to the Assistance Board and the Central Council for the Care of Cripples.

15   H. M. Devereux, *Housecraft in the Education of Handicapped Children* (London: Mills & Boon, 1965), p. 81.

16   Humphries and Gordon, *Out of Sight*, p. 61.

17   B. Harris, *The Health of the Schoolchild: A History of the School Medical Service in England and Wales* (Buckingham: Open University Press, 1995), pp. 109–10.

18   Pritchard, *Education and the Handicapped*, p. 166.

19   Hurt, *Outside the Mainstream*, p. 166.

20   TNA, ED50/271, Maudslay to the National Society for Epileptics, 19 July 1937.

21   Pritchard, *Education and the Handicapped*, pp. 57–61.

22   Charity Organisation Society, Committee for Considering the Best Means of Making a Satisfactory Provision for Idiots, Imbeciles and Harmless Lunatics, 1875 (reported 1877).

23   Pritchard, *Education and the Handicapped*, p. 61.

24   G. Sutherland, *Ability, Merit & Measurement: Mental Testing and English Education, 1880–1940* (Oxford: Clarendon, 1984), p. 19.

25   Potts and Fido, *A Fit Person to Be Removed*, p. 10.

26   Mental Deficiency Act, 1913, ch.28, Part 1, s.1 (a, b, c, d).

27   Sutherland, *Ability, Merit & Measurement*, p. 64.

28   Mental Deficiency (Amendment) Act, 1927, V, ch.33, s.1 (2).

29   Potts and Fido, *A Fit Person to Be Removed*, p. 11.

30   Education Act, 1914.

31   S. S. Segal, *No Child Is Ineducable: Special Education – Provision and Trends*, 2nd edition. (Oxford: Pergamon, 1974) (1st edition, 1967), p. 37.

32   Segal, *No child Is Ineducable*, p. 42.

33   Education Act, 1921, c.51, s.52, 2(a).

34   Board of Education and Board of Control, *Report of the Joint Departmental Committee on Mental Deficiency* (London: HMSO, 1929).

35   Stakes and Hornby, *Change in Special Education*, p. 114.

36   London County Council (LCC), *The Special Services of Education in London* (London: Hodder and Stoughton, 1929), p. 115.

37   Established in 1913, this organisation worked through local groups of volunteers to help mentally disabled people.

38   LCC, *Special Services of Education in London*, pp. 113–15.

39   LMA, LCC/EO/TRA/1/11, Training of Blind Teachers.

40   *Ibid.*

41 LMA, LCC/EO/STA/2/36, The fluidity of movement of staff between authorities, 1931–38.

42 LMA, LCC/EO/TRA/3/20, The teaching of backward children, 1936.

43 Cited in J. Cavannaugh-O'Keefe, *The Roots of Racism and Abortion: An Exploration of Eugenics* (Princeton: Princeton University Press, 2000), p. 38.

44 *Catholic Herald*, 5 June 1936.

45 F. Galton, *Hereditary Genius* (London: Macmillan, 1869).

46 H. H. Goddard, *The Kallikak Family: A Study in the Heredity of Feeble Mindedness* (New York: Macmillan, 1912).

47 Goddard, *The Kallikak Family*, pp. 114–17. By the late 1920s Goddard had reversed many of his early opinions and even voiced his new opinion that feeble-minded people should be allowed to have children, if they choose to do so. However, the Kallikak study remained a powerful ally to the eugenicist movement.

48 Cited in Stakes and Hornby, *Change in Special Education*, p. 60.

49 C. Webster, 'Eugenic Sterilisation: Europe's Shame', *Health Matters* (Autumn 1997).

50 D. J. Kevles, *In the Name of Eugenics: Genetics and the Uses of Human Heredity* (London: Penguin, 1986), p. 167.

51 *Doctors in the Third Reich* (Channel four, Documentary, Programme 1, 2005). For a discussion of racial hygiene policies under the Nazi regime see S. Bacharach, 'In the Name of Public Health: Nazi Racial Hygiene', *New England Journal of Medicine*, 29 July 2004, 417–20; D. Rosner, 'Racial Hygiene: Medicine under the Nazis', *Politics, Policy and Law*, 16 (1991), 419–22.

52 *Doctors in the Third Reich* (Channel four Documentary, Programme 2, 2005).

53 Eugenics-Watch web-site: www.eugenics-watch.com.

54 Stakes and Hornby, *Change in Special Education*, p. 61.

55 *Doctors in the Third Reich* (Channel four Documentary, Programme 2).

56 Webster, *Health Matters*, Autumn 1997.

57 Birmingham Archdiocesan Archives, BCS/M4, Sterilisation and mental defect evidence of Monsignor Newcome, 1933.

58 TNA, MH79/291, Hugh Macewen at Ministry of Health to Sir George Newman, 12 August 1930.

59 TNA, MH79/291, Sir George Newman, 7 October 1930.

60 TNA, MH79/291, letter of clarification by A. S. Molinsky, 20 February 1937.

61 Webster, *Health Matters*, Autumn 1997.

62 Humphries and Gordon, *Out of Sight*, pp. 36–41.

63 TNA, Home Office Circular 701262/8 (para. 16), 28 March 1938.

64 Ministry of Health, *Memorandum EV.4: Government Evacuation Scheme: Special Parties*, 1939.

65 *Memorandum EV.4*, p. 4.

66 TNA, ED138/56, Report of the Chief Medical Officer, Board of Education, 1939, pp. 32–3.

67 Stuart Maclure, *A History of Education in London, 1870–1990* (London: Penguin, 1990), p. 134.

68 After the war Lowndes wrote the following historical texts: G. A. N. Lowndes, *The British Educational System* (London: Hutchinson, 1955) (re-titled *The English Educational System* in 1960); *Margaret McMillan: The Children's Champion* (London: Museum Press, 1960).; *The Silent Social Revolution* (London: Oxford University Press, 1969).

69 LMA, LCC/EO/WAR/1/1, Housing Committee Papers.

70 K. A. J. Giles, 'Small World: My Memories of World War Two' (private memoirs, 2001), p. 2.

71 Thomas, *Hope for the Handicapped*, p. 118.

72 *Manchester Evening Chronicle*, 29 September 1938.

73 TNA, ED138/57, 'Handicapped and Nursery Children', from Sophia Weitzman's papers.

74 'Arrangements Complete', *Daily Telegraph*, 27 September 1938.

75 Titmuss, *Problems of Social Policy*, pp. 31–4.

76 TNA, ED 138/57, papers of Sophia Weitzman.

77 G. Avery, *The Best Type of Girl: A History of Girls' Independent Schools* (London: Deutsch, 1991), p. 344.

78 A.J.F. Doulton, Highgate *School 1938–1944: The Story of a Wartime Evacuation* (privately printed, 1975), pp. 1–2.

79 'Evacuation on the London Model', *Teachers World*, 5 October 1938.

80 Titmuss, *Problems of Social Policy*, p. 31.

81 R. Samways (ed.), *We Think You Ought to Go* (London: Greater London Record Office, 1995), p. 9.

82 LMA, LCC/EO/WAR/1/1, Housing Committee papers. Children could be compulsorily evacuated if they were 'certified to be suffering or likely to suffer in mind or body as a result of enemy attacks'.

83 Ministry of Health, *Memorandum EV.4*, p. 22.

84 *Ibid.*

85 Thomas, *Hope for the Handicapped*, p. 118.

86 TNA, ED138/49, papers of Sophia Weitzman.

87 LMA, LCC/EO/WAR/1/1, Housing Committee Papers.

88 LMA, LCC/EO/WAR/2/21, LCC Report of Education Officer, 9 February 1939.

89 *Ibid.*

90 LCC, *The Government Evacuation Scheme*, 30 March 1939.

91 LMA, LCC/PH/WAR/1/14, Assistant Education Officer at a conference of medical officers, 19 April 1939.

92 *Ibid.*

93 LMA, LCC/PH/WAR/1/14, Sir Frederick Menzies, 20 April 1939.

94 *Memorandum EV 4: Special Parties*, p. 22

95 Ministry of Health, *Government Evacuation Scheme - Special Parties*, 1939.

96 M. Parsons, *Britain at War: Evacuation* (Hodder and Wayland, 1999), p. 14.

97 Titmuss, *Problems of Social Policy*, p. 102.

98 The blind, deaf, PD and MD children, whether in day or residential schools, were included in this category.

99 Ministry of Health, *Memorandum Ev.4*, p. 4.

100 *Ibid.*

101 M. Stephens, *Evacuation* (Hove: Wayland, 1998), p. 16.

102 See notes 39 and 41. See also R. C. Boud, *The Great Exodus*; J. Gardiner, *The Children's War*.

103 R. Padley and M. Cole (eds), *Evacuation Survey: A Report to the Fabian Society* (London: Routledge, 1940), p. 145.

104 TNA, ED138/49, from Sophia Weitzman's unpublished papers.

105 Ben Wicks, *No Time to Wave Goodbye* (London: Bloomsbury, 1988), p. 82.

106 Miss Proudlove and Miss Turner, 'Evacuation of a Special School', in *The Special Schools Journal*, February 1940, pp. 19–21.

107 LMA, LCC/EO/WAR/2/21, as recommended in the Report of Education Officer's Advisory Committee on Evacuation, 22 February 1939.

108 Samways, *We Think You Ought to Go*, p. 15.

2

RESIDENTIAL SPECIAL SCHOOLS DURING WARTIME

Issues of location

The lack of large-scale accommodation in which to house disabled children presented problems for the evacuation authorities from the outset. From May 1940, however, after the occupation of Denmark and Norway, and then the Low Countries and northern France, the situation worsened. In the initial evacuation of September 1939 many children from London were evacuated to areas within the south and south-east of England, but these areas were now deemed susceptible to possible bombing raids or to invasion. Consequently, the government arranged for the able-bodied evacuees to be re-evacuated and, soon after, the local children were also evacuated.[1] For the children being accommodated in residential special schools, it was not so straightforward. Although some had returned home during the 'phoney war' between September 1939 and May 1940, there were still around 1,500 disabled children being accommodated in residential special schools, in holiday camps, on the line of coast stretching from the Wash to Newhaven.[2] Owing to the lack of alternative accommodation, the possibility of a school's relocation depended on its position, and the degree of danger in which the government perceived it to be.

In the south of England, preference with regard to accommodation was given to those situated to the east of Newhaven, in areas thought to be most susceptible to invasion, whilst those to the west were given low priority.[3] However, although the invasion never materialised, the bombers did, and the areas of danger proved more difficult to predict. Jessie Thomas was now 'commandant' of four schools, comprising around four hundred junior mixed and senior girls, evacuated to Broadreeds Holiday Camp in Selsey, West Sussex. As recommended, each school retained its own head but one was chosen to be the overall leader. In June 1940 both Jessie Thomas and officials at the

Board of Education expressed concern about the proximity to the Broadreeds camp of guns and searchlights, which could be a target for German bombers. The Board outlined its concerns to the Ministry of Health, who replied that Commands had been asked to avoid the camps unless it was absolutely necessary. The letter concluded 'While I hope that this action will have a steadying influence on the military, I am afraid that we must be prepared to lose a certain number of parties'.[4] After objections had been made, to the War Office, to no avail, arrangements were made to move the camp, on 27 August. However, on the night of 19/20 August, a bomb was dropped nearby and a thirteen-year-old boy in the camp was killed, along with a female teacher and a helper. It was decided to move the camp straight away.[5]

To the east of Newhaven, a little further inland but still on the bombers' flight path, was Tenterden camp where, on the night of 27 August 1940, some bombs had been dropped close by, killing a boy and a girl on a nearby farm.[6] On 30 August the Education Officer's department at the LCC complained to the Board of Education, 'For many weeks now we have been trying to get the Ministry of Health to consider this whole question of security and have failed'.[7] Two days later Mr Savage from the Board of Education visited some of the special schools that were thought to be in the area where air fighter squadrons would attempt to intercept German bombers:

> On 1st September I had the advantage of being within a few miles of 4 special parties whilst a fairly severe battle was being waged above. An enemy fighter aeroplane power dived a few hundred yards from me and the car in which I had been travelling. When I arrived at one part between Wrotham and Tonbridge another fighter had just crashed in the grounds of the house. The commandant told me that machine gun bullets (probably spent) had been dropping all around the premises.[8]

Despite Mr Savage's observations, many disabled children were kept in potentially dangerous areas. The following year, after his visit to the Riviera Hotel near Weymouth, HMI Mr Burrows reported that:

> The building is reached by the gates, which are strongly barbed wired and guarded by sentries. Passes have to be shown to enter. A network of barbed wire practically encloses the building. The military are permanently on guard within a few yards, and other military precautions, some within 40 yards, are actually at the very end of the school building. It would seem to me to make this building definitely a military objective. I can only feel very disquieted with regard to the future safety of these children.[9]

Soon after Burrows's report, the Board of Education requested that the Ministry of Health remove the school. However, despite heavy bombing raids on nearby Weymouth, the reply was that it would not be possible. Instead, regional transport officers were approached about moving the children if an invasion attempt warning was received in time.[10] Fortunately, this was not necessary and, despite many air raid warnings (thirty-four in April 1942 alone), the children remained safe.

The following case illustrates the dangers that could befall any group of children, whether disabled or not, even in areas deemed safe. Chatsworth House in Derbyshire housed 250 able-bodied girls evacuated from Penrhos College, a private residential school in North Wales. On one occasion two German bombers strayed off course and 'vented their disappointment by peppering the north side of the house with a few machine gun bullets'. Luckily, the girls were in the hall saying prayers at the time. On another occasion the east side of the house was machine-gunned but this time it was by nearby American soldiers taking target practice on the moor behind the house. Apparently Chatsworth House was not on their map. Fortunately, on both occasions there were no casualties.[11]

The difficulty in finding accommodation for all evacuees was an ongoing problem throughout the war and, on the whole, it would appear that the authorities did as much as they could for the disabled children, under the circumstances. Indeed, as has already been mentioned, London's Education Officer had declared that, in his opinion, 'they should have the best accommodation'. Not all government officials felt this way, however. In May 1940 there were still 450 disabled children awaiting evacuation from London, and it was proving difficult to find suitable premises. In a letter to the Minister of Health, Cecil Maudslay, one of five principal assistant secretaries at the Board of Education, wrote:

> Although it might be argued in cold blood that perhaps these disabled children are not so much worth saving as the able-bodied, yet there is a good deal of sentiment for them on the part of the population, and the Ministry and the Council might be in a very difficult position vis-à-vis the people of London if the evacuation plan were operated and these 450 blind, deaf, crippled or otherwise defective children were left behind in London.[12]

The contents of this letter are significant because they are the sentiments of a man in a position of authority. More heartening is the knowledge that 'the population' or 'the people of London' did not share Maudslay's lack of concern for the disabled. By 5 June the number of disabled children awaiting evacuation from London had risen to six hundred. Fortunately, by 21 June, a total of eight new premises had been found to house these children, as well as some of those still waiting re-evacuation from the south and south-east coasts.[13]

Three months later the minutes of a meeting of the Education Officers' department noted Maudslay's words on the subject of a further 1,300 disabled children needing to be evacuated. Again, he made reference to the people who would raise an outcry if these children were left behind, ending with 'We could not answer that we were bending our energies to saving the children most worth saving for that was discussed long ago and rightly or wrongly the government decided that the weak were as much entitled to evacuating as the strong'.[14] Again, the author's sentiments did not reflect those of the main decision-makers who, it would seem, attached as much importance to 'the weak' as 'the strong'.

As the war progressed and the shortage of large-scale accommodation became acute, more and more property owners agreed to relinquish their premises for the purpose of housing evacuated children. One such person was Colonel ffennell, the owner of Hill End Camp at Farmoor, Berkshire. Before the war, the camp had been used as a school journey centre and camp school for (able-bodied) children. After the evacuation of children from the east and south-east coasts in May 1940, Colonel ffennell agreed that the premises could be taken over to accommodate evacuated children, and the LEA spent £300 on making the building suitable for winter use. In June 1940, much to the Colonel's horror, one hundred MD children were sent there, marking the beginning of a lengthy correspondence between the Colonel and the various government departments dealing with the evacuation. Colonel ffennell wanted 'normal children' to replace the MDs because 'they would benefit more from the natural amenities of the camp'.[15] G. A. N. Lowndes, at the Ministry of Health, said: 'I can well understand Colonel ffennell's preference for normal children in whom he feels that he can take a personal interest but it would, in our view, be a real waste of this accommodation to use it as an ordinary hostel.'[16] Despite being given several explanations as to why the premises should be used for the MD children, in that they could not be billeted in individual households, ffennell pressed his appeal, leading to the following statement to the Ministry of Health:

> You yourself will admit, I think, that the lives of lunatics should be protected if it is possible to do so, but if you had to choose between the two, the lunatics and normal children, which would you save? What would be your choice? It evidently suits the LCC better at the moment to keep the MD children at Hill End, but I think that I am right in saying that, if it does so, it is probably sacrificing and certainly risking the lives of an equivalent number of normal English children who may perish.[17]

The following year, in May 1942, the authorities conceded and the MD children were sent elsewhere. The Colonel got his wish and Hill End Camp was used for weekend visits by local able-bodied children.

Another person of note who had a negative view of MD children was Sir Edward Howarth of the National Camps Corporation (NCC).[18] In November 1942 the Sheephatch NCC camp at Tilford, Surrey, became available and the Board of Education decided to send a group of 245 MD boys there. The boys had originally been evacuated to the Grand Atlantic Hotel in Weston-super-Mare, where they had experienced no trouble with the locals when at weekends they had made visits into town. They had worked on local farms harvesting vegetables and had done gardening work for the local authority. Their time at the Grand Atlantic was seen as a great success.[19]

The reason for the Board's wish to move the boys was the high charges demanded by the hotel. A month after the decision was made, a raid on Weston-super-Mare convinced some of the boys' mothers that they would be safer at home. As a consequence, the number decreased from 245 to 120. However, in a letter to the Board of Education, Howarth relayed the information that the NCC had decided that, in their three years' experience of housing evacuees, camp schools would be better used by normal children. Although another of the camps, at Horsley Green, had been successfully adapted to accommodate PD children, the Corporation had determined that any such adaptations at Sheephatch could not be undertaken at the present time. The Board decided to visit the camp to see for themselves and, in January 1943, it was found that only minor adaptations and no building work were required. Consequently, four months later the boys from the Grand Atlantic, along with boys from three other residential special schools and a few from a Derbyshire Youth Hostel, totalling two hundred, moved to the camp.

For fourteen months all went well at the camp. Reports show that there was some destruction caused by the boys, such as broken toilet seats and doors, taps and windows, but similar damage had been done by the able-bodied boys who had occupied the premises previously. All in all, the boys had settled down well and were happy and contented. However, in July 1944, the local council, the Hambledon Rural District Council, complained to the NCC about fires that had been started near the camp and letters belonging to the boys being found there. The Council enquired as to whether it was possible to 'replace these children with normal ones'. Howarth passed on the request to the Board of Education, who answered with a resounding 'No'. Meanwhile, the local press had joined in the debate over the boys, blaming them for the fires.[20] They also mentioned that the Council's senior medical officer (SMO) had informed them that the camp was unsuitable for MD boys.

After hearing of the furore over the boys, fuelled by the SMO and the local press, an Inspector of Special and Approved Schools, Mr A Waites, wrote to Hambledon Council. He questioned the evidence, stating that the fires were at a salvage dump to which discarded paper from the camp was sent. Local boys had already been prosecuted for other damage, whereas no one at Sheephatch had any such convictions. Furthermore, some of them had been working for local residents in gardens and households, and had received excellent reports. He also informed the Council that the Board of Education would take advice on the SMO's reporting, which might have far reaching consequences. Waites concluded: 'For a large number of people who have little knowledge of the character and disposition of the average educable MD, the term "mental defective" has a somewhat sinister connotation, amounting in some cases to hostile aversion.'[21] Waites invited anyone with concerns about the boys to visit the camp themselves. The matter appeared to have been resolved, but a few months later the NCC gave notice to end the tenancy on the grounds of damage done by the boys. HMI Lumsden made an unannounced visit and found some damage to the ablution blocks, which he was not surprised at as they were of light construction and easy to damage. In Lumsden's view, the NCC had never liked having the MDs in the camp, and matters were made worse by the camp manager's antagonism. Three months later Dr Bywaters of the Board of Education found that the boys were under good discipline and there was little to complain of. However, the tenure was due to end in August and, despite the LCC's request for an extension (although the war was over, many of the boys were unable to return to their homes either because their parents were dead or because their homes had been destroyed), the residual children were dispersed on 26 July 1945, and the premises officially vacated on 4 August.

Although not all camp managers and property owners held such extreme views as Sir Edward Howarth and Colonel ffennell, it is fair to say that many preferred to have healthy evacuees from private schools than the alternative. As Gillian Avery points out, 'Property owners only endured school invasion because of economic circumstances, or to avoid getting something worse'.[22] The government was aware of this preference and in April 1939, when the Minister of Health was warning of a possible requisition of large houses if a war should break out, the LCC asked him not to say that a private school might be sent because they would not be able to go back on this if the accommodation was needed for disabled children.[23]

These examples illustrate the kind of problems faced by the evacuating authorities in locating, and retaining, large-scale accommodation suitable for disabled children. Fortunately, the majority of owners or managers did not object to the 'type' of child to be accommodated in their properties and such problems were quite rare. In addition, although some children were forced to remain in areas of danger, and their degree of safety was more a matter of luck than of design, there is no evidence to suggest that the decision to leave them there was due to anything but a lack of alternative accommodation.

The staff

During the war years HMI James Lumsden and his colleagues inspected many of the camps, houses and hotels used as residential special schools, providing an insight into the day-to-day problems faced by the children and staff. It was the duty of the HMIs to report on the attitudes and abilities of the staff, and to ensure that both teachers and children were provided with essentials such as food, clothing and equipment. In doing this, they dealt with difficult and uncompromising teachers, but also met many who were hard-working and compassionate. This had also been the case in peacetime, but the conditions of war led to heightened levels of inflexibility in some, whilst others met the challenges with tolerance and co-operation.

On the whole, those in charge of the special parties appeared to be hard-working, responsible individuals whom the HMIs deemed committed and competent. Jessie Thomas, in particular, was highly respected by the Board of Education. Lumsden regarded her as 'London's best commandant as regards the physical and human welfare of the children'.[24] On 22 August 1940, just two days after the fatal bombing at Broadreeds, two hundred girls and fifty staff, including Jessie Thomas as commandant, moved to Peckforton Castle in Cheshire. The castle, which was owned by Lord Tollemache, was well equipped with an adequate water supply, electric light and lavatory basins and baths in or near most bedrooms. However, unlike the holiday camp, which was on one level, the castle had stairs, making the living conditions more difficult. Also there was poor ventilation because few windows were able to be opened, and the rooms were draughty. Obviously Peckforton Castle had not been built for the purpose of housing disabled children, and so certain difficulties were to be expected. However, as with most premises accommodating PD children, some adaptations were made and the children and staff made the best of it.

Another teacher highly respected by the education authorities was Mr Barker, head of a residential school in Yorkshire. The premises had been requisitioned by the Ministry of Health in 1939, in order to house evacuated MD boys from Leeds. Lumsden reported that the staff was excellent and the premises were remarkably clean and tidy. Although the boys were 'the difficult type of MD', they were given an amount of freedom much greater than usual. They had many hobbies, were taken on various outings and had a scout troop which had won several trophies. The boys were found to be well-mannered, free-spoken, responsive and responsible. Lumsden gave credit for the success of the school to Mr Barker: 'an excellent old man, over 65, with a most whole-some influence on his boys, to whom he devotes all his energies, hardly taking any holiday leave'.[25]

There were, doubtless, many more teachers worthy of credit. At the same time there were some who were not so committed to the welfare of the children, or who, perhaps, had not been lucky in the choice of staff with whom they had to work. The teachers and children at the Riviera Hotel, for example, were inconvenienced because of the commandants' inability, or refusal, to reprimand the kitchen staff. Lessons were taken in the same hall as the meals and, during lesson time, the kitchen staff consistently walked through the hall, sometimes smoking, and laying the tables too early. Other problems at the hotel were caused not by the staff but by the location. For example, only the 'open-air' children could go out freely because the area surrounding the building was rough and very steep. Consequently, the PD children got none of the advantages of life in the country, and not even much fresh air.[26]

In several of Lumsden's reports, the laziness of the staff was a problem that threatened the harmony of camp life. Perhaps because of resentment of the commandant, who had been singled out to be 'leader', or because alternative employment was easy to find, some of the staff lacked enthusiasm and commitment. At a holiday camp in West Sussex, the commandant hardly left the premises because he feared for the school if left in the hands of the other staff. Lumsden found that there was a general air of slackness, and that the teachers' wives did housekeeping duties because the staff was mainly male and 'does not care for these things'. Despite there being sufficient accommodation, up to three children were sharing a bed so that the staff did not have to make up the other beds. Perhaps more damning, two eneuretics occupied one bed in order to save washing.[27]

Lumsden was particularly critical of the staff at another holiday camp in nearby East Sussex, to which a total of 243 children had been evacuated from London, along with 26 teachers and 23 attendants. The commandant appeared nervous, overworked and willing, but was not firm enough with the staff and so they took advantage. There were no evening activities at the camp because she could not depend on voluntary help. Lumsden criticised the staff for grumbling unnecessarily, as they complained about the lack of baths, staff lounge and staff sick-room accommodation. Also, 'the chalets were too cold', 'it was a dull life', 'other camps have more', and 'it's on the east coast'. Never one to mince his words, Lumsden concluded that 'Their small mindedness, disguised under the pretence of acting in the children's interests, is almost unbelievable'.[28]

Not all head teachers were able to cope well with the changes brought about by running a residential school. One such teacher was Miss Virgo, who had successfully run a special day school for deaf children in Bristol. In January 1942 her school was evacuated to Ledbury Park in Herefordshire. Several weeks later the Board of Education received a request for an inspection of the premises from Bristol's Chief Education Officer, who had been concerned at the disquieting reports he had received about the arrangements made for the children. In March 1942 HMI Mrs Heap inspected the premises, which were found to be one of the most unsuitable she had seen. There were problems with ventilation, outdoor space, kitchen equipment and the sick-bay, and a lack of urinals. Furthermore, the owners of the premises, Lord and Lady Biddulph, continued to live in the house and so the school occupied only the domestic quarters. HMI Heap concluded that the owners were only interested in the business angle of letting the premises, and were without any sense of philanthropy. Their only contribution appeared to be to criticise.

Miss Virgo had only recently returned to the school after six weeks' sick leave due to a nervous breakdown. Two assistant teachers had also been ill, and a third had recently been admitted to hospital; all illnesses had been attributed to the stress and strain of the altered conditions. Later the same month Miss Virgo walked out of the school with a suitcase, giving no indication of her intentions. The following day HMI Lumsden visited the premises, along with officers from the Birmingham region of the Ministry of Health. They found that the staff were seriously overworked and in low spirits. Meanwhile Miss Virgo had returned to Bristol and had tendered her resignation. In his report Lumsden noted that she was: 'highly regarded as a head mistress both by the LEA and by myself'. Records show that improvements were subsequently made at the school.[29]

In most cases where the staff were employed by the Board of Education, Lumsden's recommendations were carried out and improvements were made. However, in some cases the schools were run, either partly or wholly, by organisations which were not used to being answerable to others. In November 1939 Lumsden paid a visit to a school camp in Glamorgan, where 299 deaf children had been evacuated from six different schools in London. As the camp belonged to the National Council of Social Service (NCSS),[30] one of the Council's own staff was in charge overall as camp manager, with the result that there was friction between him and the school staff, including the commandant. The main complaint from the staff was that the NCSS treated them as mere summer visitors, and did not agree that they should have a say in the running of the camp. In addition, although the teachers' meals were adequate, those for the children were not, either in quantity or in quality, and the kitchen was dirty. Lumsden reported that the staff were (quite rightly, he noted) indignant and in danger of losing morale, and that some of the parents would remove their children if the complaints were not dealt with.[31]

At a holiday camp in Somerset, which also had a camp manager working alongside a commandant, Lumsden found that all the work was being done by the commandant and her staff. The camp manager and the assistant teachers refused to work weekends, and did only the minimum required, doing nothing voluntarily. They blamed the commandant if they did not get whatever they requested, even though she had already acquired electric heaters, rugs, extra blankets, a wireless and a lounge, many of which were luxuries in wartime. The nurse also created problems by being unpleasant to the commandant (the local GP was afraid of the nurse!) and complaining of being overworked, even though, Lumsden reported, she had lots of help. Lumsden requested in his report that the assistants should be relieved as soon as possible as 'they are not suited to camp life and responsibility'.[32]

At the Yorkshire Residential School for the Blind in York, Lumsden had a few scathing words for both the staff and the managers. In March 1939, before the start of the war, he reported on the toilets which were a row of seats consisting of holes in a wooden plank over a trough, flushed every half hour from a tank. Lumsden reported: 'It may have been assumed that the blind do not require the privacy of separate compartments but it has been forgotten that their sense of smell and touch are unimpaired.'[33] In the same report, he called the Principal an 'all-powerful dictator'. In his next visit in 1941 Lumsden was pleased to see that seven new WCs and a urinal had been installed, but was unimpressed with the music teacher who, he said, 'is so blind that he does not see that the children are not opening their mouths or standing up'.[34] In April 1942 an air raid on York resulted in one wing of the school being destroyed. The following year Lumsden reported in damning fashion: 'Any proposal by the managers to rebuild the wing destroyed in wartime will have to be carefully examined, as they are fonder of their antique buildings than of education.'[35] The Yorkshire School for the Blind was different from many of the residential special schools discussed here because it was already established when war broke out, and the staff were able to continue rather than be uprooted and mixed with other schools. Lumsden and his colleagues monitored many schools that were privately run, including certain religious schools. On the whole, the reports of these schools show that conditions were more than satisfactory although as with all types of schools there were exceptions.

Conditions within

Whilst the evacuation of September 1938 had prepared the authorities for the initial transportation and arrival of disabled evacuees, the week-long experience had not been enough to assess any potential long-term problems. On 22 September 1939, shortly after the outbreak of war, the LCC held a special conference to discuss the camps and concluded that, 'although peacetime standards may have to be sacrificed, certain improvements must be made'. These included blacking-out procedures, heating, water services, sanitation, air raid precautions, fire protection and sick-bays.[36]

Conditions in the newly acquired residential premises, whether camps, hotels or large houses, varied enormously. Some premises were more than adequate and needed no alterations. At the Eastcourt House Residential School in Wiltshire which from 1942 to 1944 accommodated evacuated MD children from Bristol, there was central heating, electricity, well water and a telephone. The house, which was the former home of the nineteenth-century shorthand pioneer Sir Isaac Pitman, was described by the visiting HMI as 'a delightful mansion in a modern, excellent condition'.[37] The children were able to use all the grounds except the large kitchen garden, which had been retained by the current owner for cultivation under the Ministry of Agriculture. At another school, an open-air Catholic school in Surrey, most HMI visits were made unannounced and revealed the school to be 'probably one of the best equipped and well managed institutions'. The premises were clean and in good repair and the children were well fed and looked after.[38] Similarly, at an open-air home and school for Jewish children, the air raid shelters were 'astonishingly elaborate considering the relative safety of the school's position'. Also, the school premises were centrally heated, the sanitary conditions were exceptionally good, and new cooking ranges had been installed.[39]

In the majority of schools Lumsden and his colleagues found adequate, if not elaborate, equipment and safety arrangements and did not report any problems with regard to the staff. However, in some instances, premises had to be relinquished soon after occupation as, even with improvements, they were deemed unsuitable for long-term use. Such was the case at a holiday camp in Lancashire. Previously run by a voluntary society in Manchester, the camp was taken over by the Liverpool LEA at the beginning of the war, for evacuated MD boys. On inspection in December 1939 the accommodation was found to consist of detached wooden huts, in a bad state of repair and not connected by paths, and the lighting (by paraffin lamps) was inadequate. The kitchen had a leaking roof and was likely to be flooded by surface water from the playground, which was inadequately drained. The classroom was neither heated nor lit

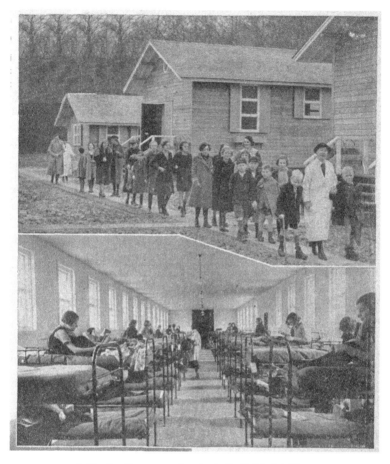

1 Horsley Green camp for physically disabled children

and many mice were present. Consequently, it was recommended that other accommodation be found.[40]

There were also incidents, in both State-run and privately run schools, where safety issues in the form of air raid shelters were less than acceptable. At the Horsley Green camp in Buckinghamshire, which housed 210 evacuated PD and delicate children, there were no shelters, and so for air raid practice the children remained in the dormitories at night and went to the trees during the day. On inspection, Dr Bywaters reported that 'Each child had been given a special tree to go to'.[41] As was so often the case, the children's safety was largely reliant on the ingenuity of the staff but, again, the lack of fatalities was more a matter of luck than of design.

A further example comes from a colony for epileptic children, also in Buckinghamshire. As there were no shelters and no sirens nearby, the children and teachers were constantly listening either for the London siren or for nearby bombs and gunfire. Apart from the disruption this caused during lessons, there were considerable physical difficulties in evacuating the children. Most were of low intelligence; some were PD, and if a child was to have an epileptic seizure he or she would have to be physically carried out. In September 1940 one of the teachers complained about the situation to the National Union of Teachers (NUT), who in turn informed the Board of Education.[42] However, construction work on the shelters did not begin for another twelve months.[43]

In many cases, the delay in constructing air raid shelters was due to a shortage of materials and labour. However, at the Royal West of England Residential School for the Deaf in Exeter, the managers, who were retired generals, refused to have shelters built. Instead, they decided to dig trenches. Hasty digging and inadequate cover with corrugated iron and earth led to them collapsing in the wet, resulting in a waste of expenditure and a continued lack of ARP. In Lumsden's final report on the school in 1943 there were still no shelters.[44]

The amount of time children spent in air raid shelters, of course, depended on the number of air raid attacks. At a school for evacuated deaf and partially deaf children in Surrey, this so-called 'shelter existence' was blamed for an outbreak of diphtheria, which occurred from August to November 1940. This was during the Battle of Britain, when there was intense air raid activity, resulting in the children and their teachers sleeping in the shelters continuously for several months. Although a programme of immunisation was in progress, not everyone had yet been protected. As a result of the intense overcrowding in the shelters an epidemic occurred; four children and one teacher died and 102 were admitted to hospital.[45]

Problems within the residential special schools, including safety measures, were remedied, with varying degrees of success, by the HMIs. After a visit to the Horsely Green camp, for example, the inspector's report was particularly critical. He noted the lack of toothbrushes; the wheelchairs were all broken and beyond repair; some beds had been broken by the boys; screens were also broken. His report appears to have been acted upon to some extent because, on his subsequent visit the following year, he was able to report that the general appearance and discipline of the boys had improved, and that they had received five new wheelchairs.[46]

Occasionally even the efforts of the HMIs were not enough to remedy problems within a residential special school. The following case study comes from an established school situated in a relatively 'safe' area. It is a most extreme case and has been included in order to highlight the degree of neglect and potential abuse that was allowed to continue, at least in this school, before, during and after the war.

Case study: Besford Court

Besford Court Roman Catholic special school for MD children in Worcester was a residential special school housing approximately 250 boys aged twelve and over; the associated school at nearby Sambourne housed the under -twelves. When Lumsden visited Besford Court on 23 September 1941 conditions were so bad that he decided to make a return visit two days later with Miss Elliott and Mr Bosworth-Smith, also from the Board of Education. On inspection they found that, whilst Sambourne was clean and reasonably attractive, at Besford Court the lavatories were dirty and repellent; the open-air dormitories were dirty and rickety; and there was a general air of neglect. The boys were not in class because of the holidays, and so they wandered about aimlessly whilst the attendants sat in the staff room. The resident manager, the Reverend Father P. F. M. McSwiney, said that it was difficult to get attendants and domestic staff, yet the school was kept full 'to keep up fee income'.[47] The inspectors regarded the dinners as sloppy, and questioned why the local butcher had got the medical officer to sign a certificate saying that the children needed more mince. Lumsden arranged another visit with Dr Gale in three months.

Owing to illness, Dr Gale was unable to accompany Lumsden to the school until March 1942. Dr E. O. Lewis from the Board of Control was also present because there were a number of boys over the age of sixteen. Lumsden found that, of the 178 boys under sixteen, who were legally entitled to an education, 50 were excluded from anything academic and spent the day in the craft workshop. Lumsden told Father McSwiney that they should have at least one day each week in school, which was still not satisfactory but, partly as a result of military service, there was a shortage of staff. The school employed just five teachers, among which, according to Lumsden, were 'three poor specimens of teachers'.[48]

Whilst Lumsden concentrated on the boys' education, Dr Gale was more concerned with their medical welfare. He found that, although the boys looked well and cheerful, there was low personal cleanliness and 'the ground around the dormitories is often soaked with urine because there is [sic] no proper sanitary conveniences for night use'. He recommended that the school should not admit boys under the age of thirteen unless they were robust and well developed.[49] It was also noted that the fee at Besford Court was, at £90 a year, higher than for any other residential MD school, and must not be increased.

Later in the year Reverend McSwiney, along with the Right Reverend Bishop Griffin and the Very Reverend Canon H. D. Yeo, were interviewed at the Board of Education by Bosworth-Smith, and Dr Rees-Thomas from the Board of Control. Dr Rees-Thomas said that the sanitary conditions at Besford Court were the worst he had ever seen. Canon Yeo said that they would have been improved but for the war.

In December 1942 Lumsden received a complaint about Besford Court from the Director of Education at Preston, who had sent boys to the school the previous year. One boy's father had employed a solicitor to investigate the conduct of the school after it emerged that the boy had worn the same vest from July to September, and was not allowed to change it. The sanitary arrangements were also questioned, as boys had been urinating in the dormitory. By this time the school was being monitored on a regular basis. In January 1943 Lumsden reported that the number of boys had been reduced, and maintenance work on the premises would soon begin. More importantly perhaps, a new headmaster, Mr Kelly, had been appointed, with whom Lumsden was very impressed. Although Father McSwiney had agreed to give the new headmaster full authority over everything connected with the boys' lives, Lumsden remarked: 'I have no fear that, out of pique at having a headmaster forced on him, he will try to undermine Mr. Kelly's authority: he is more likely to give him enough rope to hang himself if he should prove unequal to the task, which I do not anticipate.'[50] In August 1943 Lumsden reported that conditions were getting better, but in February 1944 a Miss Darwin visited the school and found that:

> The beds had no counterpanes, mattresses were old and lumpy, pillows and sheets dirty under the bedclothes. We found coal dust, cinders, peas, straw, bits of clothing and books. The top blankets and sheets had been made simply to cover the mess. The boys probably walk barefoot or in their socks about the dirty floors and to the closets along an earth path made up with cinders, and then get straight back into bed.[51]

One month later Lumsden made an unannounced visit and found that the floors were dirty and the midday meal was inadequate. The supervisors had unhelpful attitudes, and allowed the boys to behave with a lack of manners. Other than that, he said that the overall conditions had improved.

From the many HMI documents examined in regard to wartime special schools, Besford Court is by far the worst case of neglect and mistreatment. On the whole, Catholic schools, the majority of which were run by nuns, were well-managed and the children adequately cared for. Besford Court had staffing problems, but so did many such schools, and most managed to maintain a certain level of cleanliness and care. Indeed, the associated school at Sambourne was, according to Lumsden, clean and reasonably attractive. Although some improvements were made at Besford Court, the boys who were accommodated there during the war were failed by both the Board of Education and the Ministry of Health.[52] Perhaps those in charge of the school made just enough effort after each visit to satisfy the inspectors, or maybe it was due to a lack of alternative accommodation. The LEAs made payments towards the maintenance of the children, which could have been withdrawn, but this would have meant that the evacuation authorities would have to find somewhere else for the boys, which would have been extremely difficult. On the other hand, Lumsden and his colleagues did recommend the closure of certain State-run special schools, as well as the removal of teaching staff.

Although there were other staff who were less than ideal, in the majority of situations the HMIs and other officials were able to ensure that the children were adequately cared for. Besford Court was an extreme example of the neglect of disabled children during the war but the fact that the school remained open for several years after the war may be an indication of how little power the State authorities had over the Catholic Church.

Education

Despite the good intentions and hard work of many organisations and individuals on behalf of children during the war, it was inevitable that many aspects of their lives would be disrupted, and education was high on the list. Inevitably, time was lost at the outset when the children were being transferred, but this was only a matter of a few days and most settled down fairly quickly. Time spent in air raid shelters, rather than in the classroom, depended on where the school was situated. Those on the south and south-east coasts probably suffered more in this respect, unless or until they were re-evacuated to safer areas.

According to Richard Samways, education facilities for those able-bodied children evacuated into individual households were relatively satisfactory from the beginning. Classes were taken in spare accommodation in local schools, or in halls and rooms hired for the purpose. Sometimes the evacuees had to share the same premises as the local children, each receiving half-time education, but by supplementing this with other premises the system was soon converted to near full-time education.[53]

For the children evacuated into one of the residential special schools, school work tended to carry on as before the war although, as always, some schools were more successful than others. At the Delamere School for Jewish

children, which has already been mentioned for its excellent air raid shelters
and school premises, Lumsden called the school work 'dull, unreal, sedentary,
and slipshod'.[54] A maximum of two hours per day was given in secular instruction and this contained unprogressive exercises in arithmetic and English.
Individuals received no one-to-one teaching unless they were experiencing difficulties. The following year, perhaps as a result of his report, Lumsden found
that, although there was still an emphasis on manners rather than academic
work, more elementary school curriculum study had been introduced.[55]

The lack of academic subjects was not such a problem at the Springhill
Private School for Deaf Boys in Northampton. The school was noted for its
examination success, which was unique for a special school in Britain. Classes
were not rigid and pupils often attended different classes for different subjects,
thereby giving an opportunity for individual classification and attention.
However, there was no vocational training and few of the pupils entered paid
employment. Those who came from wealthy families (some 'special deserving
cases' were allowed to attend at a reduced rate) usually went into occupations
related to their father, as unpaid workers, and received payment if and when
they had proved their worth. One of the pupils had become the country's
first ever deaf person to obtain a PhD, in geology, although at the time of the
reports he was still unemployed.[56]

In the majority of residential special schools disabled children received
training primarily in vocational skills. The children of a holiday camp in West
Sussex, for example, grew their own garden produce,[57] as did the boys at a
school in Oakham, near Leicester.[58] In the latter, boys also learned how to
decorate, and were allowed to colour-wash the walls of two workshops. The
school also held classes in tailoring and, from 1941, had a qualified tailoring
instructor on the staff. Leather-work was also taught, and records show that
many boys went into the shoe trade after leaving school.

Placing children in employment at the age of sixteen was often at the
forefront of 'educational' learning, as evidenced by the number of vocational
instructors employed in all types of special schools. At a school for deaf children in Derby, for example, children were trained in a variety of occupations
and, of the sixteen children who left in the twelve month period up to 31
March 1944, the girls were placed: in factories (3), domestic service (2) and
dress-making (1); the boys: farm-work (3), engineering (1), pattern shops
(2), joinery (2), boot-repairing (1) and labouring (1).[59] The war had created
opportunities for disabled children because of the high demand for labour, but
there was concern over whether the placements would last after the war had
ended. In order to secure suitable jobs, the schools often relied on the help
of the After-Care Association. This organisation dealt with children from all

types of special schools, including day and hospital schools, and is discussed in Chapter 3.

The various problems experienced by the staff of residential special schools as a direct consequence of the war, and the abilities and shortcomings of certain individuals, have become known largely through the examination of official documents. Although these documents make mention of some of the problems of the children, it is done through the eyes of government officials. The following section includes the testimony of a teacher, as well as two former evacuees, all of whom were evacuated to residential special schools at some time during the war.

The children

When Jessica Young first saw Peckforton Castle she thought it was like a fairy-tale palace, all glistening pink stone.[60] Jessica remembers life there with fondness, but acknowledges that it was not such a positive experience for all the children, and that discipline was strict. After a group of ten-year-old runaways had been brought back to the castle, they complained that it was more like a prison. In order to show them what a real prison might be like, they were confined to their beds for two days with only bread and water. In the beginning punishment could also have been in the form of smacking, but, after a child with brittle bones was smacked and suffered a broken arm, other forms of punishment had to be used instead. Swearing, for example, was punished by biting on carbolic soap. The slipper was also used. Jessica also remembers that not enough allowance was made for 'spastics' being clumsy; jerky movements meant that they could not write properly with a pen.

Despite these negative memories, Jessica has many positive ones of life at the castle. On arrival all the girls were given a pretty flower mug that had been made by a local potter. There were many festivals and Christmas parties, and visits from American and Polish forces stationed nearby. Jessica still has the china doll she received from them at Christmas 1943. On Sundays the Americans arrived in jeeps bringing chocolate-flavoured ice cream in tall round tins kept in cold boxes. They also brought chewing gum, but the girls were not allowed to keep it because it was not 'ladylike'. Other visitors to the castle were entertainers from the radio. Nellie and Violet Carson visited once and both sang to the girls; Nellie with her big bass and Violet on the grand piano. Also, Uncles Bill, Arthur and Mac from the *Happy Hour* radio programme came to visit.

Some mothers were allowed to live at the castle, but could see their daughters only at weekends, like any other mother (although, in reality most mothers could not afford to visit every weekend). Commandants enjoyed more autonomy during the war though, and in 1941 Jessie Thomas was able to use her discretion in allowing a seven-year-old girl and her mother to live at the castle. The mother had answered an advertisement for a House Mother Assistant, and, when Jessie Thomas found out that she had a daughter who had not been accepted by any other school before because of the two braces on her legs, she agreed to accept her at the castle.

The girls at Peckforton Castle suffered from a variety of disabilities, including those caused by polio, and some that were congenital, such as deformed backs. Some were 'spastics', others had limbs missing. Jessica remembers several girls whose health had improved through being at the castle. One in particular had suffered from hip problems from birth, and couldn't walk far without pain. The hospital at Oswestry, which was mainly treating wounded soldiers at the time, agreed to operate on the girl and she was cured (and went on to become a nurse). Another hospital, at Roehampton, had an artificial limb centre and, on more than one occasion, supplied limbs to the girls. Jessica suffered through having rheumatic fever, although she didn't know that when she was first evacuated (to Broadreeds). She says, 'When I arrived, the other children asked if I was a heart case or a cripple. I didn't know but discovered that, through having Rheumatic Heart Fever, I was a heart case.'[61]

By far the biggest problem suffered by evacuees, whether disabled or able-bodied, was homesickness. An insight into how this often manifested itself is provided by a former teacher responsible for a group of physically disabled boys evacuated from Liverpool city centre to premises in Fazakerley, on the outskirts of the city. He found that on arrival the boys fell into three different groups:

> First, there was the timid child who seemed terribly afraid to move away from the haven of his bed. There he sat, his belongings on one side, his respirator on the other, a pathetic little figure. He sat on, undisturbed by movement around him, and only roused to action when definitely called upon to perform some task. As the days passed his emotional stress became greater and it was difficult to deal with him. Missing the security of his home and the close relationship of his family, he suffered very badly from home sickness. With the approach of visiting day his excitement grew until he could not settle down to work. He lived in this state of nervous tension until his visitors had departed and then he slumped. Feeling himself deserted by those he loved, his outlook became darkened and he was almost inconsolable. This condition lasted until eventually he persuaded his parents to take him home.[62]

The second group regarded the experience as an unexpected day's holiday, but then they were disappointed at having to sleep at school. Most of these went home on visiting day, whilst others lost their holiday spirit but had no desire to return to the deserted streets. The third group provided the most upheaval and were the most difficult to deal with. Most were from 'slum' homes and had probably not had a holiday before. They enjoyed the new freedom of the countryside but disturbed everyone else with their raised voices and free rein on their impulses. One month after their arrival, the remaining children moved to Llangollen, to a large country house which had been prepared for seventy PD children.

Whilst it is true that many disabled children benefited from being evacuated together with their friends and teachers, it is also true that there was a certain amount of movement with regard to individual children. Despite the best efforts of those responsible for the more severely physically disabled children, for example, it was not always possible to keep them in the residential special schools. The main reason for this was inadequate facilities, but there were also other concerns. Sometimes, their health would worsen, as in the case of two brothers evacuated to a PD camp at Bowleaze, near Weymouth. Both boys had progressive muscular dystrophy and eventually, when they could no longer help themselves, they were moved to hospital.[63] When a child suffered a double defect, the problem that could be helped most would take priority. For example, an eleven-year-old girl suffering from mild spastic paraplegia, at a school in Dorset, was given wedges for her shoes and then transferred to an MD party.[64] Sometimes children were admitted for the purpose of a short stay. A girl was admitted to the same school suffering from malnutrition and furunculosis (boils). She soon gained weight and, as her general health was good, she was discharged.[65] However, such cases were rare.

Children were also moved on when they reached school-leaving age. A sixteen-year-old girl at the school in Dorset suffered from osteitis fibrosa cystica and had a bowing of her left humerus and shortening of her right leg. As her hands were normal, it was arranged that she should be admitted to an adult centre for training in needlework.[66] Another girl, who was incontinent and could not walk, and whose mother was unable to care for her at home, was deemed fit only for an institution. Her case was referred to Public Assistance.[67]

In some schools, leisure activities were arranged for the children. A holiday camp for physically disabled boys in West Sussex had a large swimming pool in the grounds where some of the children suffering from orthopaedic or infantile paralysis had learned to swim. One boy, who could not even stand with support, had become one of the best swimmers.[68] Sometimes, the children were also encouraged to participate in local activities with able-bodied children and, in many areas, the locals made up for the lack of entertainment at the schools. At a holiday camp in Somerset, owing to the bad feeling between some of the staff, the children's leisure activities were limited to knitting, dancing and singing. However, the local vicar was very helpful and invited them to special services and talks (many of the children had not been to church before). The children were provided with free tickets by the local cinema, and the locals had promised them special treats at Christmas.[69]

On the whole, those local to the residential special schools regarded the disabled evacuees with compassion and treated them with generosity. At the school in Oakham, for example, the boys were sent a £5 gift from the boy scouts group of a nearby public school, in order to purchase some uniforms.[70] A former evacuee, Ken Giles, who suffered from hemiplegia (paralysis or weakness on one side of the body), explains why he thinks that the disabled evacuees were treated well by the local population:

> When we left the camp we tended to do so in groups. I cannot recall any adverse reaction to us as evacuees, nor as cripples. You must bear in mind that because we were housed at the holiday camp we were not forced into people's private homes; and the locals were used to the camp being occupied by outsiders because that is its function. So there were no tensions arising from invading other people's territories, and our being at the camp might perhaps have assisted the local economy.[71]

Ken Giles's view that disabled children were regarded favourably is supported by correspondence in the local newspaper in Whitchurch, to where both disabled and able-bodied children were evacuated at the beginning of the war. The following case study highlights the differences in local reaction to the two groups of children. It also provides a detailed account of the special school's evacuation to Cloverley Hall, a large country house in Shropshire. In essence the study brings together elements of each section of this chapter: location; conditions; staff; disruption; and the children's experiences.

Case study: the Lancasterian Special School

This case study has been built primarily on information and sources provided by individuals connected in some way to the Lancasterian special school in Manchester. An ex-evacuee,[72] who has not actually produced any personal recollections himself, has provided much of the material, including a handbook of information on the scheme for the evacuation of school

2 Ken Giles in 1940, aged ten

children from Manchester; a report by the School Medical Officer on the proposed evacuation of the Lancasterian school to Cloverley Hall; and an (unpublished) article written by another ex-evacuee.[73] Other useful sources have been obtained from someone who was not evacuated herself (she attended the school some years after the end of the war) but was secretary of the Old Scholars Newsletter for a while until its demise in 1999.[74] These include a History of Education essay from 1929, entitled 'The History of the Lancasterian School' and the Minutes of the Old Scholars meetings from 1933 onwards. A visit to the Lancasterian school itself yielded a CSE History Project, written by Stephen Edwards in 1980. Information gleaned from this includes letters written to the Old Scholars Newsletter (most of which have since been destroyed) during the war, by two ex-evacuees from the Lancasterian school.[75] Other information comes from a local newspaper, *The Whitchurch Herald*, and from *Farewell to Manchester*, a book of personal reminiscences including those of another ex-evacuee, who relates his experiences at Cloverley Hall.[76]

History of the school

The Lancasterian School obtained its name from Joseph Lancaster, the eighteenth-century schoolmaster and philanthropist. His aim was to educate as many poor children as possible, and so he began to raise subscriptions, many of which came from fellow Quakers, to help pay for those who could not afford the fee at his schools, the first of which opened in Southwark in 1798. At first he taught himself and was aided by an assistant, but his numbers grew so rapidly that he could no longer manage. He therefore adopted the 'monitorial system', by which older children (monitors) taught the younger ones, thereby dispensing with teachers or assistants, and so cutting costs.[77]

Lancaster's school in Manchester opened in Lever Street in 1809 or 1810 (records do not correspond as to the actual year) and for many years it was the only school of its kind in that area. However, in 1880, with numbers diminishing because of several rival schools, the management of the Lancasterian school was transferred to the Board of Education, with the premises being sold to them five years later. In 1913 the school was relocated to New Cross, where it remained virtually unchanged until 1917, when it became the Lancasterian School for Cripples.

Despite the school bearing his name, Joseph Lancaster would never know that it would be as successful as the first school for cripples, as it had been for being one of the first free schools. In the early twentieth century a group of women had started classes for crippled schoolchildren and named it the Santa Fina School, after the patron saint of cripples. In 1913, the school was taken over by the Board of Education and in 1917 it was transferred to the New Cross building, where the Santa Fina name was dropped.

In 1917 the school catered for 68 scholars, but within two years the number had doubled. Six members of staff had been added as well as a masseuse, which meant that the children no longer had to travel to hospital to receive massage treatment. In the following years additions to the staff included a gymnast who helped to train and strengthen the children by means of remedial exercise, more masseuses, cooks and nurse attendants. Physicians and surgeons of various hospitals were available, should treatment or operations become necessary.

The aim of the school had always been to make the children capable of maintaining themselves and, in order to help them achieve this, various trade classes were introduced. For the boys there were bookbinding, woodwork, metalwork and leatherwork. For the girls, needlework, machining, dressmaking and cookery lessons. For both boys and girls who wished to take up office work, shorthand, typewriting and special correspondence courses were available. At the age of sixteen, the children were expected to enter into employment.

Preparation for evacuation

By the time war broke out in 1939 the Lancasterian School was well established. The head teacher at the time was Miss Grace Nicholls, a forceful woman who went to great lengths to ensure that her pupils found appropriate employment. It was largely due to her efforts that the school had such a good reputation, and all the people who have responded to enquiries about the school have spoken in glowing terms about her work. In a letter to the Old Scholars newsletter in 1939, the old scholar Peter Ganky said 'Miss Nicholls' regime was one long period of success'.[78] Miss Nicholls had been with the school since 1915, in its days as the Santa Fina School, and became head teacher in 1917. Reference is made to her by Travis Crosby, who says that she 'held together a willing, happy, hardworking team of domestics, nurses and teachers'.[79] In 1933 she became auditor for the Executive Committee of the Old Scholars Association (formerly the Old Scholars Guild). The committee's main purpose was to conduct the arrangements of future meetings of the association and to arrange annual outings. According to the minutes of the meetings, one such outing was made to the residence of Miss Nicholls' brother, Mr Christopher Nicholls, at Cloverley Hall, near Whitchurch in Shropshire. On 22 June 1935 a party of ex-scholars were conveyed, in cars arranged by Mr Nicholls, to the Old Jack Inn at Calverhall, the small village in which the Hall was situated.[80] After a lunch at the inn, everyone made their way to the Hall where their hosts, Mr Nicholls and his wife, had arranged for the playing of bowls and tennis, and where they could relax in the grounds and by the boating lake. The day was deemed a great success and was repeated the following year.

Cloverley Hall was built in 1868, by the Liverpool banker John Pemberton Hayward. On his death, the house passed to his nephew who, being child-less, left it to distant relatives who leased it out, eventually to Mr Nicholls.[81] Although there is no solid evidence, it is not unreasonable to deduce that the close relationship between the school and Cloverley Hall, through brother and sister, was the reason behind the school's proposed evacuation there should war break out. However, the Hall first had to be checked out by the Board of Education, and on 9 May 1939 the school medical officer, along with Miss Nicholls, visited the premises for an inspection. The following information is taken from the medical officer's report.[82]

The stables, garage and loft were to be used as dormitories, as they were all at ground level. The older boys were to use the garage, which could house three rows of beds with fifteen in each row. There was suitable lavatory accommodation at one end and a room at the other end, in which several wash-bowls could be fitted. A boiler for heating water was in the adjoining harness room. There was also another room adjacent to the garage with a basin and hot and cold running water, which could be used by a nurse for the purpose of dressing minor ailments etc. Another room adjacent to this would accommodate four beds and could be used as an isolation room. There was room in the stables to accommodate about thirty children, and it was proposed that they be used for kindergarten boys and girls, and for slightly older girls. The stables were in excellent condition, being well lighted and ventilated. The loft was also well lighted and ventilated, and had an open roof fitted with electric lights. There was a WC at one end and, if a suitable staircase could be fitted (the current one was spiral and narrow and so too dangerous), there would be access to a room on the ground floor which could be converted to use as a lavatory. Under this room was an old brew house which, if the above floor was concreted, could be used as an air raid shelter. It was deemed suitable for approximately fifty girls. The maximum number of children that could be accommodated, therefore, was 125. The number of children whose parents had indicated a desire for them to be evacuated, however, was 137. It had been suggested that forty children could be housed in billets in Calverhall village, around one mile from the Hall, and obtain their schooling at the small local school, which was not currently in use. The three inspectors visited the school and found it suitable. It had two school rooms plus lavatories. The children selected for billeting would be the less severe type of cripple who had some degree of independence.

Within the Hall itself were eight or nine rooms which could be used as bed-rooms for teachers and nurses, provided that, in some cases, two shared the same room. All needed cleaning thoroughly, they would need furnishing, and some had no artificial lighting. All these problems could be easily remedied, however, and most had fireplaces, which would be useful in the winter. There was a bathroom on the same floor and lavatories could be easily reached on the floor below. Mr Nicholls suggested that all staff were welcome to use the servants' sitting room on the ground floor, but it would have to be used as a staff dining room also. The servants' dining room could be used for the children's meals, which could be prepared in the large kitchen, which contained a scullery, several larders and an Esse stove, the latter of which would have to be supplemented owing to the large numbers involved. Adaptations would also be needed in the large laundry, which was to be used as a bathing area for the children. Although there were seven fitted tubs, they were situated too high and so a board would need to be attached on which the children could sit while bathing.

The main problem for the children would be where they could carry on their schooling. It was proposed that the billiard room, once the table had been removed, could accommodate two classes. There were also two rooms above the laundry, both with no artificial lighting, one of which would need to be used as a massage room. Apart from this limited space there were the grounds although, as these was not practicable in bad weather, it was suggested that the garage be used if the beds could be piled up at one side. With regards to the number of staff, all except one of Miss Nicholls's colleagues were prepared to go. However, as the school would now be a residential school and the children would need to be supervised outside of school hours, two extra teachers and two nurses would be needed. There was also a vacancy for a good cook for the school, as the current one was not prepared to leave Manchester.

This inspection took place around four months before the war, and shows just how much preparation was being made for the welfare of the children in the event of war. Similar preparations were also being made for the able-bodied children of Manchester. In March a handbook had been produced for 'head teachers and other responsible persons', in which detailed information was given regarding the extensive planning.[83] This included the various meetings which were to be held between parents and teachers, in order that everyone should understand what evacuation entailed. The process of evacuation has already been discussed and need not be repeated here. However, the Manchester handbook is useful for highlighting any possible differences between the children of the Lancasterian School and the able-bodied children. The handbook contains specific questions and answers, which were devised to help the parents (of able-bodied) to decide if they should allow their children to go.

Where would we take them? Parents of able-bodied children would not normally be told specific details about where their children would be, so in order to be fair, the parents of disabled children evacuated in special schools would not be told the destination either.[84] Food arrangements for evacuation day were given, but no one knew if the children would be housed immediately on arrival or what conditions they would be living under. In reality, when a large group of children was being evacuated to the same place it was difficult to keep the details from the parents. Such was the case with the Lancasterian School: the parents knew where their offspring were going, and would know some details of their living arrangements.

How long would they stay away? No one knew the answer to this and no one could foresee that many children, whether disabled or not, would either return home before the war ended or would come and go as the status of the war changed. The handbook stated that it would be 'for some weeks at least'. Many of those evacuated to Cloverley Hall, like children all over the country, were away for nearly six years.

What would they do? Education was a prime concern for all children. The handbook explained that some arrangements would be makeshift. The realities of coping with educational and recreational needs during the war have already been discussed. For the children of Cloverley Hall, arrangements were made before arriving.

What would happen if they were ill? A proportion of school nurses and doctors employed by Manchester City Council would be sent out with the able-bodied children. Cloverley Hall would have its own nurses, and other medical staff would be available where required.

If you have more than one child would all the children in the family be kept together? The handbook stated that all children would be kept together and that the younger ones would go to the school attended by the eldest, or vice versa. There is no record of siblings residing at Cloverley Hall at the same time.

Would they have to pay railway fares out into the country? The government paid the expenses of all children evacuated on the government scheme, including those to Cloverley Hall.

Knowing where their child would be going, and the fact that they would be housed with their own teachers and school friends, must have been a huge relief for the parents of those taken to Cloverley Hall. The children too, must have benefited from knowing, as much as was possible to know, what lay in store for them. Margaret Tippey wrote of her expectations: 'We expected lessons would be given in entirely different surroundings, among fields in which cattle quietly graze and tall buildings do not hide away the sky.'[85]

Ten-year-old Frank Gee, who had returned early from his holiday on the Isle of Man after war broke out, remembers people on the boat being afraid of being torpedoed. Before going on holiday he, and the others at the Lancasterian School, had been issued with their 'war equipment'. He writes: 'Each child at school had been provided with a small light-green rucksack which had an extra compartment to house their gas mask. The child's name was printed on the top of the gas mask protuberance.'[86]

The evacuation of the Lancasterian Special School

On 2 September 1939 the children of the Lancasterian Special School were evacuated to Cloverley Hall. Stanley Cole remembers the day, and his statement is an example of how things looked to a fourteen-year-old, without being aware of just how much preparation had gone into the event:

> I was picked up outside my own front door and helped into a single-decker bus. Neighbours were out because there had never been a bus in our road before. It was hot and sunny when we arrived. The school staff sorted out where everyone would eat and sleep while we sat around on the grass in beautifully laid out

gardens. Everything had been done in a hurry because the authorities had been unprepared for an event like this, so everything was improvised.[87]

Margaret Tippey also remembers that day. She specifically remembers singing songs on the lawn at Cloverley Hall, and lining up waiting to be allocated to a billet in the village (the inspectors' proposals had been agreed and some of the less severely disabled were billeted in the village of Calverhall). Frank Gee was another who was billeted out, although he had initially been among those sent to the Hall. He says:

> Two weeks later my mother turned up unexpectedly at Cloverley Hall to find out how I was faring. She did not like my sleeping arrangements, and further found that I had lice in my hair for the first time in my life. She promptly took me home with her after telling Miss Nicholls that I must be billeted out or I could not return.[88]

A billet was found in nearby Willeston and Frank returned two weeks later. Every school day he was taken to the Hall by Mr Nicholls's chauffeur for his school lessons.

One day each month the children's parents would visit them at the Hall, usually by coach arranged by Frank Gee's mother.[89] There were occasional visits home to Manchester but, on the whole, the children's lives revolved around the Hall and the nearby villages. Margaret Tippey wrote in 1940:

> We have lovely times together, going for walks, collecting leaves or other interesting little things to bring back and write about. Then we organise impromptu concerts in the evenings. Our days are not dull for there is always something new to see and learn about, and at night when we are all in our beds in our respective dorms, we have great fun talking over the events of the day.[90]

Some events arranged for the children were reported in the local newspaper, the *Whitchurch Herald*. For example, Sunday 10 February 1940 was Parents' Sunday at the Hall, and a concert was put on for 160 children, parents and friends.[91] The following December the children were visited by a number of distinguished guests including the Lord Mayor and Lady Mayoress of Manchester. In preparation for the visit, the children made Christmas decorations and decorated the Hall themselves.[92] Then, on Christmas Eve a party was held at the Hall, attended by local entertainers, one of who dressed as Santa and distributed presents of books, watches and toys.[93]

Kenneth Sharman, who was seven years old when he was evacuated to the Hall, recalls gardening and woodwork in the evenings and games of football and cricket with 'village lads' at the weekends.[94] Stanley Cole remembers the

Guide and Scout groups that were set up, and the occasional trip to nearby Market Drayton. As a special treat, the children were allowed to watch the hunt assemble outside the Hall's main entrance and 'watch them ride away in splendour to hunt the local fox'.[95] There were trips to the cinema in Whitchurch, and Stanley particularly remembers watching *Pygmalion* after catching the bus from the village and 'braving the mutterings of the villagers for taking up their seats'.[96]

Attitudes towards the children

This last reference suggests that some of the local inhabitants were resentful of the children invading their community but, overall, attitudes towards the children at Cloverley Hall have been difficult to ascertain. Some insight has been gleaned from articles and 'letters to the editor' in the local press; most, however, comes from the ex-evacuees themselves. Frank Gee remembers being subjected to various 'pranks' by the local children. On one occasion he was put into a hessian sack and tied up high to a beam in the hay-loft. Another time a young farm-hand put a large toad in his mouth and held his mouth shut.[97] These experiences appear to have done no lasting damage, however, and Frank recalls his days as an evacuee with fondness.

Attitudes towards evacuees in general were often reported in the local press, especially at the beginning of the war (as the war progressed, newspapers were usually taken up with military campaigns or with recording the deaths or missing in action, of those who lived locally). The following letter to the editor of the *Whitchurch Herald* relates to the able-bodied evacuees who had arrived the previous week:

> Poverty is one thing, and filthy vermin and squalor are another. And we say without fear or favour, that it was an insulting and disgusting thing to transplant poor little helpless children, in some cases in rags and tatters, and in others alive with parasites, into the decent, respectable homes in a district like this and expect them to be re-clothed (as many of them had to be), without warning and without recompense, and without any regard whatsoever for the fitness of things, from any point of view.[98]

On 29 September 1939 the arrival of the children from the Lancasterian School was recorded, and two days later the same newspaper highlighted the fact that the Whitchurch Rotary Club had arranged entertainment at the Hall 'for the benefit of the little folks who are housed therein'.[99] Close examination of all copies of the *Whitchurch Herald* during 1939–45 has shown that, although there were only occasional references made to the children at the Hall, there was never anything of a negative context. On 9 February 1940, however, another letter to the editor appeared, again referring to the able-bodied evacuees. The author wrote that during the first two or three months of the war much was said about their lack of cleanliness, but this had died down after a teacher had given a polite but firm reply. Now, though, there was another furore because too much water was being used in the area. The author finished by asking 'Have the Lancashire evacuees changed their outlook on cleanliness, and decided to emulate the purity of Salopian children?'[100] It is difficult to ascertain whether attitudes such as this were commonplace or in a minority.

In the latter stages of the war several acts of kindness by the locals towards the children at Cloverley Hall were reported. For example, for at least two years the local coach company treated the children to a visit to the cinema, bearing the cost of both transport and the cinema tickets.[101] On 21 January 1944 the same newspaper reported that a Christmas party had been held for (able-bodied) evacuees in Whitchurch.[102] However, this was funded by the Lord Mayor of London's Air Raid Distress Fund, which obtained donations from Canada on a scheme to provide Christmas parties for children who had either been evacuated, or continued to live in a dangerous area. There were no reports of any such activities arranged by the local population.

On 4 July 1945 the children of Cloverley Hall, along with their classmates who were billeted locally, returned home to Manchester, not to its previous location in New Cross but to its new home in Cavendish Road (since renamed Elizabeth Slinger Road after the head teacher who took over when Miss Nicholls retired in 1948). The kindness shown to the children by the local population in Shropshire, as opposed to the attitudes of some of them towards other evacuees in the area, has been highlighted by references made in the *Whitchurch Herald* as well as by personal testimony. Although this school was exceptional, in the way it was arranged informally by brother and sister and then ratified and taken over by the government, the reasons for the children's positive experiences were similar to those of other disabled evacuees, in that that they were in their own environment for most of the time, and were not seen by the local villagers as much as the able-bodied evacuees. Indeed, negative recollections of the children of the Lancasterian School have been few. Kenneth Sharman says that there were some slight grievances for the first few weeks but after that 'we settled down to what seemed to me one long holiday'.[103] Margaret Tippey, who was billeted out but attended Cloverley Hall for her schooling, wasn't so impressed with winter conditions in the country. In Manchester she didn't have to go to school if it was foggy and the bus didn't turn up, whereas in Shropshire she had to walk across the fields to the Hall, fog or no fog.[104] Although it is impossible to generalise about their feelings on their evacuation experiences, Margaret Tippey perhaps sums it up best for the majority of the children: 'Though we love Shropshire with its quiet fields and friendly people, we all long for the day when it will be possible to rejoin our families, if only amid the smoke and grime of noisy, industrial Manchester.'[105]

Conclusion

The safety of disabled evacuees depended largely on the availability of premises in which to accommodate them. In this respect, they were at a disadvantage compared to the able-bodied children for whom individual billets were easier to find. Another disadvantage the disabled children had was the way in which they were perceived by some of those who had a say in where the children were to be accommodated. Cecil Maudslay, Colonel ffennell and Sir Edward Howarth were not alone in their reluctance to regard all children as equal. At a time when eugenicist ideals were widespread amongst the upper echelons of society, mentally disabled children in particular were sometimes subjected to prejudicial treatment.[106] However, owing to the efforts of others within the government, and the opinions (whether real or perceived) of the general public, fatalities were minimal and the vast majority of disabled evacuees remained safe.

Once the children had been installed in their new residential schools, whether in large houses, camps or hotels, their personal welfare was the responsibility of the commandant, and the degree of success that was achieved depended largely on that individual's personality, competence and managerial skills. As highlighted in this chapter, there was an enormous amount of stress on some teachers. Their lives had been subject to much upheaval and not everyone could cope with the pressure. Having said that, there were many unsung heroes among the teaching staff, whose compassion and abilities ensured that the children remained happy and safe. The work of the majority of these teachers went unrecognised, although in 1941 Jessie Thomas received an MBE for her services to disabled children.

Despite the efforts of the teachers, it was inevitable that previous standards of education could not be maintained throughout the war. In this respect physically disabled children were at a disadvantage. The majority of hotels and houses were not practicable for housing children with mobility problems, and lessons usually had to be taken where access allowed. Also, owing to the nature of their disabilities, getting to and from the air raid shelters (or the equivalent) took longer and so caused more disruption. Of course, conditions within all types of schools varied. In the long term, the 'practice run' of 1938 had not been as useful

3 HMI James Lumsden

as was expected. However, many of the problems that occurred were relatively minor and could be solved by one of the visiting inspectors. Unfortunately, the HMIs were not always successful in improving conditions for the children, as evidenced by the example of Besford Court. The reports of the HMIs, and of James Lumsden in particular, have yielded much information for this chapter.

For many schools, there are no personal reminiscences from which to gain a balanced view, and official reports are the only available documentation. However, as a result of the testimony of a number of teachers and former evacuees, as well as those connected to the Lancasterian Special School, it has been possible to gain a deeper insight into a number of residential special schools at different stages of the war.

This chapter includes many examples, most of which contain exceptional opinions and/or circumstances. It should be noted that, although such extremes did exist, many residential special schools, and the equivalent schools for the able-bodied, managed to operate, if not efficiently, then at least adequately.

Notes

1 For an approximation of the figures involved see Titmuss, *Problems of Social Policy*, pp. 242–5.
2 TNA, ED138/49. 'Evacuation of handicapped and very young children and their maintenance in the reception areas in special parties, nursery schools and nurseries', p. 3, from Sophia Weitzman's papers.
3 *Ibid.*
4 TNA, ED50/258, Ministry of Health to Board of Education, 8 July 1940.
5 'The Cripple Boy: Bomb Victim Who Had a Smile for Everyone', *Evening News*, 21 August 1940.
6 TNA, ED50/258, Bloomfield at Tenterden Camp to Eton at LCC, 28 August 1940.
7 TNA, ED50/258, Savage at LCC to Holmes at Board of Education, 30 August 1940.
8 TNA, ED50/258, Report of visit by Savage at LCC, sent to Holmes at Board of Education, 1 September 1940.
9 TNA, ED32/646, Report by HMI Burrows, 8 July 1941.
10 TNA, ED32/646, Ministry of Health to Board of Education, 15 September 1941.
11 N. Park, *Schooldays at Chatsworth: A Personal Memoir of the War Years* (Quick & Co., 1986), pp. 35–7.
12 LMA, LCC/EO/WAR/2/63, Maudslay at Board of Education to Minister of Health, 22 May 1940.
13 LMA, LCC/EO/WAR/2/63, documents relating to accommodation for special parties, 1940.
14 LMA, LCC/EO/WAR/2/63, minutes of meeting at Education Officers' department, 6 August 1940.
15 TNA, ED32/642, Eton at the Education Officers' department of the LCC, repeating ffennell's words in a letter to the Secretary of the Board of Education (Medical Department), 10 February 1941.
16 TNA, ED32/642, Lowndes to Strong at the Board of Education, 19 February 1941.
17 TNA, ED32/642, ffennell to Savage, 5 June 1941.
18 The NCC had been set up under the Camps Act 1939 for the purpose of providing a number of camps for short-term use by school parties and holiday-makers. In the event of war, they were to be used for refugees made homeless by bombing

raids. However, after the outbreak of war, accommodation for bombed-out refugees was not needed in the short term, and it was decided to use the camps for the purposes of the Government Evacuation Scheme.

19 TNA, ED32/666, Report by Dr Bywaters, 15 October 1942.
20 *Herald (for Farnham, Haslemere and Hindhead)* and *Alton Mail*, 8 July 1944.
21 TNA, ED32/666, HMI Waites to Hambledon Council, 21 August 1944.
22 Avery, *The Best Type of Girl*, p. 345.
23 LMA, LCC/EO/WAR/2/21, Conference for Officers of the Special Services Branch of LCC's Education Department, 22 September 1939.
24 TNA, ED50/188, Lumsden's report on Peckforton Castle, 7 January 1941.
25 TNA, ED32/871, Lumsden's reports on the One Oak Parish Residential School in Ilkley, Yorkshire, 1941–44.
26 TNA, ED50/188, Lumsden's report on the Riviera Hotel near Weymouth, 29 and 30 November 1939.
27 TNA, ED50/188, Lumsden's report on the Rustingdon Lido Holiday Club, Littlehampton, West Sussex, 3 November 1939.
28 TNA, ED50/188, Lumsden's report on the Corton Beach Holiday Camp, East Sussex, 9 and 10 November 1939.
29 TNA, ED32/334, HMI reports of Ledbury Park, Herefordshire, 4 and 12 March 1942.
30 Established in 1919, the NCSS became the largest umbrella body for the voluntary and community sector in England. In 1980 it changed its name to the National Council for Voluntary Organisations (NCVO).
31 TNA, ED50/188, Lumsden's report of Gileston School Camp at St Athan, Glamorgan, 16 November 1939.
32 TNA, ED32/188, Lumsden's report of Sand Bay Holiday Camp, Axbridge, Somerset, 29 November 1939.
33 TNA, ED32/1020, Lumsden's report of the Yorkshire residential school for the blind, York, 16 March 1939.
34 *Ibid.*
35 TNA, ED32/1020, Lumsden's report of the Yorkshire Residential School for the Blind, York, 1 December 1943.
36 LMA, LCC/EO/WAR/2/21, Conference for officers of the Special Services Branch of LCC's Education department, 22 September 1939.
37 TNA, ED32/347, HMI report of Eastcourt House Residential School at Crudwell, Wiltshire, 2 March 1943.
38 TNA, ED50/11, HMI reports of St Dominic's RC Open-Air School in Hambledon, Surrey, 3 July 1940; 18 June 1942; 23 June 1943; 22 May 1944; 30 July 1945.
39 TNA, ED32/909, Report by Lumsden and Dr Henderson of Delamere Fresh-Air Home and School for Jewish Children, 27 November 1941; 26 January 1940; and 27 November 1941.

40 TNA, ED50/188, Lumsden's report of Birkdale Refuge Holiday Camp in Southport, Lancashire, 8 December 1939.

41 TNA, ED32/1189, Report by Dr Bywaters of Horsley Green Camp Council Residential School in Stokenchurch, Buckinghamshire, 14 June 1940.

42 TNA, ED32/235, National Union of Teachers to Board of Education, 27 September 1940.

43 TNA, ED32/235, HMI report of Chalfont St Peter Colony for Epileptic Children, Buckinghamshire, 23 September 1941.

44 TNA, ED32/264, Lumsden's report of Royal West of England Residential School for the Deaf, Exeter, 21 September 1943.

45 TNA, ED32/663, Report by Dr Underwood of Banstead Residential School for Evacuated Deaf and Partially-Deaf children in Surrey, 30 October 1941.

46 LMA, LCC/EO/WAR/2/28, HMI reports of Horsely Green Camp Council Residential School in Stokenchurch, Buckinghamshire, May 1941 and June 1942.

47 TNA, ED32/827, Lumsden's report of Besford Court Roman Catholic Special School for MD Children in Worcester, 23 September 1941.

48 TNA, ED32/827, Lumsden's report of Besford Court, 10 March 1942.

49 Ibid.

50 TNA, ED32/827, Lumsden's report of Besford Court, 27 January 1943.

51 TNA, ED32/827, Report on Besford Court by Miss Darwin from the Board of Control, 8 February 1944.

52 See chapter 5 for how Besford Court fared after the war.

53 Samways, We Think You Ought to Go, p. 20.

54 TNA, ED32/909, Lumsden's report of the Delamere Fresh-Air Home and School for Jewish Children, 26 January 1940.

55 TNA, ED32/909, Lumsden's report of Delamere, 27 November 1941.

56 TNA, ED33/157, HMI report of Springhill Private School for Deaf Boys in Northampton, 18 February 1943.

57 LMA, LCC/EO/WAR/2/28, HMI report of Nyetimber Lido PD Camp, 21 October 1941.

58 LMA, LCC/EO/WAR/2/28, HMI reports of Deanscroft special school, Oakham, 7 October 1941.

59 TNA, ED32/2187, Annual report of the Royal School for the Deaf in Derby, y/e 31 March 1944.

60 J. Young, I Lived in a Castle (privately printed, 1990), p. 45.

61 Ibid., p. 38.

62 O. A. Roberts, Special Schools Journal, February 1940, pp. 10–13.

63 LMA, LCC/EO/WAR/2/28, HMI report of the Riviera PD Camp at Bowleaze, Weymouth, 29 March 1944.

64 LMA, LCC/EO/WAR/2/28, HMI report of Buckshaw House in Sherborne, Dorset, 26 August 1943.

65 LMA, LCC/EO/WAR/2/28, HMI report of Buckshaw House, 1 February 1944.

66 LMA, LCC/EO/WAR/2/28, HMI report of Buckhsaw House, 7 October 1942.

67 LMA, LCC/EO/WAR/2/28, HMI report of Buckshaw House, 26 March 1941.

68 LMA, LCC/EO/WAR/2/28, HMI report of Rustington Lido Camp for PD boys, West Sussex, 25 June 1941.

69 TNA, ED50/188, Lumsden's report of Sand Bay Holiday Camp, Axbridge, Somerset, 29 November 1939.

70 LMA, LCC/EO/WAR/2/28, HMI report of Deanscroft Special School, Oakham, 23 April 1941. The £5 came from Uppingham Public School.

71 Letter from Ken Giles to author, 18 August 2005, regarding the holiday camp at Broadreeds.

72 Ernie Jones.

73 Frank Gee.

74 Sheila Meredith.

75 Kenneth Sharman and Margaret Tippey.

76 S. Cole, 'We Slept on Trestle Beds on a Concrete Floor', in A. Jones (ed.), *Farewell to Manchester: The Story of the 1939 Evacuation* (Didsbury: Didsbury Press, 1989), pp. 85–6.

77 M. Black, 'The History of the Lancasterian School, Manchester' (unpublished History of Education Essay, 1929), p. 1.

78 S. Edwards, 'The History of the Lancasterian School, 1908–1969' (unpublished CSE History Project, Lancasterian School, 1980), p. 2. Some oral evidence has come via Sheila Meredith, an ex-scholar of the school who was secretary of the Old Scholars Newsletter.

79 T. L. Crosby, *The Impact of Civilian Evacuation in the Second World War* (London: Croom Helm, 1986), p. 73.

80 'Minutes of the Old Scholars – meetings from June 1933 onwards', 29 June 1935 (unpublished document, courtesy of Sheila Meredith).

81 'Visit to Cloverley Hall' (private video, courtesy of Sheila Meredith), 1991.

82 'Memorandum to the Director: Proposed evacuation of Lancasterian P.D. school children to Cloverley Hall, Shropshire' (unpublished document, courtesy of Ernie Jones), 15 May 1939.

83 Ministry of Health, *Air Raid Precautions: Evacuation* (London: HMSO, 1939).

84 LMA, LCC/EO/WAR/1/1, Housing Committee Papers, 1938.

85 Edwards, 'The History of the Lancasterian School', p. 2.

86 F. Gee, 'Evacuation Experiences' (unpublished article, courtesy of Ernie Jones).

87 Cole, 'We Slept on Trestle Beds on a Concrete Floor', pp. 85–6.

88 Gee, 'Evacuation Experiences'.

89 *Ibid.*

90 Edwards, 'The History of the Lancasterian School', p. 3.

91 'Calverhall', *Whitchurch Herald*, 15 March 1940, p. 3.

92 'Lord Mayor of Manchester Visits Cloverley Hall', *Whitchurch Herald*, 19 December 1941, p. 3.

93   'Evacuees' Christmas Party', *Whitchurch Herald*, 29 December 1939, p. 4.

94   Edwards, 'The History of the Lancasterian School', p. 4.

95   Cole, 'We Slept on Trestle Beds on a Concrete Floor', pp. 85–6.

96   *Ibid.*

97   Gee, 'Evacuation Experiences'.

98   The Editor, 'How Are We Shaping?', *Whitchurch Herald*, 8 September 1939, p. 2.

99   'Entertainments at Adderley and Cloverley', *Whitchurch Herald*, 1 December 1939, p. 3.

100 Letter to the Editor from G.E.R., 'Some Posers', *Whitchurch Herald*, 9 February 1940, p. 4.

101 'Crippled Children's Outing', *Whitchurch Herald*, 7 January 1944, p. 4, and 'Cloverley', *Whitchurch Herald*, 5 January 1945, p. 3.

102 'Evacuees Entertained at Whitchurch', *Whitchurch Herald*, 21 January 1944, pp. 2–6.

103 Edwards, 'The History of the Lancasterian School', p. 4.

104 *Ibid.*, p. 5.

105 *Ibid.*, p. 6.

106 For an explanation of eugenicist ideals see D. J. Kevles, *In the Name of Eugenics: Genetics and the Uses of Human Heredity* (London: Penguin, 1986).

3

SPECIAL DAY SCHOOLS, HOSPITAL SCHOOLS AND THE ROLE OF CHARITIES

Special day schools

Special day schools in neutral and reception areas managed, on the whole, to carry on as normal during the war years, while in evacuating areas they were re-established as residential schools in safer areas, as has been discussed. In some cases, however, parents of both the disabled and the able-bodied were unwilling to allow their children to be evacuated, leaving the problem of where they could be educated. As all schools were closed in the evacuating areas, initially the children remained at home. In certain areas emergency schooling schemes were quickly and effectively organised but, for most, there was no form of education until December 1939. The expected bombing raids had failed to materialise and many parents who had allowed their children to be evacuated at the outbreak of war decided to bring them home, forcing the authorities to re-open some of the day schools. When the air raids began the schools closed; with the abatement of the raids they opened again. For many schools, this went on throughout the war, with the availability of day school education being dependent upon both the frequency of air raids and the availability of premises.

Education and the level of disruption
In many ways the fortunes of disabled children remaining in or returning to vulnerable areas followed those of the able-bodied in terms of educational opportunities. Both groups lost schools because they were taken over by essential wartime services, or because they were damaged or destroyed by air attacks, and both relied on the availability of premises and staff in order to continue their education. However, the fact that physically disabled children needed accommodation that was suitable for their special needs meant that they faced even more obstacles, and so much depended on the area in which

they were situated. For example, in Birmingham and Leeds, schools usually used their own, accessible premises with their own staff, but in London and Liverpool, which had suffered more bomb damage, classes had to be held in whichever school had free, and suitable, accommodation. Added to this was the fact that most of their equipment had been transferred to the residential special schools in reception areas.

From the outset the authorities in London were concerned about the possible educational and social deterioration of children if left to their own devices and, although school attendance was no longer enforceable after the outbreak of war, teachers were encouraged to use their initiative in schemes to persuade children to return to some kind of education.[1] At the end of September 1939 there were approximately three hundred teachers left in London. Some of them, wearing official armbands, wandered the streets near schools in order to find (able-bodied) children who were willing to return to school. They then visited their parents and, once permission was granted, the teachers resumed classes, in a school where possible or in a room lent by parents. The groups were small to begin with, as few as six, but then they grew as the teachers found new premises: churches, clubs and empty rooms on housing estates. These teachers were commended for their 'excellent pioneer work under difficult conditions'.[2]

By the end of 1940 school attendance became compulsory once again, and just how concerned the authorities had been as to the behaviour of children without a school to attend is evidenced in a report to the Chief Inspector of the LCC Education Committee:

> Some had not been to school since the outbreak of war. Some had jobs they had to give up to go back to school. There were discipline problems. Some had formed street gangs looking for adventure. Some had slept for months in air-raid shelters and deteriorated in habits, manners and speech. Powers of concentration were seriously impaired. They were easily distracted, restless and noisy.[3]

The teachers of the disabled children returning to special day schools after a long absence also saw evidence of deterioration, especially in appearance and behaviour. It was noted by the HMIs that MDs were the worst offenders and the older children were worse than the younger. On the practical side it was proving difficult to obtain facilities and staff for swimming, games and physical education, domestic science, and trade instruction. It was also difficult to manage without the special facilities needed for washing and bathing. An LCC report of 1945, looking back on education in London schools during the war, noted how difficult it had been to re-establish practical and vocational instruction, which was so important in the education of older disabled children. Unlike schools for the able-bodied, these children and their teachers relied on specialist equipment, which had been destroyed or removed, and was irreplaceable in the short term.[4]

Emergency special schools in London had been set up later than those for able-bodied children, and so some children with only minor disabilities attended regular school. When the special schools eventually opened, the number of attendees grew steadily from an estimated 200 at the end of 1940, 757 in July 1941, to 1,000 at the end of 1941.[5] These figures were made up of children who had been left behind in the initial evacuation and those who had returned early from their evacuated schools. However, the number of returning disabled children was minimal compared to their able-bodied counterparts.

With the commencement of intensive air attacks, attendance in the day schools, which were usually situated in or just outside cities, inevitably fell. Regular school hours were 9.30am until noon, and 1.30pm until 3.30pm but the level of disruption to the children's education varied enormously. For example, at the Nottingham Road Special School in Bestwood, just a few miles north of the city of Nottingham, children missed many days of schooling, for a variety of reasons. At the outbreak of war the school was closed but a suitable centre in a 'safer' district was soon found. These centres were set up quite quickly and groups of children attended either a morning or an afternoon session. In all there were 14 such groups in Nottingham and the surrounding area. In April 1940 the Nottingham Road School re-opened, although only those children who were physically able to go to the shelters could return; the remainder stayed in the centres. The school tried to carry on as normal, with disruption depending on the level of air raid alerts. On 7 March 1941 the first alert was between 11.45am and 1.10pm, so the children had their dinners in the shelters. Just as they had settled back into their classrooms there was another alert, at 1.35pm, which went on until 2pm. The last alert was between 2.23pm and 2.55 pm. On that day the children could do only oral work, although some physical training was taken in the shelters in order to keep the children warm. The events of 7 March were by no means typical. Indeed, for a whole week in the same month there were no air raids whatsoever and so lessons were uninterrupted. The level of disruption usually fell somewhere between these two extremes.[6]

Another example comes from the Tottenham School for the Deaf in Phillip Lane, north London. The school was evacuated initially but in April 1940 it re-opened at the nearby West Green School, which was better protected from possible bombing raids. Between April 1940 and March 1941 the school suffered 101 air raid warnings, after which they occurred only sporadically. During the summer of 1943 the children moved back to their own premises, although some had returned to the residential special school where they had been evacuated at the beginning of the war. One year later the number of air raid warnings had grown in earnest, with 74 in just seven weeks.

Despite the disruption, the Tottenham School for the Deaf became a kind of 'showcase' during the war, playing host to a range of visitors, including students from teacher-training colleges, nurses and health visitors. In November 1944 Pathé Pictorial filmed the school at work, and after the war, in October 1946, Helen Keller paid a visit. The school continued to help with teaching methods, receiving visitors from as far away as Canada, as well as aiding researchers from the Medical Research Council in England. Pupils assisted in demonstrations of hearing tests, speech therapy and lip-reading.[7] In essence, the pupils at this school were used as 'exhibits'. During the war they were used to prove to the nation that it was possible to carry on in relative normality despite the disruption caused by air raids. It is also a distinct possibility that the film would have been used to attract charitable donations for deaf or disabled people in general. After the war the children continued to assist in demonstrations. Whilst they perhaps benefited from being at a school advanced in teaching methods it is difficult to assess, without further evidence, the degree of choice the children were able to exercise in demonstrating these methods.

During times of compulsory school attendance, children were expected to present themselves either at their day school or at their allocated emergency centre. If no reasonable explanation was forthcoming, the parents were liable to be fined. Poor attendance, said to be around one-third of pupils at the Nottingham Road School, occurred usually after an air raid. Another reason was bad weather conditions, and another was that children were kept at home to mind their younger siblings. Sometimes though, it was the school which insisted that the child should stay at home. This was usually for health reasons, such as on 11 September 1941, when four children suffering from scabies were excluded from the Nottingham Road School. The bath attendant had caught it on her hands and was off work for one week whilst receiving treatment.[8]

The shortage of teaching staff created even more disruption to lessons. At the Reginald Street PS Day School in Derby, lessons were suspended for two weeks from 2 August 1940, so that the head teacher could have a holiday. Provision was made for the pupils to attend nearby schools, but the decision lay with the parents. This school appears to have been in a particularly vulnerable position. A few days after the school re-opened it was closed again owing to the havoc caused by a bomb falling in the road outside the building. It re-opened two days later but, perhaps unsurprisingly, only three children attended. Four months later the school closed suddenly owing to the discovery of an unexploded bomb near the school building.[9] Fortunately, there are no reports of fatalities at the school during the war.

Although academic education was not usually a priority in special schools, disruption due to the war led to even fewer hours being available in day schools, resulting in children falling further behind academically. Ken Giles, who was hemiplegic and was evacuated to holiday camps at Dymchurch and Broadreeds, as well as having spells in hospital, a special day school and ordinary schools, says:

> The upheaval of the war affected all schools, but those pupils who received the least education must surely have been at the greatest disadvantage because they had less of a base of knowledge to build upon later. I most definitely found myself behind in my work compared to other pupils when I switched from special school to my first ordinary school.[10]

Ken left school (a mainstream secondary school) in 1947 with no qualifications. Fortunately, he found a job in the food industry and, after several career moves, eventually became Bacteriological Laboratory Manager for Brooke Bond Foods.

In many of HMI Lumsden's wartime reports he expressed concern over the inadequate provision of even the most basic academic education, but any corrective measures were constrained by the lack of alternative teachers and/ or adequate premises. At a day school for the deaf in Dudley, Worcestershire, he found, in February 1940, that, although the children were well cared for and lived within a good family spirit, they were receiving little education. He reported that under normal circumstances (in peacetime) he would have recommended that the school be closed but at the present time it was inadvisable to close any school in a neutral area such as Dudley.[11] On his next visit Lumsden made special mention of a particular teacher at the school who had previously disguised her own disability so well that he had never known that she was becoming seriously deaf. However, after ten years at the school, it was now evident that she was failing to notice errors in the children's speech. After enquiring about her general demeanour, Lumsden was told that she was quiet and enigmatic, but also that she could be rude, uncooperative and lazy. He recommended that a warning letter be sent to her 'so that it might stimulate her in fear of losing her job'.[12]

Another teacher who was described as inadequate was the head of Embden Street MD Day School in Manchester. The visiting HMI, Miss Withers, reported in April 1943, 'I should think her IQ is little higher than the children's'.[13] Miss Withers had found the children to be dirty and unkempt, with not enough attention given to hygiene and social training. The following year Lumsden called the head 'a plodding conscientious teacher, acting up to her rather dim lights'.[14] The premises were described as dull and drab and Lumsden described the school as unworkable. The school was closed the same year and the children were sent elsewhere.

It is difficult to determine how the HMIs managed to close down certain schools and not others. For example, in 1940 it was thought unwise to close the Dudley School but closing Embden Street School in 1944 was not a problem. It may have been because the decision on the former school was early in the war when such premises were scarce. The decision to close the Embden Street School, on the other hand, was taken later on in the war when the evacuation and education authorities were more organised. Also, by 1944 evacuees had begun to return home and so premises were not so much in demand.

The problem of 'inadequate' teaching is perhaps easier to fathom. As discussed in Chapter 1, special certificates were needed only for teachers of blind and deaf children; other teachers required only the basic elementary school teaching certificate. Without specialist knowledge and under the extra strain of war it was inevitable that some teachers would not be able to cope, and the problem was compounded by the lack of teachers in special schools. The stigma attached to special education deterred many, and the extra pay that was designed to attract more teachers may have led to some entering the profession for the wrong reasons.

Regardless of the suitability of the teachers, not much was expected of disabled children and, certainly, MD children were at the bottom of the ladder when it came to educational expectations. With mental health problems being less obvious than physical disabilities, uncertified MD children sometimes spent years in ordinary schools, where their specific educational needs went unrecognised, or were ignored. Once they were certified as educable MD and admitted to a special school, it was often too late to start training them in anything other than the most basic of tasks. One twelve-year-old boy who was transferred from a senior school to a day school for MDs in Brighton could not recognise two-letter words and could not add 5 to 16. When asked what he had been doing at senior school, he replied that he 'cleaned the sinks'.[15]

One area in which MD children benefited during the war was the Home Tuition Scheme.[16] According to HMI reports, in large classes, shy and diffident children were often held back by the lack of individual attention but in smaller groups they gained in self-confidence and benefited from the individual help and encouragement of the teacher. As early as March 1940 it was reported that the 'backward' children were making major progress, if not academically then certainly in a social context.[17] They were not pushed out of the picture by the brighter children but took their place as one of a small group, which often had the effect of restoring self-confidence.

The closer contact between teacher and pupil, and the informality of the lessons, were said to be the biggest advantages of the Home Tuition Scheme. Also, as many of the lessons took place in the children's own homes, the teachers were able to learn more about their personal circumstances. Other advantages were said to be the more intensive concentration on the '3 Rs' which, because of time constraints, were the only subjects taught.[18] However, despite the apparent success of the scheme, there were many disadvantages to not being educated in the ordinary classroom. There was a shortage of space, suitable furniture, equipment and books. Being limited to the 3 Rs was monotonous for the children and repetitive for the teachers. The scheme also suffered through being voluntary.

As we have seen, as far as was possible, given the extra duties and fewer inspectors, the HMIs managed to keep up their visits to special day schools, and their reports were mostly of the same standard as before the war. These reports show that some schools, which before the war would have been closed, were forced to remain open because of the lack of alternative accommodation. Inadequate teachers were also retained. Having said that, some teachers suffered from overwork and perhaps from the added dangers of the war or, in one case at least, from a particularly severe disability of their own. In this respect there appears to have been a lack of compassion among the HMIs, including Lumsden.

The Home Tuition Scheme proved that improvements among MD children could be achieved merely by showing individual care and attention. Some HMIs complained about the lack of academic opportunities for disabled children, including MDs, but their recommendations were constrained by what was available, and deemed necessary or appropriate at the time. Improvements in this respect would not come until the Education Act, 1944.

Arguably, the group of disabled children which suffered the most through remaining in evacuating areas was the PD children. For them as well as a lack of specialist equipment, it was often difficult to physically enter the air raid shelters; at best, it was a slower process than for others. Some children with relatively minor physical disabilities were educated under the Home Tuition Scheme. However, there was a third group of disabled children whose wartime experiences differed yet again. These children were too ill to be evacuated or to attend day school, and so were being educated in hospital schools.

Hospital schools

In 1939 there were 88 special schools in hospitals, with 7,414 pupils.[19] Education in hospital schools was, even before the war, sporadic. With hospitals, and sometimes wards, containing children of all ages and abilities, teachers often found themselves in charge of a group of children at completely different levels of education. Admissions, discharges and absence because of treatment added to the disruption.

On the outbreak of war many hospitals came under the Emergency Hospital Scheme (EHS) but the immediate mobilisation of the hospitals and their staffs to look after the expected war casualties prevented the civilian sick in London and other cities from getting the care they needed. Furthermore, as the expected casualties did not materialise for some months, beds remained empty, doctors and nurses had little to do and out-patient departments and clinics closed down. However, by the spring of 1940, when approximately 32,000 casualties and sick servicemen were evacuated from the Continent (Dunkirk), the scheme was better organised, for both civilians and servicemen. On 1 May 1940 there were 1,207 hospitals in England and Wales taking part in the EHS. These contained 406,000 beds, of which 263,000 were allotted for war casualties.[20] More was being done for sick civilians, including the many children requiring treatment and convalescence.

Despite the increase in the number of beds for civilians many children's beds were lost, although not always permanently. Under the EHS a number of children had to be evacuated in order to provide extra beds for war casualties. Those children who were unfit for evacuation were either sent home or, if beds were available, kept in hospital. As hospitals in evacuating areas closed, the more severely disabled children were transferred to hospitals in other areas, placing an even greater demand on beds, which themselves were becoming fewer. As with day schools, the number of available places fluctuated with the status of the war. As the expected bombing raids failed to materialise in the early days of the war, extra beds were made available for 'ordinary' purposes, only to be taken away again a few months later to be used by bomb-victims and returning wounded soldiers.

An example of how this impacted on children comes from the Royal Cornwall Infirmary in Truro. By July 1940 the number of disabled children at the hospital had been reduced by fifty per cent.[21] Out of the twelve children removed, one was found a place in a convalescent home; five were sent to a sanatorium; and the other six were sent home and were being visited by the 'Orthopaedic sisters' attached to the county clinic. For those remaining in the hospital, as in similar hospitals, education provision carried on almost as in peacetime, with average hours of schooling of two hours in the morning and two hours in the afternoon. Very often, only one of these periods would be used for academic study whilst the other two hours were taken up by hobbies and handicrafts. It was also usual for treatment sessions or blanket bathing to interrupt these sessions and so reducing the actual hours of schooling even further.

A problem that was common to all wartime hospitals was the safety of those children too ill to be moved to an air raid shelter. DF suffered from tuberculosis (TB) of the left hip and was a patient at the Bath and Wessex Children's Orthopaedic Hospital in Coombe Park, Bath. In 1996 he recalled his experiences during the bombing raids of 1941:

> I was always laid flat on my back. In Bath hospital there was only one floor and our ward of 20 or 30 boys had a corrugated iron roof. During the bombing the beds were brought to the centre of the ward and patients were placed underneath. All but me and one other because we were too ill to move. Because of the frame my only movement was in my arms and head. When the bombs fell my bed bounced up and down. Bullets fell on the roof. The nurses were wonderful, they held our hands. Eiderdowns protected us from splinters. We had washing bowls for tin helmets. The boys sang. It lasted 2 nights.[22]

Owing to the nature of the children's disabilities, particularly the more severe cases, most of their days were spent either in bed or in wheelchairs, and this was the same whether in peacetime or during the war. Depending on the availability of staff, those in wheelchairs were sometimes taken to the local shops and gardens. Mostly though, the children were kept within the self-contained environment of the hospital. Mrs B, who as a child had lived in a convalescent home in Compton Bishop, Somerset, was able to experience the situation as an outsider. She had moved there with her mother, a nurse, in order to escape the flying bombs in London. She says: 'We didn't know many people in the village. Not because of unfriendliness, merely a respect for privacy. Beautiful place and peaceful community. Simple village life.'[23] At the Liverpool open-air hospital school, the more ambulant children were set chores around the hospital, to relieve boredom and to prevent them from feeling that everything was being done for them. According to Lumsden, many boys and girls who had spent a considerable time in hospital subsequently complained that the 'taint of hospitalisation' held them back in life, as they had not been adequately prepared for life in the outside world.[24] With physical hardships already putting them at a disadvantage, it was important that they should acquire some kind of training so that they would not always be dependent on others.

For this reason, some hospitals provided vocational training schemes.

Perhaps the best example of such an institution is the Lord Mayor Treloar Cripples Hospital School, and its associated College School, in Alton, Hampshire.

Case study: Lord Mayor Treloar Cripples Hospital School

The idea of opening a hospital and school for the treatment, education and training of crippled children and adolescents began in 1906. Sir William Purdie Treloar had been Lord Mayor of London in 1906–7. During that time he had instigated an appeal for funds 'to train and educate boys and girls to face the battle of life with confidence and courage'.[25] The resultant funds were used by Sir Harry Twyford, who is celebrated each year on Founder's Day, to set up the hospital in 1908. Initially, treatment was solely for children crippled by TB but in 1937 a new treatment centre was opened, by the Duke of Kent, and all forms of orthopaedic cases were treated. In 1940 Lumsden called it 'one of the finest and best equipped orthopaedic hospitals in the country', with facilities including a treatment pool, massage and remedial exercises.[26] Research and Development was carried out at the hospital and students from teaching schools were able to carry out their research and postgraduate work. Patients were received from all parts of the British Isles and, according to the hospital's own literature in 1938, 'for 30 years it has eased the burden of general and children's hospitals'.[27] A separate branch, at Hayling Island, was used in conjunction with the main hospital in Alton where, in the summer, sea bathing was used as a therapeutic measure, sometimes alongside heliotherapy (treatment by exposure to light). The branch was also used for post-operative cases; children immobilised in plaster after an operation were often transferred there for healing and convalescence.[28]

By the time war broke out in 1939 the hospital's special school status was long established and the children's training and education were aimed primarily at preparing them for adulthood. On admission to the hospital, the children were put in an isolation ward for two weeks while educational abilities were tested, and the results determined to which ward they would be sent. Each ward would include a range of ages, although some limits were imposed, such as keeping seniors separate from juniors, and girls separate from boys.

On the wards, subjects taught were mainly vocational, as in other hospital schools, but group lessons were also taught in Geography, English, and History, with the latter being taught in the form of dramatisation. Wireless lessons were widely used, while talks on current events were designed to keep patients in touch with the outside world. There was a library for out-of-school hours, a school band and plays designed to encourage self-expression. Regardless of the level of ability, all children were taught skills so that they could become useful members of society after leaving hospital. These included leatherwork; embroidery; rug-making; stool-seating; weaving; paper craft; and modelling in cardboard. Girls were also taught needlework.

Between the ages of fourteen and sixteen, boys could be transferred to the Lord Mayor Treloar's Cripples College, which was on the same premises as the hospital but was, to all intents and purposes, a separate institution. To be eligible, the boys had to require only medical supervision and systematic care, and not actual hospital treatment. Rather than being taught basic handicraft skills, they could now be enrolled on courses with recognised qualifications, albeit only vocational. In the leather department, trunks, attaché-cases, bags and other forms of leatherwork were manufactured. In the boot-making department, boots were repaired and made (including surgical boots). Finally, in the tailoring department, among other things, the boys made costumes for the college Dramatic Society.

Much of the boys' academic education was inadequate owing to the amount of time spent in hospital. Therefore, part of each day (although still only one and a half hours) was devoted to academic subjects designed on suitable lines for their career. Exams were taken in arithmetic, book-keeping, and English, and in the drama department performances included not only Christmas shows but also plays by Shakespeare. In their leisure time the boys played cricket and football and the college had its own scout troop (which, in 1937, had won the Efficiency Shield for the smartest and best troop). The boys also had their own plot of garden, to encourage them to be productive. There were billiards, table-tennis and chess, and special outings to the zoo, Bertram Mills Circus, the Aldershot Tattoo and charity football matches.

When war broke out, most of the boys were at home, enjoying the last days of the summer holidays. The only exceptions were those who had no homes and had spent the summer there. The college re-opened late, on 26 September. The hospital had carried on as usual and for the first few months of the war there were not many changes in either the hospital or the college. Dark blinds were installed for the blackout; sandbags were placed along the verandas; and some side wards in the hospital were gas-proofed for the small children who could not wear gas masks. In the college the more severely disabled children slept on the verandas outside the dormitories, with a wheelchair nearby and with a 'pusher' sleeping in the next bed. On inspection in March 1940 Inspector Lumsden found the ARP arrangements were adequate.

In the same report Lumsden noted that he was impressed with the quality of trade instruction, and commended the interest shown by the staff in placing the children in employment after leaving the hospital or college. However, he also noted that the children of low intelligence, whilst being taught sufficiently in craftwork, were not receiving an adequate general education. The hospital's report for the year ended 31 March 1938 had stated that these types of children were encouraged in special aptitude, as they 'are often clever with their hands'. Lumsden, however, requested that their general education should be more carefully planned and better executed. He also requested that all the boys in their final year at the college should be taught trade conditions such as insurance, wage-rates, and social and industrial problems. This would help in their transition to the workplace. In subsequent correspondence the hospital secretary confirmed that all recommendations were being carried out.

By June 1940 there were 45 EMS beds for children from bombed areas, and overcrowding had become a problem. Also, wireless lessons had ceased and, because of the extra children, some were not receiving any instruction at all. As the war progressed, the lack of available materials brought an end to some of the trade classes, and others were replaced owing to a change in needs during wartime. For example, fancy leather and case making were regarded as a luxury trade and so were replaced by leather splint-making. Despite the problems, most children who reached the age of sixteen at the hospital or college were satisfactorily placed in jobs, because of the training they had received in the workshops.[29]

In September 1944 the college was only half-full. The reason given was that finding employment had become easier, even without a trade. Therefore, some of the children were leaving at the age of fourteen. Also it was thought that the courses offered, in boot-making and tailoring (the leather department was now closed), were no longer interesting to the boys, and so it was recommended that new skills should be introduced, such as watch and clock making and repairing. In the hospital it was found that the children had progressed academically because more hours had been given to reading as a result of the difficulties in obtaining handicraft materials. As with the college, the numbers had reduced, from 390 in 1942 to 326, probably owing to the evacuees returning home.[30] By May 1945 the hospital was almost back to prewar conditions, at 276 patients, one teacher for each ward, one in the college and one for convalescents in the classroom.[31]

Overall, the war appears to have had a bigger impact on boys at Lord Mayor Treloar School and on those aged fourteen and over. Although all children were affected by air raid precautions and overcrowding, and those in hospital schools were forced to forgo their wireless lessons, it was the college boys who were affected most. It can also be said that those boys had an impact on the war as, instead of learning how to make luxury items, they were now making and repairing items needed for the war effort. As jobs became easier to acquire, however, some of the boys left the hospital before learning a trade which, after the war when jobs became scarce again, would have had a detrimental effect on their future employment prospects.

As with all official records, there is a serious lack of information on the emotional state of the children. The following is the personal testimony of Ann Rattue, who was a patient at Lord Mayor Treloar Hospital during the war.

Ann was a 'normal' five-year-old when the war started, and was evacuated along with her classmates, and her brother, from London to Maidenhead. Ann's foster-parents in the billet did not treat her well. When the teachers noticed that her brother was carrying her to school on his back because she had a problem walking, they summoned her mother, who took her home. Ann was diagnosed with TB of the hip and spent several months in Great Ormond Street and Tadworth hospitals, before being evacuated back to Maidenhead, this time to more caring foster-parents. However, complications due to the TB resulted in another spell in Great Ormond Street, and from there Ann was sent to convalesce at Lord Mayor Treloar Hospital at Alton. She was there for just under two years, before being sent home in 1944. Between the ages of ten and eleven she attended a special day school in Maida Vale before being 'signed off' from special education in 1945 to attend a 'normal' grammar school.

As we have seen, Lord Mayor Treloar Hospital received many positive reports from visiting officials. Ann knew nothing of the hospital's excellent facilities and reputation, however. More than anything, she remembers the attitude of the nurses who, she says, were over-strict and lacked compassion; in front of the matron 'the children literally laid to attention'. She soon began to wet the bed on a regular basis so was sent to the babies' ward as punishment, whilst the other children had handicrafts, listened to stories and sang. Her left leg was plastered from waist to toe, and her right leg from waist to knee. This was called a 'double-hipped spiker' and, because she was still growing, it had to be changed every so often. Once, the nurse clipped her skin when removing the spiker so Ann screamed. She was told off for making a fuss. She was also reprimanded for crying when being wheeled (in her bed) into the babies' ward, and says that she was treated as a leper for being in pain after spraining her ankle once she had started to walk again.

Ann doesn't remember much about her time in Great Ormond Street or Tadworth hospitals, so believes that her experiences there could not have been as bad as those at Lord Mayor Treloar. She likens her stay there to being in an orphanage. A world of isolation, yet not lonely because of the other children. Parents could visit only once each month, although not during January, February or March because of the fear of bringing in infection (this was before the use of antibiotics). Children were not allowed their own clothes or toys and, when parents brought toys in, they were confiscated after the visit and

placed in a communal cupboard. She still has vivid memories of wearing hospital clothes which, she says, were clean but rough and itchy. Three months after
leaving the hospital, Ann's bed-wetting stopped but she couldn't bear to see or
hear the name of Alton for years. Even at the age of seventy-two, she says it was
by far the worst experience of her life.[32] With regard to her physical well-being
Ann may have benefited from her stay at Lord Mayor Treloar. After all, the
hospital had excellent facilities and the treatment she received was successful.
However, as Ann herself testifies, the emotional scars have never healed.

Although Lord Mayor Treloar Hospital School, led the way in preparing
disabled children for adulthood, many other hospitals also had adequate
facilities for teaching them a trade. At the St Vincent's orthopaedic hospital
in Pinner, Middlesex, the children were being taught engineering as well as
the usual boot-making and tailoring.[33] At the Liverpool open-air hospital
school, workshop staff included a joiner, a blacksmith, a (female) leather-
worker, a splint-maker and two cobblers. In fact, all surgical appliances
needed at the hospital were made on the premises.[34] At a hospital school
in Bedfordshire, both boys and girls were taught knitting and embroidery.
There was also cane and leatherwork. The craftwork was said to be excellent, although limited in scope, and academic work was said to be adequate.
Drawing was found to be of a remarkably high standard, with the children
excelling at map-making. Children could also join the Guides and the
Brownies, and in the summer of 1944 the hospital was visited by the Chief
Guide, Lady Baden Powell.[35]

From the available records it appears that as much as was reasonably possible was done for the children in hospitals. Although provision for their academic education was questionable, their medical care and vocational training
seem to have been more than adequate given the difficult times through which
they were living.

Overall, the welfare of children in hospital schools, as with those in residential and special day schools, depended largely on the attitude of the staff.
Indeed the relationship between primary carer and child was more intense
in hospitals where the child was often bedridden and unable to interact with
others. This discussion on hospital schools has recorded the testimonies of
Ann Rattue and DF, who had vastly different experiences during their hospital
stays. Lord Mayor Treloar's, with its up-to-date equipment and facilities and
its excellent reputation, conjures up nightmarish memories for Ann. On the
other hand, DF's overriding memory of his time in Bath hospital, rather than
being one of fear of the air raids, is of the kindness of the nurses. As expected,
the more seriously disabled children were in a more precarious position than
most because of their need to stay in bed. However, as DF and the various

government reports show, the nursing staff improvised quite well in order to keep the children safe.

As with other groups of disabled children, there is a serious lack of personal testimonies, although the personal accounts that are included show the contrast between experience and official reports very clearly. However, the limited number of first-hand accounts necessitates greater reliance on other sources, such as government reports. The most revealing information in the reports of hospital schools is with regard to 'training'. As was usual at the time, academic education did not feature prominently on the curriculum for disabled children. Instead, most children learnt craftwork, with the older ones being trained for a vocational career. Some academic education was given but, apart from the very basics, subjects such as book-keeping and English were designed to help the children in their vocational career, rather than an academic one. As the war went on, some trade classes suffered through a lack of materials. There was also a change in the type of goods needed. Consequently, many hospital workshops were producing and repairing items such as surgical boots, thereby becoming almost self-sufficient and helping towards the war effort.

As with other groups of disabled children, conditions for those in hospital improved once the authorities had had time to become better organised. Many beds were taken away from 'ordinary' patients (i.e. those not injured by war) initially but within several months the management of hospital beds became better structured and many children were able to return to hospital. The one group who were not catered for by the State, however, and who in effect were 'left behind', were the severely physically disabled children, who were denied a place in the official evacuation parties and for whom no hospital bed was available. For these children, as well as the many children who needed only convalescence, or therapeutic treatment, or even merely advice, the help given by the various charitable organisations was invaluable.

The role of charities

There were numerous charities, of all sizes, set up for the welfare of disabled children before the Second World War. Some were concerned solely with the provision of hospital treatment and/or education. Others were also involved in other aspects of the children's lives, such as leisure and religion, and the problems they might encounter on a day-to-day basis, especially if they were permanently at home. During the war the services of these charities were in demand more than ever. As discussed in Chapter 1, children with serious physical disabilities were excluded from the initial Government Evacuation

Scheme and continued to be so throughout the war. Although disabled evacuees were generally treated with kindness and generosity by the general public there was hardly any interest shown in this particular group; a point not unnoticed by a Manchester physician who believed that opinions were influenced by the belief that 'spastic cripples do not repay the time, trouble and expense of their own care'.[36] It would seem that the question of whether certain children were 'worth saving' continued to be asked during the war.

In the absence of an official scheme to help this most vulnerable group, it was left to those organisations whose personnel had an appropriate level of knowledge and experience and, more importantly, who managed to continue to operate during the war years. One such organisation, a relatively small charity, was the Birmingham Catholic Cripples Care Society. Founded in 1906, the Society's aims were: to supply each child with a visitor who would watch over their health, and ensure that they received proper religious instruction; to provide nourishment, clothing, fares, surgical instruments (other than those which should be provided by an institution); to give parties and country holidays; and to co-operate with other agencies engaged in work for Catholic crippled children.[37]

The Society's home visitors saw religious education as being of primary importance and frequently arranged for children to be sent to a Catholic school, as well as persuading the parents to return to their religious duties. In 1938, with 119 cases on the books, the Society sent two children to Lourdes, had a summer outing to Southam and arranged a Christmas party at a local boys' school. In 1939, with 117 cases on the books, and with a decrease in income, the Society still managed to send three boys to a farm for two weeks, sent a 'helpless little girl' to the country with her mother and provided a summer party for 46 boys. During 1940, the activities of the Society were curtailed due to the conditions of war. Regular visiting became impossible, not only because of transport difficulties but also because the Society's members and visitors had other important work to do. For the rest of the war Sister Agatha of St Chad's Cathedral in Birmingham continued to visit the children, mostly giving only practical advice. When the Society eventually resumed its regular activities in 1947, there were only fifty children on the books.[38]

In wartime, when human and financial resources were scarce, it is perhaps inevitable that charitable organisations struggled or even folded altogether. One organisation, however, experienced the reverse; rather than diminishing, the work of the Invalid Children's Aid Association (ICAA) grew during the war. That said, the association was already one of the most prominent disabled charities before the war, as will become evident.

The Invalid Children's Aid Association

The ICAA was founded in 1888, by the clergyman Allen Dowdeswell Graham, in order to help poor children who were either seriously ill or disabled.[39] Graham organised a group of home visit volunteers who took food, bedding and medicine to children and their families, and helped arrange admissions into hospitals and convalescence homes, holidays, apprenticeships and the loan of spinal carriages, wheelchairs and perambulators. Royal patronage was established in 1891. As the association grew, volunteers were gradually replaced by professional social workers, and 'homes of recovery' were set up. When war broke out, the ICAA had eight homes under its own management, as well as several beds in other homes on their 'approved list', all of which they used solely for children from London.

During the Munich crisis in 1938, when the LCC was evacuating disabled children to residential special schools in safer areas, the ICAA was asked to provide for those who were unfit to join the school parties. This included: children in general hospitals recovering from recent accidents but who had been discharged owing to the pressure on bed space (Category A); children suffering from chronic asthma and similar illnesses, who also could not be accommodated in individual billets (Category B); and those already in convalescence homes but whose parents preferred them to join their evacuated school parties (Category C). Again, as with the LCC's evacuation, lessons were learnt from this 'practice run' and the ICAA were prepared when their services were called upon again the following year.

When the order came to evacuate in September 1939, children in categories A and B were gathered in a centre in London, pre-arranged and staffed by ICAA workers, from where they were taken by cars to a home in East Grinstead. From there they were taken, again by cars (all the cars had been lent by the Women's Voluntary Service) to various convalescent homes further afield. In all, around two hundred children were evacuated in this way. Those same cars that had been used to transport the evacuated children were now used to return some of those in category C to their parents, so that they could be sent either to the residential special schools or to friends or relatives, in safer areas. At the beginning of the war there were around 1,700 children in convalescent homes placed there by the ICAA. Five of the association's own homes were told straight away that they would be taken over by the EMS and so the children were moved elsewhere.[40] However, two months later there was a change of mind and so children were moved in once again.[41] Despite this, many convalescent beds were taken over by the EMS, which led to a serious shortage.

As the war progressed, the duties of the ICAA workers grew. According to its own annual report for 1940, the association's wartime aims were: to look after delicate children still in and around London; to provide periods of convalescence and surgical appliances to those in London and in reception areas; to ensure that the children didn't have to return to a danger area after their convalescence; and to keep in touch with the parents of evacuated children, who were usually already known to the ICAA.[42] After the capitulation of France in June 1940 the ICAA lost a further eight hundred beds in convalescent homes on the south and south-east coasts. Independently of the Ministry of Health and the local authorities, and therefore relieving them of the responsibility, the ICAA and managers of other voluntary homes on the association's approved list, took action to find alternative homes in other areas. Two new units were opened in houses lent for the purpose, and furniture and equipment were transferred from the abandoned homes.[43] The relative ease in which these charities were able to find alternative accommodation when the evacuation authorities were struggling indicates that there was a private agreement, perhaps pre-arranged, with the property owners. It is also likely that the new accommodation was already in use as convalescent homes.

Some voluntary societies who managed convalescent homes for children before the war were unable to keep them open because of wartime conditions; safety and staff shortages were just two of the problems they encountered. The ICAA however, was extending the reach of its operations. Rather than its being concentrated in London and south-east England, the war led to branches or affiliated societies all over the country. Unlike the evacuation of 1938 children in need were now situated throughout the country. Rather than dealing solely with children in general hospitals and convalescent homes, the workers now also dealt with those in ordinary billets who fell ill or who, for various reasons, failed to make progress in them.[44]

The ICAA provided a link between parents, countryside and seaside hosts, billeting officers and others concerned with the children's welfare. They intervened in cases where children in billets were suffering because of an overdue operation, and they provided children with special shoes that were easy to acquire in London, but not in the provinces. In 1943, when the staff problem became acute because more and more workers were being called up, the ICAA still managed to help over ten thousand children. Over four thousand went to convalescent homes for an average stay of ten weeks; 750 were provided with surgical boots and appliances; and 2,800 were visited in their own homes, where the workers' duties ranged from advice to changing bandages. The ICAA also provided escorts for children needing to be transferred to or from hospital or convalescent homes. In this, they were helped by railway companies as well as by voluntary car pools.

In 1943 the shortage of convalescent beds became so serious that, in the spring of that year, the Ministry of Health released six British Red Cross auxiliary hospitals. The following year, with the intense flying bomb and rocket attacks on the south of England, the situation worsened. Again the British Red Cross stepped in and provided emergency vacancies. Also, some of the provincial societies federated to the ICAA offered vacancies in their convalescent homes in the north of England.[45]

The success of the ICAA, and indeed the many other charitable organisations that managed to operate throughout the war, was largely due to the hard work of the staff, many of them volunteers. There were many instances of collective and individual bravery among these workers, especially the ones who remained in dangerous areas to help the children who, for whatever reason (many were too severely disabled to be moved, even into the air raid shelters), remained there. The work of the vast majority of these workers went unrecognised, although in 1940 King George VI awarded the George Medal to a Miss Ratenbury (former secretary of the Bermondsey ICAA) for driving women and children to safety through dangerous conditions during an air raid attack. Miss Ratenbury was subsequently seconded to the Ministry of Health.[46]

Another reason for the success of the ICAA was the financial and material help given by a wide range of individuals and organisations. As one of England's most prominent charities, the ICAA was a recipient of the many gifts and donations from both at home and abroad. The American Red Cross and the British War Relief Society of America both gave generously to disabled children, with the latter donating over £3,500 to the ICAA in 1941 alone. In the same year gifts of food and clothing came from the Anzac Fellowship of Women, Canadian Red Cross, Personal Service League and the Royal Empire Society.[47] The following year Queen Mary accepted, on behalf of the ICAA, £1,000 from 'Americans on behalf of the English Speaking Union'. Also Princess Elizabeth received a shipment of dried bananas from South America and sent a crate of them to the two convalescent nurseries run by the ICAA.[48]

The British public was also generous to those less fortunate. In 1940 there was a BBC appeal for a million pennies; the London ICAA received £3,462 and the ICAA in the provinces, £1,400.[49] In 1942 the Duchess of Portland made a personal appeal on behalf of the ICAA which raised £450, and later the same year the association was allowed a share in a BBC appeal made by 'Uncle Mac' on the *Children's Hour*.[50] In a slightly different vein, which was more to do with kindness than with finance (but was probably equally, if not more, important to the children involved), at Christmas 1944 Queen Mary sent an autographed Christmas card to boys at one of the ICAA's own homes, in return for the card they had sent her, and which they had designed and painted themselves.[51]

Many of the achievements of the ICAA during the war were made possible by the co-operation of other organisations, including the WVS, Red Cross, the railway companies and the Hospital Almoners Association, whose personnel assisted in home visits. Without this help and without the donations they received, the ICAA workers would not have been able to help as many children, and parents, as they did. Their achievements also show the extent to which the government was reliant on the expertise and voluntary personnel of charities to look after some of its most vulnerable citizens. Despite their best efforts, however, not all children received their help. One child, with what we now call cerebral palsy, lived at home with his mother; his father was in the services. He says: 'Many times the bombs would be dropping and the sirens would be going off all over Cardiff. My mother would have to carry me to the air raid shelter at the bottom of the garden ... my mother was responsible for all the care I needed.'[52] For some children the situation was much worse. Their mothers were at work or queuing for food when the air raids began. Occasionally an ICAA worker would be visiting at the time and would stay with the child, putting their own lives at risk. Sometimes, though, the child would be alone.

The records of the ICAA do not contain any criticism of the evacuation authorities. Indeed, in many instances they worked well together. But when discussing the plight of the more seriously physically disabled children a simple statement spoke volumes: 'Query: Should not some provision have been made for them?'[53] The lack of facilities for seriously physically disabled children, whilst not being of great concern to government officials and the general public, was recognised by one of the most prominent organisations at the time in relation to the welfare of 'cripples' and during the war a school was opened especially for them.

Hinwick Hall

The Central Council for the Care of Cripples was formed in 1919 by the Surgeon Sir Robert Jones in order to organise a national scheme to deal with 'cripple problems' in both children and adults, throughout the UK.[54] Specific aims included investigating causes and promoting measures for their elimination, and encouraging the formation of local associations, which could become involved in the treatment, employment and other aspects of the cripples' lives. In 1935 the Council acknowledged that provision was still inadequate and that serious financial difficulties were threatening any further progress. However, a donation of £125,000 from Lord Nufffield in the same year secured the Council's immediate future.

In late 1941 and early 1942 the Council arranged a conference of representatives of societies interested in cripples. It was emphasised at the conference that LEAs were consistently asking the Council for advice on how to accommodate bedridden cripples and chronic incontinent children, as their present arrangements were 'pitifully inadequate'.[55] One of the societies at the conference was the Shaftesbury Society, which ran its own convalescent homes. The Society subsequently informed the Board of Education that, if the Council could raise the necessary capital, approximated at £10,000 (of which £3,000 had already been promised), it would open and maintain a residential school in order to meet this urgent need. The proposal was approved and, in May 1942, HM The Queen sent for the project a donation of £1,000 which had been placed at her disposal by the Bundles for Britain charity in America.[56]

In January 1943 the school, called the Hinwick Hall Residential School for Seriously Crippled Boys, opened in Wellingborough, Northamptonshire. There was accommodation for fifty boys but a strict criterion was adhered to. No MDs or borderline cases were admitted and patients were required to be seriously crippled and unable to benefit from further treatment. Some were incontinent but none was entirely bedridden, and they were all to be clothed each day.[57]

The school was quickly established and after the first inspection, in June 1943, Dr Bywaters reported that the village and neighbourhood were taking a great interest. Local cadets visited at weekends to help and to entertain the boys, and the nearby American camp gave surplus food and provided entertainment. Dr Bywaters deduced that the villagers considered the children as belonging to them and they always made a point of including them in their fetes, parties and other events. The boys were taken out as much as possible, in wheelchairs, cars or ambulance, the latter of which belonged to the school and was also used to take the boys to the nearby clinic or hospital. In suitable weather they were carried outdoors for lessons. Nature study was popular but craftwork was difficult owing to the severity of disabilities. Academic subjects were taught and the doctor was told that arithmetic and geometry were to be given more space in the timetable.[58]

Dr Bywaters's next visit was not until March 1945, when she found vast improvements in accommodation and facilities. At the time of the previous visit, improvements to the buildings could only be carried out when the builders were not needed for emergency work. Since then, however, an extra classroom had been built (for existing pupils, not to increase numbers); a new central heating system had been installed; and an electric lift, which had been gifted to the school, was about to be fitted. Films, concerts and other forms of entertainment were still being arranged by the locals, and a disabled scout troop had been organised by an outside leader. At the time of the visit, the staff were considering how the new full-size billiard table (another gift) could be used by those in wheelchairs.[59]

In October 1945 HMI Mrs Loch visited the school and found it 'a delightfully run school'. A pleasant feature of the school she noted was that every boy had his own locker in his dormitory and no member of staff was allowed to disturb the contents without the boy's permission. She concluded that the success of the school was due to the wise, pleasant and understanding leadership of Mr Riding (Superintendent) and his wife (SRN Matron).[60]

Hinwick Hall was an experiment which both the Ministry of Health and the Board of Education deemed successful. The school provided a programme of physical, educational, recreational and spiritual welfare. The children received adequate food and they appeared happy and relatively healthy. Dr Bywaters recommended a letter of commendation for keeping the incontinent children clean and free from the smell of urine. More importantly, the children had remained safe; in December 1944 bomb blasts had broken several windows but there were no casualties.

Despite the good work carried out at Hinwick Hall, there was always the problem of where to send the children after reaching the age of sixteen. Only those who would benefit educationally or domestically were admitted to the school and so, in theory at least, all were capable of contributing to society in some way in adulthood (although some did prove to be ineducable and were sent home or to a mental institution). The frustration felt by Dr Bywaters and Mrs Loch in this matter is evident from their reports. As Dr Bywaters pointed out in March 1945, there was nothing for the boys after reaching sixteen except to be sent back to where they came from, to stagnate. At Hinwick Hall they had a few short years of care and happiness; they were taught to appreciate cleanliness, good habits, organised leisure and companionship, but then they were thrown back to a bed on a senile ward in a public assistance institution. Mrs Loch said that the school was known as 'the medical museum' because no one would ever go out into the world; all the boys would require institutional care for ever. Sheltered workshops and a home were needed.

It is evident that employment prospects for the more seriously physically disabled children were virtually non-existent. On the other hand, those whose disabilities were not so serious and who were attending either residential, day or hospital schools were often trained in some type of vocational work. Subsequent employment was procured through either the school itself or through the After-Care Association.

After-care and employment

In 1900 Mrs Humphry Ward, who had been involved in setting up the Tavistock Place School, the first public day school for PDs, formed a small committee to supervise the after-care and training for industrial life, of those leaving the school. This was the parent of the After-Care Association, which played such an important part in the lives of disabled school-leavers during the war. By early 1944 the association held records of over two thousand firms covering eighty different occupations where they had placed cases. Evacuation made keeping in touch with the children difficult, and enemy action meant that the majority of interviews with the children took place in shelters. Despite this, there were over 1,500 visits to children and parents in the twelve months up to 31 March 1944, with very few left unemployed.[61]

The object of any after-care programme was to ensure that disabled children who were able to work were given the opportunity to gain wage-earning employment after leaving school, in order that they could become self-supporting. Many schemes, as with the After-Care Association, started through the efforts of one philanthropist, or perhaps a small committee of philanthropists. In 1925 Miss Sweet, who was skilled in needlework, opened the School of Stitchery and Lace for Crippled Girls. Initially she taught in her own home in Leicester and her first two students were disabled ex-army nurses who were unable to earn a living and were struggling to survive on their small army pensions. Three years later, after having trained sixty disabled girls and women, all of who had been kept in employment, she moved to a mansion in seven acres of land in Great Bookham, Surrey. Miss Sweet had managed to secure a loan of £5,000 in order to purchase the property, probably helped by the fact that the Royal Family were among those to whom she sold her finished goods. As for the girls, there were many orthopaedic hospitals more than willing to employ them to teach disabled girls in their charge.[62]

After the Second World War broke out, it became difficult to purchase raw materials and those that were available were too costly. Fortunately, the school was able to survive by using up the large amount of materials in stock at the beginning of the war. In November 1942, after a short illness, Miss Sweet passed away. Although a new principal was soon found, the school began to experience severe difficulties. Miss Sweet had never taken a salary but, of course, the new principal did. Also, the stock of materials was running out. In June 1943, when the financial problems became critical, the relevant authorities (the school had been recognised as a vocational training centre for crippled girls since 1938) agreed to increase the fees and the school was able to operate throughout the rest of the war.

Much of the work done by the girls during the war was repair work to military equipment such as tents, respirators and haversacks. The outbuildings at the school were taken over by Southern Command for use as a Chief Repair Depot and in 1941 Dr Bywaters learnt that the girls worked more quickly than the men, and that they were all paid the same rates.[63] When the girls finished their training, they were able to stay on at the school, providing they paid board and lodging. However, this meant blocking the school, thereby making it impossible to accept new cases. In some instances the girls would be sent to a Public Assistance Institution where their training would be wasted. For those girls who were bedridden but were able to return to their own homes, work would be sent to them. In 1942 there were between twenty and twenty-five 'home-workers'.[64]

Another organisation that was formed especially for the after-care and employment of cripples was the John Groom Crippleage (incorporating the Flower Girls Mission), which was established c. 1866 for the homeless 'flower girls' of London.[65] In 1939 around 250 girls and women were living and working at the Crippleage in Edgware. The work, making artificial flowers, was carried out in Groom's factory, and cottages were provided as living quarters. The money earned by the girls helped to pay for their keep and extra money came from donations and subscriptions, legacies, fetes and the interest and dividends earned on investments.[66]

During the war the flower-making was maintained, although on a smaller scale owing to the shortage of materials. Some of the workers did other jobs, contributing to the war effort, and charitable income appears to have remained consistent throughout these years. The factory itself was in a particularly dangerous area and the workers spent a lot of time in the air raid shelters. According to their own report in 1941, they narrowly escaped the bombing on several occasions, but on one particularly precarious night four girls were killed and four others injured by a bomb which wrecked a house outside the Crippleage grounds, where the girls were living.[67] Unfortunately, records of the Crippleage after 1943 have not survived.

The role of the Central Council for the Care of Cripples, the 'Council', was mentioned briefly in a previous section. The Council was heavily involved in bringing awareness to the plight of crippled children but it also exercised a hands-on approach, and training colleges were set up in order to prepare the children for life after special school. One such college was the St Loyes Training College for Cripples in Exeter. Before the war the college ran three courses, each with an average of twelve months' training. These were in horology, handyman duties (usually houseboys for schools) and gardening.[68] However, during the war the college came under the Essential Services

4 Female power-machinist with double above-knee amputation, trainee at St Loyes
Training College for Cripples

Division of the Ministry of Supply on account of its production of supplies
of national importance.[69] In 1940, in order for the college to meet wartime
requirements, a grant of £10,666 was made by the trustees of the Lord Nuffield
Fund for Cripples.[70] Consequently, in the following year the college opened
departments in production making (hairsprings and collars) and electrical
instrument making. In the horology department, between seven and eight
thousand hairsprings were being produced each week.[71] In 1942 a women's
section opened and production expanded to include parachute-making; the
girls also trained as canteen store-keepers, control clerks and in needlework
and cooking.[72]

Another college run by the Council, and therefore along the same lines,
was the Queen Elizabeth Training College for the Disabled, in Leatherhead,
Surrey.[73] As with other colleges of this type, the Queen Elizabeth College
relied heavily on voluntary contributions. Prior to the outbreak of war, the
college received annual donations from charitable events, such as the Fitness
Festival at the Royal Albert Hall which in 1939 was to be in the presence of the
Queen. However, as with many other such events, this was cancelled, which
was an enormous financial loss to the college (although the Queen did make

a private donation of £25).[74] Some charitable occasions prevailed, however, and the occasional large windfall managed to keep the college in operation. In 1940 the same Trust that had given a grant to St Loyes granted £12,000 to the Queen Elizabeth. Then in 1942 'Uncle Mac' (Derek McCulloch, a well-known radio personality) made a BBC appeal on behalf of the Queen Elizabeth College and the St Loyes College, which raised £1,230 between the two.[75] Also, as both colleges admitted children under sixteen (but with a minimum age of fourteen), a contribution to their training was paid by LEAs. For those aged sixteen or over, the fees came from Public Assistance or, more commonly, from the Ministry of Labour under the Cripples Training Scheme.

As with St Loyes, the trainees from the Queen Elizabeth's College made a valuable contribution to the war effort and, in its report for 1941, the College declared that, since the outbreak of war, nearly 350 trainees had gone into munitions work. As early as December 1939 the Ministry of Labour acknowledged that 'It is satisfactory to note that so far disabled young people have been well able to hold their own under war conditions'.[76] Yet, in 1941 the same department expressed doubts as to whether men who had become disabled as a result of war should mix with those at colleges such as St Loyes and the Queen Elizabeth. According to a report by the Ministry of Labour, trainees at the colleges were, for the most part, difficult and subnormal in many respects. He went on: 'Furthermore, it is apparently true that the handicap which cripples from birth has a tendency to make them embittered and difficult to live with and, in addition, creates a sub-normal moral attitude.'[77] In his view this might have had an adverse effect on the war disabled and, if the colleges were to be used, the two types of trainees must be segregated. According to one official at the Ministry of Labour and National Service Training Department, this negative view of the 'ordinary cripple' was shared by Dame Georgina Buller, one of the founders of the colleges, who reportedly said that 'permanent cripples are difficult to deal with due to their sub-normal aspect on life'.[78] Even with an increasing shortage of accommodation, the Ministry of Labour was reluctant to send the war disabled to fill the small number of vacancies at St Loyes.

It is evident that the State was more involved in the training and employment of disabled adolescents during the war. This was not as a result of a new awareness of disabled people's desire to feel useful but rather a need for labour. Again, when dealing with disabled children and adolescents, the State relied heavily on the co-operation and initiatives of charities.

As we have seen, the role of charities during the war depended on a variety of factors. The activities of smaller organisations tended to be seriously curtailed owing to staff shortages, lack of funds, transport difficulties and aspects of safety. Some organisations were forced to cease operations altogether whereas the larger, more well-known charities were more likely to benefit from the many charitable appeals, both at home and abroad. Inevitably, their roles changed in order to accommodate the conditions of war, and some, such as the ICAA, expanded both in duties and in areas served. The level of success achieved by charities during the war depended largely on their collaboration with other organisations, including other charities. The evacuation of disabled children from London in 1938, and again in 1939, is testament to this. The relationship between charities and the State was also important. In many ways this was a continuation of the prewar situation when the various voluntary bodies both complemented and supplemented State efforts.

Arguably the most significant role of charities during the war concerned the more seriously physically disabled who were unable to be evacuated as part of the special parties. For these children, who were in effect 'abandoned' by the evacuation authorities, the staff of the various charities provided a vital link with the outside world. Yet even they regretted that more could not be done.

The example of Hinwick Hall is yet another example of expertise residing with charities rather than with the State. It also illustrates the lack of employment opportunities for those children and adolescents with serious physical disabilities. Again, this is a continuation of the prewar situation when both the State and to some extent the charities were unable (and perhaps unwilling) to offer the children a future other than institutional care.

Conclusion

As with residential schools, the reports of HMIs have made it possible to gain an insight into the wartime lives of children in special day schools and hospital schools. Inevitably, those remaining in or returning to vulnerable areas suffered serious disruption to their education. Unsuitable premises, a shortage of teachers and equipment, and time spent in air raid shelters compounded the problems within an already inadequate system of special education. One positive outcome of the disruption was the social benefits gained by the MD children.

For those spending significant periods of time in hospital, disruption mainly affected the type of handicraft the pupils could work on, owing to the lack of materials. In some cases this led to the pupils working on items relevant to the war, thereby making their contribution to the war effort. For others, ironically, the lack of materials meant more time spent on academic subjects, something that the HMIs frequently strove for in all types of special schools. Regardless of the level of education, however, the main determinant of how the children have looked back on their wartime experiences was the attitudes of the staff. Ann Rattue and DF testify to this.

In addition to the reports and correspondence of the various government departments, the records of certain charitable bodies have provided invaluable information on the activities of those working on behalf, or independently, of those government departments responsible for the welfare of disabled children during the war. The vital part played by charities such as the ICAA and the Central Council for the Care of Cripples, and many other smaller bodies, is most evident in the case of the seriously physically disabled children. Without the help of these organisations, Hinwick Hall would not have been established and those children remaining at home in vulnerable areas, often confined to their bed, would not have received the same level of care and advice provided by the home visitors. Of equal importance, perhaps, these visitors let both children and their parents know that they had not been totally abandoned.

As shown in the previous chapter, the attitudes of government officials towards disabled people, including children, was ambiguous throughout the war years. This chapter has discussed special day schools, hospital schools and training colleges, and it appears that it was with regard to the latter that negative perceptions were most evident. Although there was general agreement that disabled adolescents were 'holding their own' in contributing to the war effort, it was thought unwise to allow those disabled by war to be trained alongside long-term disabled people due to the latter's 'sub-normal moral attitude'. For those within the colleges, who probably would have been unaware of this prejudice, the conditions of war presented an opportunity to make a significant contribution to the war effort, one aspect of the war that went some way towards changing perceptions of disabled people in general.

Notes

1 LMA, LCC/WAR/1/238, minutes of Board of Education meeting, 21 February 1940.
2 *Ibid.*
3 LMA, LCC/WAR/1/238, Report to the Chief Inspector of the LCC Education Committee, 31 December 1941.
4 LMA, LCC/WAR/1/238, LCC report, 20 June 1945.
5 *Ibid.*
6 Nottinghamshire Archives (NA), SL159/2/1, Nottingham Road School Logbook.
7 Smith, *Still Unique after All These Years*, pp. 25–7.
8 NA, SL159/2/1, Logbook, 11 September 1941.
9 Derbyshire Archives (DA), D384/2, Logbook, 22 January 1941.

10 Letter from Ken Giles to author, 13 September 2005.

11 TNA, ED32/829, Lumsden's report on the Dudley Day School for the Deaf in Worcestershire, 27 February 1940.

12 TNA, ED32/829, Lumsden's report on the Dudley Day School, 17 March 1943.

13 TNA, ED32/1121, Report by HMI Miss Withers on Embden Street MD Day School in Manchester, 7 April 1943.

14 TNA, ED32/1121, Lumsden's report on Embden Street MD Day School, 24 February 1944.

15 TNA, ED32/1006, HMI reports on Hollingdean MD School, Brighton, 1932–44.

16 The Home Tuition Scheme was education provided outside the classroom, usually in surroundings familiar to the child, and formed part of the overall Emergency Schooling Scheme.

17 TNA, ED10/252, Report on the working of the Home Tuition Scheme in Hendon from October 1939, by HMI Cox, 8 March 1940.

18 The '3 Rs' was a term used for the basic lessons of reading, writing and arithmetic.

19 Ministry of Education, *Pamphlet 30: Education of the Handicapped Pupil 1945–55* (London: HMSO, 1956), p. 22.

20 Titmuss, *Problems of Social Policy*, pp. 183–5.

21 TNA, ED32/1054, Secretary of the Hospital School to the Secretary of the Board of Education, 13 July 1940.

22 Imperial War Museum (IWM), 96/55/1, personal memoirs of Dennis Ford, 1996.

23 IWM, 92/9/1, personal memoirs of Mrs Balister, 1986.

24 TNA, ED32/1052, Lumsden's report on the Liverpool Open-Air Hospital School, 16 October 1943.

25 TNA, ED32/352, Hospital report for the y/e 31 March 1938.

26 TNA, ED32/1092, Lumsden's report on Lord Mayor Treloar Cripples Hospital School and College School, Alton, Hampshire, 5 March 1940.

27 TNA, ED32/352, Hospital report for the y/e 31 March 1938.

28 This, and the following information on Lord Mayor Treloar's Hospital and College, comes from the establishment's own reports for 1940: TNA, ED32/352.

29 TNA, ED32/352, report by Dr Bywaters, included in the hospital's own papers, 25 June 1942.

30 TNA, ED32/352, report by Dr Bywaters, included in the hospital's own papers, 27 September 1944.

31 TNA, ED32/1092, report by Dr Bywaters, 29 May 1945.

32 As told by Ann Rattue to the author, 21 March 2006.

33 LMA, SC/PPS/093, Hospital's own report for 1944.

34 TNA, ED32/1052, Lumsden's report of Liverpool Open-Air Hospital School, 16 October 1943.

35 TNA, ED32/1041, HMI reports of Alexandra Hospital School, Luton (formerly Swanley), 1939–45.

36 TNA, AST7/283, 'A Neglected Group' by William Hodgkins, Central Council for the Care of Cripples Newsletter, April 1942.
37 St Chad's Cathedral Archive, Birmingham, BCCCS2 – Miscellaneous papers 1930–89.
38 *Ibid.*
39 LMA, 4248/D/01/006, Annual report of ICAA, 1943.
40 LMA, 4248, from the ICAA's own papers.
41 TNA, CAB102/786, from the ICAA's own papers.
42 LMA, 4248/D/01/006, Annual report of ICAA, 1940.
43 TNA, CAB102/786, from the ICAA's own papers.
44 LMA, 4248/D/01/006, Annual report of ICAA, 1940.
45 LMA, 4248/D/01/006, Annual report of ICAA, 1943.
46 TNA, CAB102/786, from the ICAA's own papers.
47 LMA, 4248/D/01/006, Annual report of ICAA, 1941.
48 LMA, 4248/D/01/006, Annual report of ICAA, 1942.
49 LMA, 4248/D/01/006, Annual report of ICAA, 1940.
50 TNA, CAB102/786, from the ICAA's own papers.
51 LMA, 4248/D/01/006, Annual report of ICAA, 1944.
52 'An Active Life, Against the Odds' by Graham Reginald Bevan. Go to www.bbc.co.uk and then follow the links to 'Southeast Wales war stories'.
53 LMA/4248, from the ICAA's own papers.
54 LMA, AST7/283, National Assistance Board, 'Co-operation with the Central Council for the Care of Cripples', 1936–42.
55 TNA, ED32/1039, Secretary of the Shaftesbury Society to the Secretary of the Board of Education, 27 February 1942.
56 TNA, ED32/1039, Press Communique from the Central Council for the Care of Cripples, 9 May 1942.
57 TNA, ED32/1039, Report of Hinwick Hall residential school for Seriously Crippled Boys, Wellingborough, Northamptonshire, by Dr Bywaters, 8 June 1943.
58 *Ibid.*
59 TNA, ED32/1039, Report of Hinwick Hall by Dr Bywaters, 8 March 1945.
60 TNA, ED32/1039, Report of Hinwick Hall by HMI Mrs Lock, 30 October 1945.
61 TNA, CH/M/8/5, Bi-annual report of After Care Association, y/e 31 March 1944.
62 TNA, ED62/140B, Dr Bywaters to Mr Elliot, both of the Board of Education, 22 July 1938.
63 TNA, ED62/140A, Report on School of Stitchery and Lace for Crippled Girls by Dr Bywaters, 15 August 1941.
64 TNA, ED62/140A, Report on School of Stitchery and Lace by Dr Bywaters, 27 June 1942.
65 LMA, 4305/3/31, Records of John Groom's Crippleage.
66 LMA, 4305/3/31, Organisations own report for 1940.
67 LMA, 4305/3/31, Organisations own report for 1941.

68   TNA, ED62/100, Report on St Loyes Training College for Cripples, Exeter, by Dr Bywaters, 18 August 1938.

69   TNA, ED62/100, Report of a meeting between Dame Georgina Buller (Chairman), Maudslay, Marshall and Dr Bywaters, c. 1940.

70   Central Council for the Care of Cripples, 'Training of Cripples', *The Times*, 11 October 1940.

71   TNA, ED62/100, Report on St Loyes Training College by Dr Bywaters, 13 May 1941.

72   TNA, ED62/100, Letter from St Loyes Training College to unknown recipient, 14 July 1942.

73   Prior to 1941 this was known as the Cripples Training College but after her visit in that year the Queen asked that the name be changed from 'Cripples' to 'Disabled'.

74   TNA, ED32/764, Old Members Annual Report, y/e 31 December 1939.

75   TNA, ED32/764, Old Members Annual Report, y/e 31 December 1941.

76   TNA, LAB19/59, Ministry of Labour, notes for the inspector by Secretary Miss Winder, December 1939.

77   TNA, LAB18/460, Report on disabled training colleges, by Mr Rouse, 15 August 1941.

78   TNA, LAB18/460, Watson-Smythe to Gomme, 21 August 1941.

4

HOSTELS AND INSTITUTIONS

The 'ineducable' and the 'difficult'

In order to have been evacuated as part of the government's special parties, a child had to have been certified as both disabled and educable. In the years since the end of the Second World War, advances in the diagnosis and treatment of mental health problems have led to an increased understanding of the different types of disorders. We now know that some children, far from being ineducable, simply have specific 'learning difficulties' that are unconnected to intellect. Someone with dyslexia, for example, merely has a problem processing language:

Learning disorder	*Particular difficulty*
Dyslexia	processing language (reading)
Dyscalculia	mathematics
Dysgraphia	writing
Dyspraxia	fine motor skills
Auditory Processing Disorder	hearing differences between sounds
Visual Processing Disorder	interpreting visual information

However, under the 1921 Education Act, a child's intellect was defined by its ability to learn, and assessed under a strict IQ test upon which a disorder of one or more of these learning skills would have had a considerable effect. This led to many children being wrongly diagnosed, either as feeble-minded or, perhaps more likely, as imbecile. Either diagnosis could have resulted in the child being denied an education. Officially, children assessed with an IQ of below 50 were deemed ineducable, whilst those whose score was 50–70, the feeble-minded, were allowed to attend special school. In reality, the feeble-minded were split into two further groups: high-grade MD (educable) and low-grade MD (ineducable). Some of the former group were included in the special parties for MDs; others were sent to mental institutions, or colonies, where they came under the LEAs. The low-grade feeble-minded children, however, were treated in a similar way to the idiots and imbeciles. It is this group of children, the ineducable – those who were denied a place in the official evacuation special parties (along with those who were included 'by mistake') – who will be the focus of the first part of this chapter. Also discussed will be children suffering from epilepsy, who spent their war years in special institutions, or colonies, and many of whom, as discussed in Chapter 1, were deemed to be imbecile.

The second group to be discussed is the children suffering some form of emotional disturbance. In 1939 there was no legal definition for these children, but they will be referred to as 'maladjusted' (as subsequently defined in the Education Act, 1944). Many of these children were evacuated into one of the special hostels for 'difficult' children that were established at the beginning of the war under the Government Evacuation Scheme (but not as part of the 'special parties'). The hostels, which were administered by the local authorities in the reception areas, catered both for children with long-standing psychiatric problems and for those whose difficulties came to light only after being evacuated into ordinary billets. These hostels will be contrasted with independent homes and schools for the disturbed child that were already in existence at the outbreak of war.

The underlying theme of this chapter is how change was brought about for children defined as having mental health difficulties, and the extent to which the war contributed to these changes. In order to make an informed assessment, all wartime developments need to be seen in the context of earlier instigations, and the recognition of inadequacies that, owing in part to the lack of funding, remained unresolved. Although a certain amount of prewar mental health provision was discussed in Chapter 1, the ambiguity and confusion surrounding mental health issues warrants a further examination of the social and political climate in the years leading up to the outbreak of war.

A call for change

Although some prior concern over the treatment of children suffering mental illness had been raised by private individuals and charities, the first official recognition of the issue was not instigated until the late 1890s. In 1898 the report of the Sharpe Committee, which had been set up by the government after pressure from concerned organisations, teachers and members of the medical profession, indicated a particular concern for children who were being teased and harassed by their more able peers.[1] The committee recommended that more special schools be established in place of some of the special classes in ordinary schools, and that the term 'feeble-minded' be dropped. Although none of these recommendations was incorporated into the subsequent education act (Elementary Education (Defective and Epileptic) Act, 1899), the Sharpe Committee had heard evidence from teachers, doctors, educational inspectors, administrators, and representatives from the welfare services, placing the care and education of disabled children on the public agenda for the first time.

After further pressure a Royal Commission was set up, reporting in 1908.[2] Again evidence came from concerned professionals, but this time the subsequent act (Education Act, 1913) made positive changes by developing a uniform national system of provision for disabled children (except for the lowest grade of feeble-minded).[3] However, the act was not implemented; the First World War and a lack of adequate funds were important factors, but the prevailing attitudes towards the mentally ill, and the idea that mental illness was hereditary, was also to blame. In line with eugenic thinking, the Royal Commission recommended the continuance of separate provision for children whose disabilities were described as genetic. In 1924 the Board of Education and the Board of Control set up a joint departmental committee to report on aspects of mental deficiency, with parts one and two of the report dealing specifically with the mentally defective child. Known as the Wood Committee, it published its report in 1929.[4]

One of the duties of the committee was to report on the number of mentally defective children at the time, and to assess how many would need to be dealt with under the Mental Deficiency Act, 1913. The committee reported that the total number of MD children was 105,000, which was three times the number estimated by the LEAs. This included thirty thousand idiots and imbeciles, which amounted to two and a half times the number estimated by the LEAs. It was also noted that no fewer than 77 per cent of the educable MD children were attending ordinary public elementary schools. The conclusion of the committee was that the inadequacy of special provision for the children meant that the system had broken down.[5]

Included in the Wood Report was the recommendation that all educable MD children, and the dull and backward children (who were not deficient) should be treated as a single educational group of 'retarded' children, and that the school system should be modified to provide for them. The committee further advised that all-age special classes should be abolished, and that separate classes should be provided for children over eleven years of age. Also, children who had not made substantial progress by the age of eleven, and needed care and supervision, should be the responsibility of the local MD authority, although the LEAs should make special provision for them. Significantly, the committee recommended that education provision should also be made for the imbeciles and idiots, who would continue to be under the care of the MD authorities. The committee members also felt that the educational criteria for ascertaining the status of children were inadequate, and that the real test should be 'the need of care and control'. They were concerned that all children who needed the services of the MD authorities should be found, and made special mention of those children in poor law institutions and Home Office schools, who might at the present time be denied adequate provision.

Despite the changes called for by the Wood Report, there were substantial obstacles to its implementation. The committee acknowledged that there was an inadequate number of special schools but was also aware that the funds needed to extend the system would not be available. Its recommendations that the elementary schools should be reorganised in order to provide for MD children caused confusion, and led some to believe that special schools were no longer needed. In 1933 George Newman was forced to clarify the continuing need for such schools in his annual report, and reiterated that it was the duty of the LEAs to provide them.[6]

One of the most significant recommendations of the Wood Committee was the abolishment of certification. A number of teachers in special schools opposed this, perhaps because they might lose some pupils and so face unemployment.[7] However, the stigma surrounding children receiving special education made certification unpopular with both parents and teachers alike, and sometimes prevented them from notifying the relevant authorities. It was the legal duty of each LEA to ascertain which children in the area were defective and capable of receiving benefit from instruction in special classes or schools, and to make provision for such education.[8] By definition this did not include those who were idiot or imbecile; under the Mental Deficiency Acts, 1913–27, it was the duty of each local authority to constitute a committee for the care of ineducable MD children in its area, and to provide suitable supervision. This might be in the form of supervision at home with parent or guardian, in an institution or in some other place under guardianship.

Another possible reason for the decline in notification was the controversy surrounding certifying officers and the method of certification. In April 1939 the *Daily Telegraph* and *Morning Post* reported that a Mr Keasley had been successful in his efforts to have his eleven-year-old son's certificate quashed. The next day *The Times* also reported the case in its 'Law Report'. The boy had been at a council school for some years, but in 1937 the father was told that his son was to be examined with a view to sending him to a special school. The father's doctor said that the child was fit for an ordinary council school, and this was later confirmed by a specialist. However, in 1938 he was certified imbecile and it was suggested that he should go to a mental institution. The father's contention was two fold. Firstly, the second doctor (two doctors had to sign the certificate) had never examined the boy, and secondly, as it was a borderline case, it should have been decided by the Board of Education (under s.31 of the Mental Deficiency Act, 1913).[9] In May 1939 the *Education Journal* contained a full explanation of why the father had won his case. The fact that one of the doctors had signed the certificate without seeing the boy, whilst seeming unsatisfactory, was not illegal. What decided the verdict was the fact that the case had not been put before the Board of Education.[10] Consequently, the certificate was quashed.

Misdiagnosis or the failure to place a child in the correct environment was relatively common before the war. There were cases of children wrongly admitted to mental hospitals or colonies, and cases of children who, under current legislation, should have been admitted to such institutions, but remained in a special school, an elementary school or even an approved school. During the war the problems continued, and were compounded by the effects of the war and the disruption of the evacuation. That being said, MD children, as with other disabled groups, became more visible during the war, forcing the authorities, often belatedly and not always adequately, to provide for them.

The 'wrong institution'

Problems surrounding ascertainment and certification, together with a decreasing number of available places in both residential special schools and mental institutions, meant that an increasing number of children were being sent to approved schools. In peacetime it was usual for each child remanded by the courts to see a medical officer, who was also a psychologist. However, during the war, with more and more doctors being sent to war, children's mental health difficulties were often missed. In 1942 the Board of Education, the LCC and the Children's Branch of the Home Office attempted to address the problem. Ascertainment was initially the responsibility of the LEAs but, again, too many doctors were being lost to the fighting forces. The Board of Education explained the situation:

> In present conditions, we cannot induce the LEAs to be more active in carrying out their duties towards MDs. It is accepted that they do not carry out their statutory duty in respect of ascertainment and education ... there is no use ascertaining if there is no accommodation.[11]

The Board enquired whether the Home Office would be prepared to concentrate, in a few approved schools, those children with a low IQ who required special attention and care. The response by the Home Office was that they should not have to be 'saddled with the responsibility' although they would try to meet the children's particular educational needs.[12]

In London at least, the problem seems to have been somewhat alleviated a short time after. The LCC announced that 'measures are in place to ensure that no certified MD child is committed to an approved school'.[13] However, the same arrangements were not as easy to secure outside London, because the majority of approved schools were conducted by voluntary bodies, and few were brought within the school medical service of the LEAs.

The courts were not the only ones to experience problems with detecting mental health problems. It sometimes happened that a child was sent to a special school, but was subsequently deemed ineducable and so had to leave the education system altogether, as the following example highlights. RC, who was aged twelve in 1942, was bullied at his regular council school. He could sound and name some letters and could copy from the blackboard, but could not read. Consequently, he was spat on by his classmates and told that he belonged in a lunatic asylum. He was examined by the LEA and was found to have normal speech, hearing and sight, was affectionate and clean and his behaviour was excellent. However, he was backward for his age. He was ascertained feeble-minded educable and sent to a residential special school. One year later, when he had still not learnt to read, he was certified ineducable and was forced to leave the school.[14]

In cases such as this, unless the child had committed an offence, it was usually the decision of the parent whether to care for the child at home or to have him or her committed to a mental institution. Sometimes though, the parents refused to accept the diagnosis and disputed the classification of their child, as the following example demonstrates. PAB, aged twelve, was certified feeble-minded ineducable in 1944 whilst at a special MD school and, at first, the mother agreed to send her to an institution. However, the father disagreed and they entered into a lengthy correspondence with the authorities to try and keep the girl in school. Their request for re-examination was agreed but the diagnosis did not change and the girl was sent home. Several months later the girl 'slipped through the net' and was evacuated to a residential special school. Once there, she was certified imbecile and sent home. The staff at the school complained that she had dirty habits and refused to speak. The mother replied that she must have been neglected. The local county council tried to reassure both parents that the girl would be better off, and safer, in an institution in the country, but to no avail. In June 1945 their parliamentary candidate wrote to the education committee asking for the family to be helped in some way. However, in March 1946 the girl was examined yet again and was found to be a 'Mongol' with a mental age of three. The parents finally had to concede and the girl left the education system.[15]

As in the prewar period, many low-grade children during the war were kept in special schools, instead of being certified ineducable and thereby being forced to leave the special education system. Some teachers may not have realised the seriousness of a child's problem; others, as already discussed, were reluctant to involve the MD authorities. Undoubtedly, the circumstances of a school and its pupils relied, to a considerable degree, on the reports and recommendations of the visiting HMIs. HMI Miss Moodie, for example, reported in 1940 that most children at the Hollingdean MD School in Brighton were of a relatively low grade, but did not recommend their removal. In 1943 she noted that not much had changed. The children were interested in current affairs and most were capable of doing jobs in school, shopping, gardening and boot-repairing but education had not really been affected because they were low-grade children who were 'not capable of doing much'.[16]

HMI Lumsden, on the other hand, almost without fail, recommended that low-grade MDs should be removed from special schools. After visiting a MD school in Oldham in 1932 he had reported that 'The headmistress has a soft heart and although some are undoubted imbeciles, unless a child is a nuisance, she keeps it'.[17] Lumsden requested that assessments be carried out, so that those of a low IQ could be notified to the MD authorities, and those with an IQ of 70 or above could be decertified. There were no further inspections of the school until 1941, when it was reported that only educable MDs were admitted.[18]

On this occasion Lumsden had been successful. However, with an overstretched inspectorate, and with not all inspectors being as 'conscientious' as Lumsden, it was inevitable that some low-grade MD children would remain in the special school system throughout the war. One such case was that of PW, a boy who was sent to Pontville RC MD School in Lancashire. He entered the school in 1938. In 1949 the Board of Control visited the school to inquire into the number of ineducable children still there. This is a particularly poignant case and is best explained in the words of the inspector:

> This is a low-grade Mongolian imbecile, who is unable to speak but says odd, badly pronounced words and utters animal noises. Physically, he is very immature. He comes from a good home and has been at Pontville since the age of 3 years. His parents pay for him and he sleeps in the convent – used to sleep in a dormitory. He does not attend school and plays by himself all day long in a corner of the garden or in the convent. The Sisters 'love' him and expend much of their maternal affection on him – and he is a repulsive looking lad. Since he is in the convent by a private arrangement between the Mother Superior and his

parents and is not at school and no longer occupies a dormitory bed, I suggest no action be taken. When he gets older the Sisters will have to discharge him, but they hope before that happens that 'the good Lord will take him to Heaven'.[19]

For some reason, there was only one inspection at this school during the war. This was done by Lumsden in 1943, when, as usual, he recommended that all ineducables be removed.[20] Obviously, PW was not removed, but his case may have been helped by the fact that his family could afford to pay for his care. Indeed, the financial aspect, rather than legislation, could determine the type of child that was sent to an institution, as the following case highlights.

The Mary Dendy Home and Council School for MD children at Great Warford, Sandlebridge, was initially owned by the Incorporated Lancashire and Cheshire Society for the Permanent Care of the Feeble-minded. When Lumsden made his first visit, in September 1941, he found that despite Mary Dendy's policy of limiting admissions to the feeble-minded, a large number of imbeciles had been admitted. Lumsden concluded that this had occurred because the LEAs had sent them there under the 1921 Education Act for the purpose of obtaining a grant, instead of notifying them to the MD authorities. Also, that the Committee had accepted Board of Education cases without much scrutiny. Lumsden recommended that the feeble-minded should not continue to mix with the imbeciles, and that the Medical Superintendant should re-examine the children.[21] In his next report nine months later, sixty children had been re-examined and it was found that almost all had been graded too high.[22] Despite this, the Committee decided that the children would stay where they were: 'Classification is difficult because low and high grades had been together for some years before the council took over, and the high grade looked after the low grade. So the low grades are attached to where they live.'[23] It must be remembered that HMI Lumsden was an employee of the Board of Education, and part of his responsibility would have been to ensure that the Board was not paying grants for children who were ineducable. In the majority of cases, he recommended that such children be removed from a special school. However, as alternative accommodation became increasingly difficult to find, it became acceptable to the Board for the children to remain in the school, as long as the mental health authorities, and not the Board of Education, paid for their care. This was the case at Mary Dendy's, and also at a residential special school in Liverpool, where approximately twenty-five per cent of the children proved to be ineducable. Ironically, in this case it was the head teacher, and not Lumsden, who insisted on discharging the children.[24]

One way of solving the problem of where to rehouse ineducable children without having to find additional accommodation was to 'exchange' them with educable children wrongly placed in mental institutions. It is not known how frequently this occurred, but at some point during the war an exchange was arranged between two institutions in Birmingham. When Monyhull Colony opened shortly after the end of the First World War, the only other institution for mentally disabled children in Birmingham was Erdington House, an institution for idiots. As only a small number of places were available for children at Erdington House, a large number of ineducable children were admitted to Monyhull. When the Board of Education began inspecting the school in 1940, there was a large range of intelligence among the children. Out of the 360 children in the colony, 240 attended the special school, and these were organised into two streams: low grade and high grade.

HMI Lumsden found that the work of some of the high-grade children was of the same standard as children in ordinary MD schools. On the other hand, the low grades, whilst seeming busy and happy, were capable only of occupational work. It was found that some of these children were of a lower grade than those at the nearby Marston Green mental institution. Although Lumsden inspected Monyhull each year, it is unclear exactly when the ineducable from Monyhull were exchanged with the educables from Marston Green but, by January 1944, when the Superintendent of Monyhull reported to the school sub-committee, he said that as a result of the exchange 'there are only a few unsuitable children who remain and the HMI is more satisfied'.[25]

Epileptics

Arguably the most difficult category of disabled child to accommodate appropriately was the epileptic. As discussed in Chapter 1, the epileptic child was often thought to be suffering from a mental illness. In 1932 the problem was raised at a conference of representatives of schools for epileptic children, where it was agreed that there should be no epileptics in special schools if they were of a low mental grade. Although the accommodation situation improved slightly after 1932, there were still waiting lists in special schools when war broke out, leading eventually to the Liverpool conference of 1943, in which representatives of colonies for epileptics brought the problem to the attention of the Board of Control and the Board of Education.[26]

The four main epileptic colonies during the Second World War were Chalfont St Peter, David Lewis, Lingfield and Maghull. The largest of these was the Chalfont St Peter Epileptic Colony in Buckinghamshire which, in 1939, contained five hundred men, women, boys and girls in houses of approximately forty each. The children's quarters were arranged in houses providing a dormitory, feeding and play rooms for 37 children and each with a classroom

opposite.[27] No MDs were officially accepted at Chalfont, but a limited number
of blind epileptics were. When Lumsden inspected in 1944 he found that one
of the blind epileptics was also an imbecile. However, on this occasion there
is no evidence that he recommended the child's removal.[28] Another relatively
large colony for epileptics was the Maghull Home in Liverpool. Opened in
1935, the colony was made up of several houses, of which children used two.
Despite the rules regarding MDs, Lumsden found that at least twenty per cent
of the children could be classed as such, and ten were ineducable. Again, there
was no recommendation to remove anyone.[29]

An obvious difference between Lumsden's reports on special schools and
those in epileptic colonies is his attitude towards the MD children. It is likely
that his failure to recommend the removal of MD epileptics was due to the
lack of alternative accommodation for them. Although there was a shortage of
accommodation for all groups of disabled children, places for epileptics who
were also MD were virtually non-existent outside the epileptic colonies.

The problems associated with children being wrongly placed, both before
and during the war, were both financial and practical. For example, the Board
of Education did not want to pay for ineducable children, and it was difficult to
teach a group of children made up of different levels of ability. Whilst it was the
duty of the HMIs to ensure that these children did not remain in the special
education system, they were not always successful. Although not all children
who were denied a place in a special school spent their war years in a mental
institution (some remained at home with parents or guardians), many did. The
following section examines the level of disruption suffered by these children
and how the authorities reacted to the problems of safety and the shortage of
bed space.

Children in mental institutions

According to the Board of Control, there were ample places in MD colonies
in the prewar period, but they were getting increasingly difficult to fill, and
the Board queried the fact that imbeciles were still being educated in schools.
By 1939, despite the efforts of the HMIs and certifying officers, there was a
real concern within the Board of Control regarding the fall in numbers notified.[30] In sharp contrast, during the Second World War, all mental institutions, including the MD colonies, experienced severe overcrowding. In all,
more than 25,000 of their beds in England and Wales were taken over by the
Emergency Medical Services.[31] Bomb damage, and the necessity of relocating
patients on the south and south-east coasts, served to worsen the problem.
That said, unlike the special schools that had been evacuated into established

residential premises, the majority of mental institutions were able to carry on in their original premises during the war. However, life didn't always carry on as normal, and the children were very often affected by war conditions, as highlighted by the following examples.

At the Meanwood Park Institution and Colony in Leeds, the Board of Control reported that war conditions had imposed a considerable burden. The colony, which opened in 1920, was re-organised in 1932 into the 'villas system', which was designed to prevent people losing their identification, and to give a community spirit.[32] Along with the six villas, the colony also contained a school. During the war, part of the colony was commandeered by the EMS, which requisitioned 270 out of the 481 beds.[33] Although no serious harm was done to the long-term patients, medical and admission work was made complicated by the detailed attention which had to be given accommodating both British soldiers and German prisoners of war; their segregation was made easier because the premises were already designed to segregate the sexes. Although the colony and its air raid shelters suffered overcrowding, no real damage was caused by the war. Indeed, it has been found that, although this was officially forbidden, patients and British soldiers did mix and the newcomers brought variety, interest, opportunities and supplies.[34]

In contrast to Meanwood Park, life in the Monyhull Colony in Birmingham went on more or less as normal, although the risk of air raids had forced the use of dining rooms as dormitories. This had caused overcrowding, but no serious epidemics, and Lumsden found that the children's health was generally good.[35]

By March 1941 the Board of Control had surrendered approximately twenty-five per cent of its mental institutions to the EMS and fighting services. At this time, with a serious threat of a German invasion, the Civil Defence and the Ministry of Home Security were discussing what to do with the three asylums in and around Colchester. All were within a mile or two of the 'defended line' (Colchester formed an important defence centre in the event of invasion) and the authorities were worried about the patients being used as a screen by the Germans.[36] Another concern was for the local population in the event of the patients being released. In a letter to the Ministry of Health, an official at the Board of Control wrote: 'I know of no way of rendering dangerous mental patients harmless, unless you regard a machine gun or strychnine as permissible methods.'[37] It was agreed to move the more dangerous patients if the need arose.

A particular problem faced by the mental health authorities during the war, and at the Meanwood Park Institution in particular, was the high number of absconders. This was blamed on the abnormally high proportion of delinquents being admitted and, while it was accepted that a mental institution was unsuitable for them, it was seen as unavoidable because of the lack of alternative accommodation.[38]

The issue of delinquency was the subject of many debates during the Second World War. Some children, rightly or wrongly, were sent to approved schools, as has been discussed. Others were labelled merely as 'difficult' and sent to hostels from where, after a period of 'treatment', they were (re)billeted in ordinary households. A number of children suffered from some form of emotional disturbance and were labelled 'maladjusted'. The following section discusses the possible causes of the illness, the various ways in which it manifested itself and the ways in which it was treated. The section argues that the treatment of emotional disturbance was an area in which there was considerable innovation during the war. As children became more visible, their mental health problems became more recognised, and it soon became apparent that the hostel system, introduced at the beginning of the war for children deemed too difficult to billet normally, as well as the Child Guidance Service, would need to be expanded.

Emotional disturbance

Although there was no official recognition of 'emotional disturbance' as a category of disability in any of the legislation passed prior to 1944, during the late 1920s the needs of such children were recognised by the establishment of the Child Guidance Council. The Council had been formed in 1927 'to encourage the provision of skilled treatment for children showing behavioural disturbances and early symptoms of nervous disorder'.[39] It was thought that by methods of play therapy, careful observation and attention to the child's physical and mental weaknesses and to his or her home conditions, the child could be helped to develop those qualities necessary for life in society which he or she had previously lacked.[40]

During the 1930s there was a steady growth in child guidance clinics (CGCs), from just two in 1930 to 54 in September 1939. Of these, 22 were provided, wholly or in part, by LEAs.[41] Fully staffed clinics were composed of psychiatrists, educational psychologists and psychiatric social workers (PSWs), and referrals were usually made by care committees, hospitals, parents, teachers or probation officers attached to juvenile courts.[42] Under s.35 (2) of the Children and Young Persons Act 1933, it was the duty of each LEA to furnish the court with a report of the child's home surroundings, school record, health and character. The clinics were frequently used by juvenile courts as an alternative to detention, whereby a probation order would be issued with the condition that the child attended a CGC for treatment.[43]

The importance of CGCs and the high esteem in which they were held at the outbreak of the Second World War is perhaps best summed up by an article, entitled 'Cured by Kindness', which appeared in the *Times Educational Supplement* (*TES*) in July 1939:

> Child Guidance Clinics, with their insistence on psychological study of children, are in a great measure responsible for the changed attitude towards delinquency that is to be found among a large part of the population. London child guidance clinics have treated and often cured children and have helped to educate public opinion in the theories that lie behind the treatment. The difficult child is not merely naughty but suffering from unconscious disturbance causing asocial or neurotic behaviour.[44]

Early in 1939 the Mental Health Emergency Committee (MHEC) was formed by national organisations for mental health (including the Child Guidance Council) in order to formulate and carry out a co-ordinated policy of action with regard to mental health problems in time of war. The duties of the committee were to assist government departments, local authorities, the community and individual cases of mental and nervous disturbance. This included children who had previously attended CGCs or who needed their help after evacuation, through becoming difficult or unbalanced.[45]

Experts at the time disagreed on the level of impact that would be caused by the evacuation. Shortly before the outbreak of war Dr John Bowlby of the North London CGC wrote that 'there is no evidence that normal children over 5 are likely to suffer serious psychological harm from being sent away, although already unstable children may get worse and the normal children may be unhappy and homesick'.[46] Some mental health workers, however, advised that there would be severe emotional disturbances among nervous children, unstable defectives and unstable and unbalanced adolescents if war were to break out.[47] The child psychologist Susan Isaacs agreed and in the first week of the war wrote to the President of the Board of Education expressing concern for the mental health of young evacuees, as already symptoms such as sleeplessness, night terrors, ill-health and difficult behaviour were showing and could later develop into inability to learn and delinquency.[48] The Board members were themselves concerned, warning that 'if we neglect the mental health of childhood we cannot escape its results in many kinds of mental ailment – dull, backward, neurotic, "difficult" or delinquent children'.[49]

Despite the concerns raised, in the early stages of the war 18 of the 43 clinics recognised by the Child Guidance Council were requisitioned or closed.[50] However, the evacuation soon highlighted the large number of children who were unbilletable owing to their disturbing behaviour and were in need of psychiatric and psychological services. As a result, by August 1940 old CGCs had re-opened (but not in London), five new ones were established (including one at a London hospital) and four temporary ones opened.[51] In addition, the MHEC offered the services of its educational psychologists to LEAs with the hope that much could be learnt about the causes of bad behaviour.[52]

One particular group which was concerned that the evacuation was having an adverse effect on the mental health of vulnerable children, which believed strongly in the work of the CGCs and which appears to have had some considerable influence was the Joint Committee of Working Women's Organisations.[53] At the end of 1941 the committee wrote to R. A. Butler MP to relay its concerns about the lack of CGCs. Members who had experience of social work in their localities, and especially in the children's courts, felt that wartime conditions made the provision of child guidance more urgent than ever before.[54] At that time LEAs differed widely in their attitude towards child guidance: 'Some regard it with the suspicion which psych-analysis arouses in many of us; others attach the highest value to it.'[55] However, the Board of Education agreed to help finance additional CGCs and, by end of 1942, there were 62 CGCs in reception areas.

The following year the Provisional National Council for Mental Health (provisional NCMH) was established. This was a new central voluntary body whose aim was to co-ordinate the activities of the voluntary mental health organisations, including the Child Guidance Council and the work of the MHEC. One of the first undertakings of the new body was to form the Child Guidance Committee, and one of the aims of the committee was to establish new CGCs. In the first year another six clinics were opened; by the end of the war there were 79 clinics, 75 per cent of which were supported entirely by LEAs.[56]

The type of emotional disturbance dealt with in CGCs during the war was broader than in the early days of the service. In the beginning 'the existence of problem children, as distinct from children with problems' was appreciated by few.[57] Consequently, it was children whose behaviour presented problems for others who were likely to be referred. Indeed, the modern child guidance clinic began with the study of delinquents.[58] Gradually, the teaching and medical professions, and parents, came to recognise that the unnaturally quiet, withdrawn, child also required psychiatric help. The extent of the problem, however, was not realised until the evacuation.

One symptom of emotional disturbance, or 'maladjustment', was bed-wetting and, whilst for some this was regarded as merely the poor hygiene habits of the urban working class, for others it was evidence of emotional trauma and should be treated as such. An article sympathetic to this view appeared in the *Medical Officer* shortly after the outbreak of war, asserting that it wasn't surprising that children wet the bed in the excitement of the evacuation, and that most had been cured by patience and understanding.[59] Evidence was to show, however, that enuresis was one of the most frequent problems amongst 'disturbed' evacuees. One example comes from a CGC in Cambridge where, in a study of 155 evacuated children referred to the clinic, it was found that over sixty per cent suffered from some kind of incontinence, mainly of the bladder. Troublesome behaviour and quarrelling were the next most frequent symptom about which complaints were made (7 and 8 per cent respectively). Other 'bad' behavioural habits included disobedience and temper-tantrums. The more 'nervous' children tended to experience home-sickness, sleep-disturbance, crying, anxiety, speech difficulties, babyishness, worrying and fearfulness.[60]

Attitudes towards the disturbed child were ambiguous in the early days of the war. The fact that urban children did not necessarily act the same as their rural counterparts was reason enough for some to be labelled delinquent. In April 1940 a Mr David Wills addressed the Howard League for Penal Reform on the difficulties faced by evacuees. It was his belief that in many cases the evacuation had exposed the children as delinquents because, for example, it was more difficult to escape detection when stealing from the village shop than from a stall in the street. Also, Wills went on, conversation allowed at home was suddenly frowned upon by foster parents, as indecent and wicked. He believed that this change in attitude in adults, by suddenly reacting differently to actions which the child had regarded as normal, caused emotional disturbances.[61]

It was recognised early on that treatment on an out-patient basis would not be sufficient to meet the needs of all emotionally disturbed children. Less than a month after the outbreak of the Second World War the Board of Education held a meeting with members of two of London's CGCs to discuss behaviour problems amongst evacuated children.[62] Two types of difficulty had emerged in the reception areas for children who, it was agreed, would need some kind of residential accommodation. The first concerned children with emotional problems due to separation from home, aggravated by 'mal-billeting'. The second related to children whose behaviour problems probably already existed in their own homes. Some of these children perhaps already attended a CGC. In 1939 the use of residential accommodation for the emotionally disturbed child was uncommon but not unknown. In 1931 the Northamptonshire Home for Girls in Dallington (later known as the Dallington Home for Maladjusted Girls), formerly a female orphanage, became a home for difficult girls.[63] The girls attended the local elementary school but the home provided social and occupational interests, and psychiatric treatment was provided. However, the Dallington home was not regarded as a great success, and in February/March 1939 it was reported that the home was doing more harm than good. The girls were said to run riot, they were institutionalised and aggressive towards the staff.[64] By February 1940 only a handful of girls remained at the home; because of the closure of CGCs there had been a lack of referrals. Soon after, the home closed and the lease, owned by the LEA, went to the Church of England's Waifs and Strays Society.[65]

Another establishment that catered for the disturbed child at the beginning of the war was the Red Hill School in West Chistlehurst, Kent, a private boarding school. Unlike the one at Dallington, however, this school had not been approved by the Board of Education and so did not qualify for government funding under s.80. In 1935 the school had been denied approval mainly because of the visiting inspector's uneasiness at the headmaster's attitude and his lack of precaution in keeping the sexes apart in lavatories and bedrooms.[66] In July 1938 the school was visited again, this time after an application had been made to the Joint Register of Foster-Homes and Schools for Nervous, Difficult and Retarded Children, which had been set up by the Child Guidance Council and the CAMW to help place disturbed children. Again the headmaster, Mr Shaw, gave a bad impression and the application was rejected.

Neither the headmaster of the Red Hill School nor any of his staff had any academic qualifications in psychology or training at CGCs. Before the war Mr Shaw was described as evasive, unpleasant and defensive, giving no proper answers on his methods. However, when war broke out, the Ministry of Health sent evacuees there, and the Board of Education's inspectors suddenly gained a more favourable impression of him. In June 1941 the school was approved (under s.80) and a girl was sent there by the education authorities. The following year, after a visiting inspector was denied access to the girl, she was moved to another school. The inspector reported, 'we feel there are grounds for an inquiry and will not be sending any more children there'.[67] Five weeks later Lumsden and Dr Bywaters, both from the Board of Education, made an unannounced visit but everyone, including Mr Shaw, was on a picnic. The teacher who greeted the two officials answered questions on school work, but was evasive on other things, especially admissions policy and methods of treatment. Despite this, children began to be sent there, and seven months later, after a visit with notice, the same two officials reported the school as satisfactory. By this time there were 49 children at the school, including 19 sent there by LEAs. The following month the total number had risen to 60, most of who were said to suffer sexual difficulties. In many reports, both before and during the war, visiting officers mentioned Mr Shaw's 'preoccupation with sexual matters'.[68] The last report was made in 1944 when 61 children resided at the school, including 46 sent from LEAs, and the school was said to be satisfactory.[69]

From the available evidence it would seem that the school was used by the education authorities only because of the lack of alternative accommodation. The headmaster's evasive attitude and his preoccupation with sexual matters were noted both before and during the war but it was only before the need for places became urgent that the school was seen as unsuitable. This case has many similarities with Besford Court (see Chapter 2) and is perhaps another example of the conditions of war having a detrimental effect on disabled children.

The examples of Dallington and Red Hill show that the number of residential places for emotionally disturbed children was extremely small in the prewar period. That said, it was recognised by the health and education authorities that such places were needed. The Dallington Home's prospectus described the type of child who would benefit as being: 'The child who creates social difficulties by repeated abnormal behaviour as a result, in most cases, of failure of adjustment in reaction to home environment'.[70] In September 1939 a similar kind of system was required for the child evacuees who were of the same type, and then also for the many whose problems came to light only after they had been evacuated to individual billets. As a direct response to this need, the Ministry of Health set up a number of 'hostels'. At first they were established under the Government Evacuation Scheme but in 1941 they were taken over by local county councils and became a separate entity.

Hostels for 'difficult' children

The primary purpose of the hostel system was to fit children suffering behavioural problems with life into an ordinary community. Initially it was thought that children merely needed a period of special care or supervision, but it was soon realised that many would also need a steady rebuilding of their stability and confidence. In order to do this, it would be necessary to foster an environment of community, rather than institution, and to provide individual affection, understanding and opportunities for growth.[71]

Although the Ministry of Health had foreseen the need for hostel accommodation, the number of places required was underestimated at the initial evacuation planning stage.[72] Consequently, as places were limited, it was necessary to make their stay short-term. In 1940 the Ministry of Health published a review of the evacuation scheme to date, advising that more hostel accommodation should be provided and that disturbed children should remain in hostels only until they were judged to be fit for ordinary billeting.[73] It had come to light that some hostels had retained children even after successful treatment in order to avoid the difficulties of rebilleting, with the result that other cases could not be admitted.

Although the concept of residential accommodation for disturbed children was not entirely new, the type and scale of the hostel system during the Second World War was unprecedented. As a result, mistakes were made; some children received the wrong treatment, others received no treatment at all and many became institutionalised. Many hostels accepted children of all school ages, all types of difficulty and both sexes. With time, however, the hostel scheme improved; its value to the disturbed child was realised, and wardens and psychiatrists began to understand more about the causes of abnormal behaviour.

In 1944 the Ministry of Health published the results of a survey of hostel experience under the evacuation scheme, which had been carried out in July 1943.[74] The aim of the survey was to examine how the hostel system had evolved between September 1939 and July 1943, and to assess the ways in which children had been affected. It was hoped that the results would be of benefit to both voluntary and official bodies, during the war and in normal times, which might need to provide groups of children with a similar type of care. Out of the 215 hostels in England and Wales, 48 were selected for the survey.

The surveyed hostels accommodated children with an age range of five to sixteen. A broad mix was included, with some hostels catering only for girls, some for boys and some for both. The children's behaviour was also mixed. For example, according to the survey, 'in general hostels do not specialise in one type of problem, and it has been found unsatisfactory to have too many children who, say, pilfer or behave aggressively'.[75] The survey, taken after four years of evacuation, highlighted the degree of improvement that had been made in assessing the child's need for this kind of care. In the early days there was little or no investigation into a child's background. By 1943, however, the child's particular difficulties would determine to which hostel he or she would be sent. Some children responded best in a small hostel, where the matron could give individual attention and 'mothering', whereas others might be more suited to a larger hostel, where there were many interests and activities, and perhaps a male warden acting as a father figure. The main purpose of the hostels was to help the child reach the stage where he or she could be billeted out with a family, and the hostel staff aimed to provide a sense of community where the child could develop a sense of self-respect and responsibility. The children were encouraged to mix with local children and to join organisations such as the Guides, Brownies, Scouts and Cubs.

One of the most important considerations for a successful hostel was the choice of staff. As this type of hostel was in its infant, or experimental, stage there were no clearly defined or recognised qualifications that applicants should possess. Fortunately, though, it was found that the most important skills needed were sympathy and understanding. Having said that, most of the staff did hold practical qualifications of some kind, such as catering or household management, and some were qualified nurses, teachers or social workers. Also, the Ministry of Health organised courses and conferences for the staff. Here the emphasis was on the causes of children's difficulties, advice on occupational activities and forms of play. It was also advised that, although the children suffered from some form of behavioural problem, the hostel should be run on a relaxed basis, giving the children as much freedom as possible. In one hostel, accommodating 26 boys aged nine to fourteen, the regime was restricted and there was a policy of segregation. This had a bad effect on the boys' discipline and, consequently, on their reputation in the village. However, a new warden was found, the boys responded to their new-found freedom and their standing in the community was reinstated.[76]

An example of just how demanding caring for 'difficult' children could be is given in a report by the matron of a hostel near Bradford.[77] The matron joined the school in July 1941, one month after it opened. On arrival she found six extremely difficult children in an unsuitable house in the middle of the village and too close to the river, and with no adequate garden. The children were very hostile; they frequently threw stones at the staff and would sit on the dinner table with one foot in the food. One day they tried to run away. The matron said she would join them, and escorted them in hot sun and thunderstorms. After two hours the children had had enough and went back to the house. The matron said it was a turning point in their relationship, although some problems remained.

The children at the Bradford hostel were unpopular with the locals, who suggested physical violence. The matron said that this was not her way, and that she preferred activities to keep the children occupied, even though that often led to destruction. The views of the local community were important for the success of the hostels and, according to the survey, most were supportive of the scheme, and their children were often invited to the hostels to play with the children. In one area, a local lady invited eight to ten boys to tea at her house every week. In some areas, locals became involved in the hostel, helping out with mending, bathing the children or staying overnight when a resident staff member was on leave.

It was usual for the children to attend a local school with other evacuees, either together with the local children or as a separate group. Sometimes, though (as in eight out of the 48 hostels surveyed), hostel children were educated separately. This was due to local conditions and had mixed results. On the positive side, being a smaller group, they received more attention and enjoyed a freer curriculum. On the negative, they were more isolated, adding to their sense of being different.

In the 48 hostels surveyed, deliberately selected in order to provide a balanced view of the system, differing degrees of psychiatric treatment and/or advice were available in all but eight and, if any child needed psychiatric help in those hostels, they could be transferred to one where such help was available. By the time of the survey most children were being sent to hostels from ordinary billets rather than straight from home. Sometimes it was thought to be unnecessary to remove the child from the billet, but the decision whether to send an evacuee to a hostel depended largely on whether the foster-parents could cope with the child's 'abnormal' behaviour. For example, although enuresis was one of the most common symptoms of emotional disturbance, it did not automatically result in being sent to a hostel. According to the Ministry of Health, 'a boy who wets the bed should not be moved for this reason alone as it gives no clue to the real nature of the problem, and moving him might make more problems for the hostel and for the child'.[78] In these cases, if the foster-parents were agreeable, the child could remain in the billet and attend a CGC.

By July 1943 there were more than 3,400 children in 225 hostels in which psychiatric services were, in varying degrees, available.[79] These hostels were run by the local authorities; others were run by private or charitable organisations. For example, in November 1941 the Friends Relief Society opened the Chaigley Manor Hostel for maladjusted children from Liverpool. Unusually for hostels, this establishment also provided education, although members of staff were unpaid except for fifteen shillings per week pocket money. At first the children were the nervous and delicate type who had proved unsuitable for ordinary billets. However, after twelve months children were admitted with differing degrees of maladjustment. Many of these came from homes 'which are unfavourable to normal development'.[80] As some of the children were paid for by the Board of Education, the hostel was subject to inspection. In June 1944 HMI Lumsden inspected the premises and found that the atmosphere was conducive to healthy child development, but there was overcrowding in the dormitories and there was a tendency to accept children with no maladjustment but who merely needed care and protection. As was usual when he found that the wrong type of child was being accommodated in an establishment, Lumsden noted that there was a 'need to make adjustments'.[81] On the whole, though, the Chaigley Manor hostel was deemed a success.

In addition to the hostels run by the State and by private organisations, a number of schools for difficult or maladjusted children opened up during the war. However, as was the case before the war, those schools were not always successful, as highlighted by the following example. The Little Becketts Farm School for difficult boys at Saffron Walden, Essex, was approved by the Board of Education and the Home Office in June 1942. In January and February 1943, officials from these departments visited the school after complaints had been made by the Essex Education Office. The visitors found the whole situation 'disquieting' but had to decide whether to continue to approve the school. Conditions had greatly deteriorated since the school's initial approval, and there had been an unauthorised increase in numbers. The report read: 'we would normally advise against approval by the Board but with the lack of alternative accommodation, should be approved under certain conditions'.[82] One week later the Board of Education received the report of a hospital doctor who had been acting as the school's MO for two years, and had recently visited the children:

> I have only paid occasional visits but I feel I want a bath when I go there. I cannot think the boys will improve. One of the boys was in my hospital for a few weeks. [He was] supposed to be a hopeless enuretic and also incontinent of faeces. When in hospital he never wetted the bed and was the brightest boy in the ward. As soon as he returned to the school all the abnormalities returned and he was as bad as ever.[83]

The doctor concluded by describing the situation at the school as 'unreal and phoney'. In the same month as the doctor's visit, an officer of the Children's Branch of the Home Office reported a conversation he had had with a probation officer (PO), who had taken a boy to the school but had been so depressed by the conditions that he almost took the boy home.[84] Parents also complained: 'filthy clothes, torn; no washing and cooking facilities; dirty beds, only one blanket each; lack of discipline; lessons not compulsory, no books'.[85] The PO questioned how the Home Office could have approved such a school. In contrast to the Besford Court and Red Hill establishments, the Little Becketts Farm School had its Board of Education and Home Office approval withdrawn (March 1943) and all children referred by them were removed by the end of the following month. Rather disturbingly, however, Mr Casteel, who ran the school and, incidentally, had previously worked with Mr Shaw at the Red Hill hostel, was allowed to continue taking in private pupils.[86]

A more successful private organisation that accommodated difficult children during the war was the Caldecott Community. Although not officially part of the Government Evacuation Scheme, the Community received help with its evacuation arrangements from the Home Office in July 1941. In return, the Honorary Director Miss L. M. Rendel, agreed to accept a group of 'toughs'. Home Office cases seemed to fall into three types – toughs, neurotics and delinquents – and Miss Rendel usually preferred to treat the latter two groups only. The Caldecott Community hostel did not offer any special psychiatric treatment, preferring instead to manage on 'commonsense lines' and with apparent success. Apart from Home Office cases, the Community accepted the Board of Education's difficult or maladjusted children and all the children appeared to mix well together. Dr Bywaters from the Board of Education found that although some children (mainly the Home Office children) were difficult to manage, all were well dressed, in good health and seemingly happy.[87]

Regardless of the successes and failures of individual hostels, much was learnt during the war about the emotional needs of children. Awareness was raised of the objective reality of children's losses and traumas, and how their behaviour reflected the sense of loss and rejection they experienced when parents failed to write or to visit.[88] According to Clare Winnicott, a social worker who supervised five Oxfordshire hostels during the war, many believed that adjustment to hostel life would be easier if the child's contact with the past was severed. Many parents rarely communicated with their child, and social workers were often their only link. The children's expectant, almost desperate, reaction to any kind of contact with their parents made social workers realise the need to respect the child's attachment to the parents, no matter how distant or problematic.[89]

Winnicott also had a retort for those who believed that all a child needed in order to be good was a good home: 'the answer is not so simple. They cannot enter into a good home and become part of it until the idea of a good home has first been created or revived in them.'[90] Often the children, especially those from the worst backgrounds, tended to create the ideal home in their mind, a fantasy that they would never be able to find. Children who were sent to hostels from billets rather than straight from home suffered a second rejection, and Winnicott noted that those children often brought with them a deep sense of failure and guilt. She regarded an important function of the hostel as helping the child to reconstruct the past, however good or bad it had been.

The work done in hostels during the war by Clare Winnicott (née Britton) and her husband, the renowned psychiatrist Donald Winnicott, along with that of Susan Isaacs, was part of several initiatives into emotional disturbance stimulated by the crisis of war and the evacuation. Anna Freud, for example, studied the behaviour of nursery children; and John Bowlby analysed the behaviour of delinquents.[91] After the war Bowlby, Isaacs, Donald Winnicott and Clare Britton (as yet unmarried) were interviewed about their work by the 'Care of Children Committee' as part of the Home Office's inquiry which reported in 1946 (known as the Curtis Report) and led to the Children Act, 1948.

The hostel system was largely experimental, and occurred as a direct consequence of the war. The concept of residential care for emotionally disturbed people (as with a number of other disabilities) was seen as beneficial and, as will be seen in the following chapter, was adapted and extended after the war. Another wartime experiment that involved the treatment of emotional disturbance, although not arising as a result of wartime conditions, was Brambling House, a special day school in Chesterfield, Derbyshire. Initiated by the Board of Education in 1936, and opened in July 1939, the school was the first to accommodate physically defective, delicate and emotionally disturbed children.

Case study: Brambling House

Brambling House was set in extensive grounds, and was designed to accommodate both an open-air school and a children's centre (essentially a CGC). The house and grounds were bought by Chesterfield education authority for the sum of £3,000, but over £10,000 was subsequently spent on renovations. In the grounds, school buildings were erected with provision for 125 children and, once finished, the premises comprised five detached classrooms of the open-air type, a large combined rest and recreation room, dining room, shower baths, medical inspection room, cloak rooms and accommodation for the staff.[92] The following extract from a 1939 Board of Education publication describes the principles of OA schools:

> They receive the PD or delicate child who, for the time being, is unfit for education side by side with healthy school fellows; they cure or ameliorate the child's ill health, at the same time providing education suitable to his individual capacity; in the majority of cases they restore the child to normal health and enable him to be transferred back to the public elementary school, there to continue his education.[93]

For the children's centre, the house was adapted to provide rooms for consultation, diagnosis and treatment, with waiting rooms, and facilities for the staff. Accommodation was also made for a residential caretaker, cook and gardener. From the start the centre and school worked in close co-operation and some of the children referred to the centre also attended the school.

The experiment was not supported by all officials at the Board of Education. The Principal Assistant Cecil Maudslay, for example, tried to discourage the Director of Education from going ahead because Chesterfield was a small

5 Brambling House special school and child guidance centre, Chesterfield

town, and the modern practice was to accommodate 'higher grade MDs and the dull and backwards' in public elementary schools.[94] It is possible that at the time (1937) Maudslay was unsure as to the type of child to be treated at the children's centre. This was clarified by HMI Lumsden before the opening in 1939, when he stated that the school and centre were not for the dull or MD who does not respond to treatment. Only the physical and mentally disabled who were capable of recovery would be admitted.[95] The aims of the experiment were laid out, quite succinctly, in a report by the Education Department:

> Brambling House Open Air School and Children's Centre was designed as an experimental attempt to combine the physical, intellectual and psychological approaches to children's problems. This arrangement makes it possible to do away with the usual distinction between the delinquent, the nervous, the retarded and the ill child, and to regard all sorts of varied conditions such as nervousness, chronic headaches, stealing, rheumatic pains, temper tantrums, bed-wetting, shyness, asthma, lassitude, school failure etc. merely as symptoms that something is wrong with THE CHILD; and to pursue investigations along three lines simultaneously to discover whether that something is physical, intellectual, emotional or, as is so often the case, a combination of all three. When the condition has been diagnosed, this arrangement makes it possible for treatment to be carried out simultaneously along any or all of the three lines.[96]

In line with the progressive nature of the experiment, the members of staff were employed as much for their forward thinking as for their individual skills. The headmaster of the school, Mr Frank Merifield (after whom the school and centre would later be named), was said to have 'a progressive outlook and is keen on experimental work'. The six young assistant teachers had made 'certain investigations and done experimental work in the borough' and the senior woman assistant 'has made a close study of modern methods and is fully capable of supervising the work of the girls'.[97] The children's centre employed a fully qualified play therapist,[98] a psychiatric social worker, a psychologist who could be consulted as required and a psychiatrist for two sessions per week (later reduced to one session). The latter was a Dr H. S. Bryan, who was also employed as Assistant School Medical Officer for Derbyshire County Council. Dr Bryan was a pioneer of child guidance in Derbyshire. In the early days, before child guidance was officially recognised, he persuaded the Medical Officer, who had recently established a Minor Ailments Clinic, to provide him with the space and money to supply the bare necessities of equipment. Thus, Dr Bryan started child guidance in Derbyshire as an activity of the Minor Ailments Clinic.[99]

A great advantage of Brambling House was that, by having the school and children's centre side by side, no time was lost by children travelling elsewhere for psychiatric treatment. This was a particular problem in special schools specifically for PD or delicate children who attended outside CGCs during school hours. Perhaps more importantly, as all children in the school suffered some form of emotional difficulty, there was no obvious stigma attached to the attendance of the children's centre.

In March 1941 Brambling House was taken over by the EMS. A local factory owner, Alderman P. M. Robinson, offered his private house, Rye Flatt House, for both school and centre. The LEA agreed to pay half the rates, half the upkeep of the gardens and the cost of alternative accommodation for his family. The house had the usual disadvantages of any private house, such as small rooms which were difficult to arrange for resting and dining, but it was modern and well ventilated, and had well lit rooms, and grounds of one and a half acres. The tennis courts were used as a playground, the garage as a rest room; there was a swimming pool, and small rooms for the CGC. The Ministry of Health paid £1,600 for reconstructions and alterations, and the transfer took place on 21 March 1941.[100] Although conditions were more cramped, the work of both the school and the CGC was able to continue throughout the war.

In 1943 Brambling House was extended to incorporate a hostel for maladjusted children. Holly House hostel opened in March 1943, and worked in conjunction with the CGC at Rye Flatt. The house and grounds, which incorporated approximately two acres, were purchased by the LEA for £3,000 and, when adapted, comprised residential accommodation and playrooms for 18 children (boys up to eleven and girls up to fifteen). Resident staff included a warden and house mother (husband and wife) and a general assistant. A psychotherapist made weekly visits.[101]

The degree of success which Brambling House achieved is difficult to ascertain. Any successes in the school were said to be largely as a result of accommodating children with a range of emotional disabilities. In addition to being either PD or delicate, some were over-shy and did not disrupt the class. Others were noisy and/or uncooperative, and it was found that the class could be conducted successfully only if these children were kept to a maximum of three in a class of 25. Only then could the teacher maintain the conditions in which he or she could deal with the varying needs of individuals. The degree of success achieved in the children's centre is best illustrated by a sample of cases. The following children were treated at the centre (and the school) during April 1939 to March 1944.[102]

EJ, Boy aged 9, IQ 95. Suffered from eczema; and from asthma attacks when taking subjects he disliked. He had been tied to his bed or pram for the first three years of his life. Parents were co-operative but would not admit to a psychological cause. EJ was secretive, negative, and inattentive in class and without friends. He was treated at the children's centre for two years, in which time both the eczema and asthma attacks became less frequent. He became 'normal' and a hard worker.

VE, Girl aged 5, IQ 113. Suffered from enuresis and asthma and was in poor general health. She was 'dull-looking' with no life and no initiative; anxious over school work and would not join in. Her mother was nervous and very proper. After two years, treatment at the children's centre, during which time the mother herself had interviews with the psychiatrist, VE became lively, confident and healthy, was clear of enuresis and asthma, and was good at her school work. However, she became unpleasant, domineering and selfish. Therefore, treatment continued.

TW, Boy aged 7, IQ 126. TW suffered from poor health arising from no apparent grounds. He could develop severe bronchitis with a high temperature within an hour. His sister had attended the centre some years previously for enuresis, nervousness and timidity. The mother was very delicate, with a neurotic attitude to illness. TW was treated at the children's centre for 18 months, during which time he became robust and healthy, with a creative mind. However, he became unpleasant and domineering and so treatment was continued.

Although these cases demonstrate rather ambiguous results, especially the ones where the child's personality changed from one extreme to the other, they were not seen as failures. This is not surprising, given that the vast majority of information comes from government records. The only negative comments about the centre come from HMI Lumsden. After visiting Rye Flatt House in March 1945 he reported his suspicion that children were being kept at the centre for unnecessarily long periods.[103] Certainly the sample cases highlight the lengthy periods in which children who were initially admitted for only a limited time were treated. However, no irregularities could be proved and nothing came of Lumsden's suspicions.

What is evident from the sample cases is the link between the physical, intellectual and emotional health of the child. This alone is a vindication of the decision to open the school and centre. The particulars of psychiatry and psychology are beyond the scope of this study. What is important here is the fact that such an establishment was allowed to continue throughout the war, giving an indication of the extent of interest in the emotional difficulties of children at such a difficult time.

Conclusion

This chapter has focused on the wartime developments in provision for two groups of children: the low-grade mentally defective and the emotionally disturbed. The prewar activities of those seeking to make changes for these children have been examined, and some examples have been given in order to highlight the reasons behind the calls for change. With regard to the low-grade MDs and feeble-minded, prewar debates focused mainly on the issue of segregation. In line with the beliefs of eugenicists, the various bodies involved in the care of these children followed the recommendations of the Royal Commission of 1908, that they should be separated both from society and from the opposite sex. In the midst of this thinking however, the Wood Report was published. Although some of its information was used to further the cause of eugenicists, the report was notable for its concept of community care and other progressive ideas. The timing of the Wood Report, during an era of financial stringency, was unfortunate and its many recommendations were not enacted until after the Second World War. It did, however, exert an influence over wartime thinking. Various government reports were published during the war, and these will be discussed in the following chapter.

Before the outbreak of war, individual events were already bringing awareness of the problems faced by mentally disabled children. The Keasley case, for example, brought the issue of certification to public attention. However, the need to evacuate certain children during the war led to all children becoming even more 'visible', both to the government and to the general public. Problems relating to misdiagnosis were highlighted as was the role of the parent. The case of PAB, for example, shows the lengths to which the authorities went to help when pushed by the parents.

For most disabled children, their new-found visibility and the raised awareness of their problems did not lead to change until after the war. The inevitable difficulties caused by wartime conditions, such as the lack of accommodation and of finance, prevented any radical change. That said, visiting HMIs were obliged, as far as was possible, to ensure that children deemed ineducable did not occupy a place in a special school, whether evacuated or not. In this respect, as with many aspects of the children's care, HMI Lumsden featured heavily. His professionalism in insisting that each child should be treated and accommodated according to current legislation is evident. Other government officials do not appear to have been as concerned. This may be seen as a lack of professionalism, an acceptance of the situation in difficult circumstances or, in some cases, a display of sympathy for children who were happy staying where they were. As we have seen, however, even Lumsden did not, or could not, find alternative accommodation for epileptic MDs. Residential places for these children in particular, were scarce both before and during the war and, despite the 1943 conference which raised awareness of the problem, the situation did not improve.

The hostel system for difficult children was a direct consequence of the war, and of the evacuation. Along with the CGCs, these establishments led to a new understanding of child psychology and were, on the whole, seen by the government as a huge success. The experiment at Brambling House, which provided the focus for the case study in this chapter, was also deemed a success. Of course, without a comprehensive study of the individuals who attended the schools and hostels, it is difficult to assess the degree of real success.

We now know that many children did suffer emotional trauma through being separated from their parents. Dr Bowlby foresaw this for nursery schoolchildren and warned that it would cause delinquency. Others said that the consequences would affect children of all ages. Were they right? That is, perhaps, for a separate study. Certainly, there are many different personalities among children, and much depended on how they coped with the separation as well as how they were treated by their 'foster-parent'. With regard to those children whose difficulties came to light during the war it is likely that access to mental health professionals early on reduced the degree of trauma suffered later in life.

A large part of this chapter has been devoted to maladjusted children. Although the condition was recognised to a certain extent before the war it was perhaps the aspect of mental illness that gained the most attention during the war, and after the war it became an official category of disability for the first time. In a climate of eugenic thinking, it is probable that the emotionally disturbed were regarded more kindly that the low-grade MDs because they were more likely to recover and to become 'normal' citizens.

Notes

1 Stakes and Hornby, *Change in Special Education*, p. 19.
2 Board of Control, *The Royal Commission on the Care and Control of the Feeble Minded* (London: HMSO, 1908).
3 *Ibid.*, p. 21.
4 *Wood Report*: Parts I and II; General; Child, 1929.
5 *Ibid.*
6 *TES*, 5 August 1939.
7 Stakes and Hornby, *Change in Special Education*, p. 64.
8 Under s.55 of the Education Act, 1921.
9 TNA, ED50/268, Law Report in *The Times*, 27 April 1939.
10 'Education in the Law Courts: Mental State of Child – Doctors Certificate Quashed', *Education Journal*, 5 May 1939.
11 TNA, ED50/173, Bosworth-Smith, Board of Education, to Odgers, Home Office (Children's Branch), 20 April 1942.
12 TNA, ED50/173, Odgers to Bosworth-Smith, 13 May 1942.
13 TNA, ED50/173, Eton, LCC, to Bosworth-Smith, Board of Education, 7 August 1942.
14 LMA, LCC/EO/SS/8/7, 'Children reported on under MD Acts 1913–1927': individual cases (no. 432).
15 LMA, LCC/EO/SS/8/7, 'Children reported on under MD Acts 1913–1927': individual cases (no. 98).
16 TNA, ED32/1006, Report of Hollingdean MD School, Brighton, East Sussex, by HMI Moodie, 1 April 1943.
17 TNA, ED32/1124, Lumsden's report on Chaucer Street MD School, Oldham, 13 December 1932.
18 TNA, ED32/1124, HMI report on Chaucer Street MD School, 24 September 1941.
19 TNA, ED32/1602, Board of Control report on Pontville RC MD School in Ormskirk, Lancashire, 30 August 1949.
20 TNA, ED32/958, Lumsden's report on Pontville RC MD School, 21 January 1943.
21 TNA, ED32/244, Lumsden's report on the Mary Dendy Home and Council School for MD Children at Great Warford, Sandlebridge, 17 September 1941.

22 TNA, ED32/244, Lumsden's report on the Mary Dendy Home, 23 June 1942.

23 TNA, ED32/244, Board of Control to the Cheshire County Council, 7 October 1942.

24 TNA, ED32/950, Report by Lumsden, Dr Henderson and HMI Laird of the Board of Control, on the Allerton Priory RC Residential School in Liverpool, 27 May 1943.

25 TNA, ED32/1015, Report by the Superintendent of Monyhull Colony, 25 January 1944.

26 TNA, ED50/271, Maudslay to the National Society for Epileptics, 19 July 1937.

27 TNA, ED32/235, HMI report of Chalfont St Peter Epileptic Colony in Buckinghamshire, 19 January 1939.

28 TNA, ED62/99, Lumsden's report of Chalfont St Peter Epileptic Colony, 2 January 1944.

29 TNA, ED32/954, Lumsden's report of the Maghull Home for Epileptics, Liverpool, 20 January 1943.

30 TNA, ED50/266, Board of Control to Board of Education, 11 March 1939.

31 Titmuss, *The Problems of Social Policy*, p. 497.

32 Potts and Fido, *A Fit Person to be Removed*, p. 26.

33 *Ibid.*, p. 98.

34 TNA, MH95/39, Board of Control reports of Meanwood Park Colony, 7 and 8 April 1943.

35 TNA, ED32/1015, Lumsden's reports of Meanwood Park Colony, 13 and 14 May 1941.

36 TNA, MH79/485, Civil Defence to Ministry of Home Security, 6 March 1941.

37 TNA, MH79/485, L. G. Brock to Mr Hickinbotham, 6 February 1941. It is not known if the official included children in this 'solution' to the problem.

38 TNA, MH95/39, Board of Control report, 15 February 1944.

39 TNA, ED50/273, Report of the Child Guidance Council, 1935.

40 H. A. Mess, *Voluntary Social Services since 1918* (London: Paul, Trencher & Trubner, 1947), p. 125.

41 Swann, *The Practice of Special Education*, p. 99.

42 *TES*, 22 July 1939.

43 Mess, *Voluntary Social Services since 1918*, p. 125.

44 'Cured by Kindness', *TES*, 22 July 1939.

45 TNA, ED50/273, MHEC to Board of Education, 19 April 1939.

46 J. Bowlby, 'Phychological Aspects', in R. Padley and M. Cole (eds), *Evacuation Survey: A Report to the Fabian Society* (London: Routledge, 1940), pp. 186–96.

47 'Billeting Misfits', TES, 28 October 1939.

48 Gosden, *Education in the Second World War*, p. 175.

49 Board of Education, *Suggestions on Health Education: For the Consideration of Teachers and Others Concerned in the Health and Education of School Children* (London: HMSO, 1939), p. 38.

50 Modern Record Centre (MRC), MSS.378.APSW/P/20/5/7, Report of the Association of Psychiatric Social Workers, 26 October 1939.

51 MRC, MSS.378/APSW/P/20/5/19, Child Guidance Council, 'Notes on present activities', August 1940.

52 'Billeting Misfits', *TES*, 28 October 1939.

53 This group campaigned and advised the national executive committee of the Labour Party on matters affecting women, including improved social services for children.

54 TNA, ED50/274, Joint Committee of Working Women's Organisations to R. A. Butler, MP, 2 December 1941.

55 TNA, ED50/274, Report of interview between Joint Committee of Working Women's Organisations, President of the Board of Education and the Parliamentary Secretary, 7 May 1942.

56 Leff and Leff, *The School Health Service*, p. 201.

57 TNA, ED50/273, Report of the Child Guidance Council, 1935.

58 MRC, MSS.16C/5/0/60, William Healy, Institute for Juvenile Research, 1934.

59 *The Medical Officer*, 62 (1939), 144, quoted in John Welshman, 'Evacuation and Social Policy during the Second World War: Myth and Reality', *Twentieth Century British History*, 9:1 (1998), 51.

60 S. Isaacs (ed.), *Cambridge Evacuation Survey: A Wartime Study in Social Welfare and Education* (London: Methuen, 1941), p. 119.

61 'The Delinquents Abroad', *TES*, 13 April 1940. Mr Wills was superintendent of a hostel for difficult children.

62 TNA, ED50/273, Board of Education memorandum, 30 September 1939.

63 As no such category of disability was recognised under Part V of the Education Act, 1921, those sent by the LEAs (the home was run by a charitable trust) were paid for under s.80 of the same act.

64 TNA, ED32/696, Board of Education interview memorandum, 25 February 1939; and Report of the Superintendent, 1 March 1939.

65 TNA, ED32/696, Dallington Home Prospectus.

66 TNA, ED32/384, Visit by a Kent inspector of elementary schools and a psychologist, to East Redhill School, September 1935.

67 TNA, ED32/384, LCC to Ministry of Health, 11 March 1942.

68 TNA, ED32/384, Report by Education Officer, LCC, 16 December 1942.

69 TNA, ED32.384, Report by Dr Bywaters, 21 October 1944.

70 TNA, ED32/696, Dallington Home Prospectus.

71 Ministry of Health, *A Survey of Experience under the Evacuation Scheme: Hostels for Difficult Children* (London: HMSO, 1944), p. 9.

72 Gosden, *Education in the Second World War*, p. 176.

73 Ministry of Health, *Memorandum EV8: Government Evacuation Scheme* (London: HMSO, 1940).

74 Ministry of Health, *Hostels for Difficult Children*.

75 Ministry of Health, *Hostels for Difficult Children*, p. 4.

76 Ministry of Health, *Hostels for Difficult Children*, p. 10.

77 TNA, ED50/274, Regional Psychiatric Hostel for Difficult Children in Burley-in-Wharfedale, Bradford. Matron's report for 1942–43.

78 Ministry of Health, *Hostels for Difficult Children*, p. 6.

79 Gosden, *Education in the Second World War*, p. 176.

80 TNA, ED32/247, Secretary of Friends Education Council to Bosworth-Smith, 9 May 1935.

81 TNA, ED32/247, Lumsden's report on Chaigley Manor Hostel for Maladjusted Children from Liverpool, 5 July 1944.

82 TNA, ED122/21, Report of visits by the children's branch of the Home Office and the medical branch of the Board of Education to Little Becketts Farm School for Difficult Boys, Saffron Walden, Essex, 22 January 1943 and 5 February 1943.

83 TNA, ED122/21, A. G. Salaman to the Board of Education, 12 February 1943.

84 TNA, ED122/21, Children's branch of the Home Office to Dr Glover, 16 February 1943.

85 TNA, ED122/21, Parent to Bedfordshire County MO, who passed it on to the Board of Education, February 1943.

86 TNA, ED122/21, Mr Casteel subsequently changed his name to Kasteel and the last available record on his activities showed him to be running a school for maladjusted children at Skenfrith, Monmouthshire, in December 1946, and under investigation by the Monmouthshire County Council Child Life Protection Service.

87 TNA, ED32/391, Report by Dr Bywaters on the Caldecott Community hostel, 15 July 1941.

88 Gosden, *Education in the Second World War*, p. 176.

89 Joel Kanter, 'Residential Care with Evacuated Children: Lessons from Clare Winnicott', Cyc-online, Issue 80, September 2005, www.cyc-net.org/cyc-online/cycol-0905-kanter.html. Viewed 1 November 2008.

90 *Ibid.*

91 See Dorothy Burlingham and Anna Freud, *Children in War-time* (London: Methuen, 1940); and John Bowlby, 'Forty-four Juvenile Thieves: Their Characters and Home Life', *International Journal of Psycho-Analysis*, 25 (1944), 207–28.

92 Board of Education, *Report on a Five Year Experiment in the Combination of Open-Air Medical and Psycho-Therapeutic Treatment in a Midland Town*, 24 March 1945.

93 Board of Education, *Suggestions on Health Education*, p. 46.

94 TNA, ED133/8, C. W. Maudslay to the Unemployment Assistance Board, 25 October 1937.

95 TNA, ED32/254, Note on Brambling House by Lumsden, 1939.

96 Board of Education, *Report on a Five Year Experiment*, p. 2.

97 TNA, ED32/254, Report of the Chesterfield Education Committee, 29 December 1938.

98 In 1945 the child psychotherapist Phyllis M. Traill published an account of the

type of play therapy employed at Brambling House, known as the 'Lowenfeld Technique'. The examples used in her paper came from the Birmingham Chid Guidance Clinic, where she practised before the war: P. M. Traill, 'An Account of Lowenfeld Technique in a Child Guidance Clinic, with a Survey of Therapeutic Play Technique in Great Britain and USA', *Journal of Mental Science*, XCI:382 (1945), 43–78.

99 Sampson, *Child Guidance*, p. 17.
100 TNA, ED32/1057, HMI report on Brambling House, 23 July 1940.
101 Board of Education, *Report on a Five Year Experiment*, p. 8.
102 Board of Education, *Report on a Five Year Experiment*, p. 10.
103 TNA, ED137/23, Lumsden's report on Brambling House, 15 March 1945.

5

POSTWAR CHANGE

The end of evacuation

By the end of the war many evacuated children, both disabled and able-bodied, had already returned to their homes. As the evacuation was voluntary, parents had been free to take their children home at any time, and some returned before the official arrangements had been made. The majority of those remaining in reception areas in May 1945 were able to go home soon after. Some, however, were unable to return because their parents had been killed, or because their home had been destroyed and their parents were unable to care for them at this time.

For the disabled children who were still in residential special schools when the war ended, who had previously lived at home and attended a special day school, their return was effected as soon as was practical. In London, for example, the government arranged a scheme whereby the return would be staggered over several months. Arrangements made for the closure of the schools began in September 1944, and by the end of the war two lists had been produced. The first contained those schools which would be vacated between 11 August 1945 and 22 December 1945; the second list, between 24 November 1945 and 19 January 1946.[1] Other local authorities made their own plans for their schools' closure.

Some children needed continued residential care because their particular disability prevented them from living at home, but in the immediate aftermath of the war there was a serious shortage of premises in which to accommodate them. This was mainly due to the war damage caused to premises which otherwise could have been used, but also some of those buildings which had been used previously had been requisitioned by the military or by other essential services, and had not yet been vacated. When they eventually became available, the premises often needed extensive repairs and alterations.

This is illustrated by the experience of the Bethesda Home for crippled children in Manchester, whose residents had been evacuated to the Tanllwyfan Convalescent Home in Wales. When the war ended, the RAF had been in residence at Bethesda for some time and did not move out until October 1946. Some decoration and alterations were needed before the children could move back and, in 1947, it was decided that an extension should be built on to the property. The whole project would cost £15,000 and would take many months to complete. In the meantime the children remained at Tanllwyfan. It was not until October 1949 that they returned home to Manchester.[2]

Fortunately, the Homes in both Manchester and Wales were run by the same charity organisation (The Boys' and Girls' Refuges) and so there was no undue pressure to vacate the premises in Wales. However, this was rare; usually the lack of suitable premises created many problems, not just for the authorities and the children but for others, who suffered the knock-on effects. This is highlighted by the example of the White Heather Home in Old Colwyn, Wales, which was run by a charitable organisation as a holiday home for the blind.

During the war the Institute that used the Home the most was itself evacuated and White Heather was used for evacuated MD girls from Liverpool. At the end of the war there were 35–40 children still at the Home; about half were due to return home soon, but the rest needed continued residential care. The Liverpool LEA informed the White Heather Fund that there was nowhere else to send the girls at the moment, but there were plans to purchase a building in which to accommodate them. In the meantime the girls would have to stay where they were.

The building in question was Oakfield, the private home of a Lieutenant General, who planned to put the house up for sale at an auction in July 1945. The Liverpool LEA prevented the auction and subsequently made a Compulsory Purchase Order on the property. An amount of £5,000 plus costs was agreed but the sale was delayed, resulting in serious financial difficulties for the owner. The owners of White Heather were also unhappy; they were told that the necessary adaptations were soon to begin on Oakfield, but they had still not begun by April 1946. By this time some of their subscribers were drifting away. Despite the intervention of R.A. Butler, MP, and Colonel Sir Joseph Nall, MP (for Liverpool), the matter was not resolved until August 1946, when the girls eventually moved out and White Heather reverted to its original use.[3]

The main reason for the delay in making repairs and/or adaptations to school buildings was the shortage of labour and raw materials. This problem affected all building projects in the postwar reconstruction phase, and the subject will be revisited later in the chapter when discussing the expansion of special schools. The problem of limited resources was not the only obstacle that the education authorities had to contend with; they also had to deal with the reorganisation of the whole education system. This was due to the implementation of the new Education Act, 1944, which, in turn, was largely due to changing perceptions not only of educational provision but also of the 'worth' of disabled children.

Changing perceptions

The change in attitude with regards to disabled people began, to a large degree, after the outbreak of the Second World War, for two reasons. Firstly, as Julie Anderson points out, 'men who were disabled or disfigured tended to be seen as romantic heroes, fighting for their country'.[4] Douglas Bader, who suffered a double amputation but still managed to fly his Spitfire against the Germans, is perhaps the best illustration of this. Secondly, with a shortage of labour, disabled people were recognised as being able to contribute to the war effort, and were no longer seen an inevitable drain on resources. Government-produced 'information films' were shown to promote a positive image of disability. For example, one film entitled *Blind Farmer Carries On* showed 'Blind John' carrying on with his farm-work and delivering milk to his local community.[5]

One incident that occurred during the war stands out for the way in which the gradual change in the use of labels became visible in a public way, perhaps reflecting existing change as well as encouraging it. In 1941 Queen Elizabeth visited the Cripples Training College at Leatherhead, Surrey, which was going to be renamed in her honour. The Queen requested that 'Disabled' should be incorporated into the name of the college instead of 'Cripple' and the college was renamed The Queen Elizabeth Training College for the Disabled.[6]

The terminology used to describe a certain group of individuals is vital when attempting to alter people's attitudes towards them. The Education Act, 1944, made a significant change in this respect. However, the incident at the Queen Elizabeth Training College took place some years prior to the act and suggests how changes were already taking place. With its royal connection, the event would have been well publicised and a useful vehicle for influencing the general public.

Changing how society regards a certain group of people can be a slow process and is made more difficult if the attitudes of the group itself are slow to change. Prior to the Second World War society had generally seen disabled, and physically disabled people in particular, as 'unfortunates'. Some individuals, perhaps because they had been 'conditioned', saw themselves in this way. It must be remembered here that it is very difficult to get access to the views of the disabled people themselves at that time. That said, in 1941 the editor of the *National Cripples Journal (Leicester)* who, in the title of the journal, described himself as a 'lifelong cripple' wrote the following editorial:

> All over the country there are folk who will always be sick. Amongst these men and women are cripples and incurables – brave courageous souls who are condemned to a life of pain and inconvenience. It is wonderful to see how cheerful these people are. Pain seems to give them a joy denied to those who are fit and well. They seem to see beauty where others see nothing; they obtain an outlook on life which gives them contentment and peace.[7]

Perhaps the author thought this was the best way of getting people to buy his journal, or perhaps he really did view disability in this way; at the time, disabled people were seen largely as objects of pity. Also, there was the perception amongst certain people of a divide between deserving and undeserving disabled people. For example, during the First World War the Ministry of Pensions was established and one of its duties was to assess who was eligible for a free wheelchair. From then on, only the paraplegic veterans and double amputees (with at least one leg amputated above the knee) would qualify. Those who did not receive a free wheelchair from the State had either to pay privately or to rely on charitable gifts and donations.[8]

Whether 'deserving' or not, some people continued to regard disabled people as a burden and questioned their rights as members of society. In November 1946 Edie Rutherford wrote, in a diary that became part of the Mass Observation Archive:[9]

> I don't think Gordon Richard Long should be hanged for ending the life of his imbecile daughter. Poor wretch. Even if spared, his life is not worth much to himself, yet I'm sure he felt he was doing right. It must be awful to live with a child of the kind his daughter was, day after day, week after week, month after month, for seven years. How dare we judge the man and condemn him?[10]

Without knowing the facts of the case it is, indeed, difficult to judge the man. What interests us here is the extent to which Edie Rutherford's sympathies lay not with the daughter but with the 'poor wretch' of a father. She obviously believed that the girl was a burden, and made no mention of the possibility that she could have been taught in some way in order to lead a productive life. Of course, only snippets of Edie's life are given in her letters and diaries, and a further entry on 5 October 1945 suggests that her attitude was perhaps more ambiguous than her earliest entry suggests, or simply that she viewed different types of disability very differently:

In library porch yesterday I was interested to read that those industries who can employ cripples will be obliged to employ a percentage. Husband objects, says it's against nature. As I pointed out, we go agin nature at every point of civilisation – that it is obvious that crippled folk are better off themselves and for the community as a whole if they learn a trade and follow it.[11]

Another way of assessing contemporary attitudes is through film and television. In 1952 Ealing Studios in London made *Mandy*, a film about a deaf-mute child whose middle-class parents found themselves unable to cope, and so placed her in a special school. The film (based on a real case) portrayed all three characters sympathetically, and highlighted the difficulties faced in raising a disabled child. The teacher, played by Jack Hawkins, was seen as a dedicated professional, struggling with the obstacles caused by inadequate funding. Two years later, the British Information Services produced a twenty-minute documentary entitled *Thursday's Children* (from the old nursery rhyme in which 'Thursday's child has far to go'). The film was made without sound, except for a limited amount of narration by Richard Burton, and featured the Royal School for the Deaf in Margate. The main feature of the film was the determination of the children and the joy they showed when able to communicate. The film was extremely successful, winning an Oscar for Best Documentary-Short Subject and a BAFTA for Best Documentary Film (both in 1955).

Both productions were critically acclaimed and were popular with audiences. They were also intentionally moving and, the documentary especially, were designed to provide an insight into the children's lives. Walter Goodman of the *New York Times* said of the children in the documentary: 'we share the joy of their successes without being able to forget their lifetime apartness'.[12]

Whilst it is true that many disabled children remained 'apart', it is also true that legislation had been introduced with the aim of integrating disabled children, particularly within the education system. This was the Education Act, 1944. The degree to which the act was a continuation of prewar thinking, as opposed to the result of wartime developments, continues to be debated. It is most likely that it was a combination of the two.

The new Education Act

In some ways the Education Act, 1944, was the result of 'unfinished business' from the interwar years. S. J. Curtis describes the act as representing the 'logical outcome of the lines of thought which had been expressed in the Hadow and the Spens Reports'.[13] Stakes and Hornby agree that these reports contained the philosophy and direction behind the 1944 act, but suggest that changing attitudes towards the education of disabled children did not appear until the publication of the Board of Education's *Education after the War* (1941) and *Educational Reconstruction* (1943).[14]

The Hadow Report of 1926[15] had advocated the end of all-age schools, and the introduction of a post-primary stage of education where all children would be able to follow a variety of types of secondary education suited to their abilities. It was also suggested that it should become compulsory for children to remain at school until the age of fifteen.[16] In 1938 the Spens Report[17] emphasised the need for a treble-track system of secondary education,[18] but its recommendations were set aside as children were evacuated, schools closed and school buildings requisitioned.[19] Although disabled children were not mentioned specifically in these reports, when the recommendations on secondary education were eventually put into practice in the 1944 act, disabled children were included.

Despite the inevitable upheaval in educational provision due to the conditions of war, a reorganisation of the system continued to be discussed. In *Education after the War*, also known as the Green Book, apart from two pages in the 'summary of main suggestions', the 76-page booklet contained a mere five pages on the subject of disabled children. However, the stipulations within these pages were to make a considerable difference to disabled children's lives after 1945. The Green Book was prepared by a number of officers of the Board of Education who were presenting their personal views on the ways in which educational reforms might be affected.[20] Although there is no evidence of consultation between the authors and experts in special education, it is possible, given his position at the Board of Education, that HMI Lumsden had some kind of input. In line with the recommendations of the Wood Report, the authors of the Green Book suggested that the requirement of certification should be reconsidered for children requiring special education. Also, it was reiterated that a new category of maladjustment should be provided for, along with a small number of residential special schools. Acknowledgement was made of the fact that, with regard to MD children, little had so far been done to carry out the recommendations of the Wood Report, and that residential provision for these children was 'gravely inadequate'.[21] However, it was suggested that for the majority of such children, along with the delicate, provision should be made within the public elementary system. The Green Book stimulated wide-ranging debate on postwar education and, in July 1943, the Board's White Paper *Educational Reconstruction* was published.[22] In the same year an Education Bill was introduced, based on the White Paper and, on 3 August 1944, the new Education Act became law. Many of the changes put in place by the act came from the recommendations from 1941 and 1943. The act came into force on 1 April 1945.

In essence, the act was intended to extend the opportunities for, and improve the quality of, education. In place of all-age schools, the education system was divided into primary and secondary, with the latter being further divided into the 'tripartite' system of grammar, technical and modern. The abolition of fees in the grammar schools meant that children could gain access to high-quality education based on their educational ability, rather than on their parents' ability to pay.[23]

The 1944 act was the first educational legislation that did not treat disabled children as a separate group. In the 1921 act they had been excluded from the general provisions of education, and treated as a distinct category.[24] Under the new provisions, it was recognised that physical and mental disability exists in all degrees, from the slight to the serious, and that special educational treatment (SET), as it was now called, should be suited to the needs of the individual child. The 1944 act changed, and extended, the official categories of children's disability. However, it did not define the new categories; it merely empowered the Ministry of Education (the act changed the Board of Education to the Ministry of Education, and its President became the Minister) to do so, and this was done in *The Disabled Pupils and School Health Service Regulations*, 1945. The eleven categories of disability, with their full definitions, were:

a) Blind Pupils, that is to say pupils who have no sight or whose sight is or is likely to become so defective that they require education by methods not involving the use of sight.

b) Partially Sighted Pupils, that is to say pupils who by reason of defective vision cannot follow the ordinary curriculum without detriment to their sight or to their educational development, but can be educated by special methods involving the use of sight.

c) Deaf Pupils, that is to say pupils who have no hearing or whose hearing is so defective that they require education by methods used for deaf pupils without naturally acquired speech of language.

d) Partially Deaf Pupils, that is to say pupils whose hearing is so defective that they require for their education special arrangements or facilities but not all the educational methods used for deaf pupils.

e) Delicate Pupils, that is to say pupils who by reason of impaired physical condition cannot, without risk to their health, be educated under the normal regime of an ordinary school.

f) Diabetic Pupils, that is to say pupils suffering from diabetes who cannot obtain the treatment they need while living at home and require residential care.

g) Educationally Sub-Normal Pupils, that is to say pupils who, by reason of limited ability or other conditions resulting in educational retardation, require some specialised form of education wholly or partly in substitution for the education normally given in ordinary schools.

h) Epileptic Pupils, that is to say pupils who by reason of epilepsy cannot be educated in an ordinary school without detriment to the interests of themselves or other pupils and require education in a Special School.

i) Maladjusted Pupils, that is to say pupils who show evidence of emotional instability or psychological disturbance and require special educational treatment in order to effect their personal, social, or educational readjustment.

j) Physically Disabled Pupils, that is to say pupils, not being pupils suffering solely from a defect of sight or hearing, who by reason of disease or crippling defect cannot be satisfactorily educated in an ordinary school or cannot be educated in such a school without detriment to their health or educational development.

k) Pupils suffering from Speech Defect, that is to say pupils who on account of stammering, aphasia, or defect of voice or articulation not due to deafness, require special educational treatment.[25]

The 1944 Education Act disregarded the term 'defective', preferring instead to use the more sympathetic 'disabled'. Neither was the terms 'imbecile' and 'idiot' used to describe the section of mentally disabled children thought to be ineducable. Instead, children of below average IQ were deemed educationally sub-normal (ESN). In 1944 this term was seen as a step forward in lessening the stigma attached to mental disability, but eventually even this fell out of use.

The new provisions for disabled children were due, in part, to the recommendations of the Wood Committee and the reports of the committees of inquiry on the partially blind and the partially deaf.[26] All three committees had stressed the importance of bringing the special schools within the general education framework, and had been concerned with the stigma attached to special schools. As a result, certification was abolished; in future a certificate would only be given where the parents demanded it, or where the LEA required it for the purpose of enforcing attendance at a special school.[27] Medical officers would no longer decide who was to attend special school, but would merely advise the LEA, who would make the final decision. Also, from then on, teachers and others who were in a position to judge the ability and aptitude of the child would also have a say in his or her future.

In 1945 the Ministry of Education published a document suggesting how the LEAs should go about their duties under the new act. It was their responsibility to find and provide education for children who were being impeded in their educational progress. The seriousness of carrying this out successfully was emphasised:

The uneducated and untrained, blind or deaf person is practically unemployable; the educated one can support himself and a family. The uneducated mentally retarded child grows up into an unemployable or unstable casual worker; the educated one into a more dependable and useful citizen. The uneducated cripple is a burden to his family; the educated one may become a useful worker. This applies to every category of the disabled. It is a matter of common prudence as well as humanity to do everything possible to equip these children to take their places as self-reliant and responsible members of the community.[28]

As already stated, the new legislation advocated educational inclusion wherever possible, and stipulated that, for certain children requiring SET, education could be provided in a school other than a special school.

'In any school'

When the new Education Bill was being passed through Parliament, it was made clear by the Secretary of the Board of Education that the issues surrounding the education of disabled children should be carefully worded. Where possible, a more inclusive approach would be implemented, and it was important that separate provision in a special school would not be the 'usual' provision.[29] Consequently, the wording was as follows:

The arrangements made by a local education authority for the special educational treatment of pupils of any such category shall, so far as is practicable, provide for the education of pupils in whose case the disability is serious in special schools appropriate for that category, but where that is impracticable, or where the disability is not serious, the arrangements may provide for the giving of such education in any school maintained or assisted by the local education authority.[30]

However, not all disabled children would be allowed to attend ordinary school:

Unless the Minister otherwise determines in the case of any particular disabled pupil, every pupil who is blind, deaf, physically disabled, epileptic or aphasic, whether or not he also falls within some other category of disabled pupils, shall be educated in a Special School, and if the pupil is blind or epileptic the school shall be a boarding school.[31]

The only recommendation for teachers of disabled children in ordinary schools was that they should provide 'special attention'.[32] However, certain conditions within the classrooms were to be met. For example, where needed: a favourable position in the classroom; the provision of special furniture, apparatus and equipment; and adequate tuition and supervision.[33] A maximum class size was also stipulated:

(a)   deaf; partially deaf; speech defect: 10
(b)   blind; PS; maladjusted: 15
(c)   ESN; epileptic; PH: 20
(d)   delicate; diabetic: 30[34]

The regulations allowed for these numbers to be exceeded in certain conditions, such as a lack of teaching staff or a lack of school accommodation due
to difficulties arising out of war conditions, or out of conditions occasioned by
the coming into operation of the act.

Apart from the blind and epileptic, all disabled children requiring SET in
a special school could, depending on location and personal circumstances, be
educated in either a day or a boarding school. After 1945 the number of special
schools increased. Before discussing the numbers involved, it is necessary to
give a brief summary of the main changes that occurred for each category of
disabled children.

Blind and partially sighted children

Under the 1921 act, blind and partially sighted children were treated the same,
but the 1944 Education Act created two distinct categories. The policy of separating blind from PS children, and of educating PS children in ordinary schools
wherever possible, both of which had been advised as long ago as 1934,[35] was
finally put in place after the war. The new act also stipulated that blind children
should be educated in boarding schools. With more PS children attending ordinary schools after the war, the number of special school places decreased, especially in special day schools. For the children who still needed special education,
such as those whose visual defects meant that they were not suited to education
in an ordinary school, and who lived too far from a special day school, boarding
accommodation was needed. Although some boarding schools existed for the
PS after the war, most were still being run by voluntary bodies.

In January 1946 there were 16 schools for the blind and 14 which accepted
pupils who were either blind or PS (this is in addition to the PS schools). In
1949 there was still only one such school maintained by a LEA: the Blenheim
School in Leeds.[36] However, in 1951, an LEA-maintained boarding school
especially for PS children was opened, at Exhall Grange near Coventry. With
accommodation for 240 PS pupils, about half the LEAs in England sent their
pupils there. By 1955 there were 22 blind schools, all boarding, and three that
accepted both blind and PS children.[37] Of the latter, one was in the process of
being reorganised and the other two had special dispensation to remain mixed
(one was the only blind/PS school in Wales and the other the only Catholic
blind/PS school in England and Wales).[38]

Deaf and partially deaf children

During the immediate postwar years, there was an increase in the number of deaf children needing SET. This was partly due to the German measles epidemic in 1940, and the subsequent rise in babies being born deaf, and partly due to the realisation that they should be educated from as young an age as possible. The 1944 Education Act made it possible for deaf children to be educated from the age of two, and lowered the compulsory school age from seven to five. The ruling that deaf children should not attend ordinary schools meant that more special school places were required. As with the PS, schools for deaf and partially deaf children could be either day or boarding schools, but, for those children who did not live near a day school, the only option was to attend a boarding school. By 1949 there were eight such schools run by LEAs, and twelve by voluntary bodies.[39]

The ruling that all deaf and partially deaf children should be educated separately became impossible to enforce for many years after the war. In Bolton, Lancashire, for example, the Thomasson Memorial School continued to be used for both deaf and partially deaf children until the early 1950s, when the latter group was transferred elsewhere.[40]

As some categories of disability incidence were too low for a single authority to provide for its children only, it was a common and well established practice for an authority to provide a special school which also served other areas. Unlike the building programme for primary and secondary schools which allocated resources individually for each authority, the special schools programme made allocations on a regional basis.

In the West Midlands, as at 14 January 1950, there were 75 partially deaf children waiting for a special school place, and 42 others being educated in a deaf school. In 1947 approval had been given for the purchase of Rangemoor Hall in Staffordshire. In excellent condition, with 70 bedrooms, 15 bathrooms and 40 WCs, the property could accommodate 150–200 partially deaf children, catering for the whole West Midlands. The building (which was subsequently named Needwood Boarding School because it was near Needwood Forest, and because the name 'Rangemoor Hall' was reserved to the vendor, Baroness Burton) was bought for £41,710, with another £31,000 estimated for adaptations. The project was included in the 1951/52 Building Programme, but was put on hold when it was discovered that the stable block had been omitted from the estimate, raising the total for adaptations to £60,000. The premises eventually opened on 25 January 1954, at a total cost of £116,705.[41]

Delicate and diabetic children

The 1921 act had grouped the delicate children and the diabetics together with the physically defective children, but the 1945 Regulations separated them into three distinct groups (the physically defective, or PD, now becoming the physically handicapped, or PH). The delicate children, of course, had previously been accommodated in open-air schools and, for some, nothing changed; in the short term, those who could not attend ordinary school continued to attend open-air schools. However, from the beginning of the 1950s questions were asked about the continuing need for such schools; since the end of the war there had been fewer children suffering from malnutrition and other conditions caused by poor home conditions. The Report of the Chief Medical Officer of the Ministry of Education for 1950/51 declared that there was still a need for some schools of this type, especially in industrial areas where respiratory problems were more common, but that there was no real need to expand the number of schools.

The diabetic children, on the other hand, had been grouped during the war with the children classed as 'difficult to billet' and, where possible, had been evacuated to special hostels, and attended ordinary schools. This arrangement was deemed successful and was allowed to continue for those who needed boarding accommodation. These were the diabetic children who needed a modified diet, supervised injections of insulin and training in the 'diabetic way of life'. They were taught how to become self-reliant by giving themselves injections, carrying out the necessary urine tests and learning how to detect problems related to abnormal blood sugar levels.[42]

Since the discovery of insulin treatment in 1922, diabetes was no longer a death sentence, and the majority of diabetic children were able to live at home and attend ordinary school – so much so that from 1953 they were no longer classified separately but included in the general category of delicate pupils.[43]

Educationally sub-normal children

Despite the emphasis on 'inclusion', one group of children remained outside the education system after the 1944 act. Children deemed ineducable were the responsibility of the local health or hospital authorities and, as such, are not discussed here.[44] It is evident from the previous chapters that the category of mental disability was the most diverse and complex of all disabilities and, on the whole, it was this group of children who were most affected by the new education legislation. Apart from the abolition of certification (with exceptions, as previously noted) a child would no longer have to be considered feeble-minded before being allowed a place in a special school. The new definition, of ESN, was deliberately broad in order to incorporate all children who were markedly failing in their school work; this did not have to be due to low intelligence but also incorporated those who had suffered educationally through physical ill-health. The 1945 Regulations did not mention the degree of educational retardation that should be present in order to qualify for SET, but the following year the Ministry of Education suggested a guideline of 20 per cent or more below the average.[45]

In the postwar years special school places for ESN children were seriously lacking. In the five years from the end of 1949 to the end of 1954, for example, the number of children requiring a place increased from 15,483 to 22,895, but the number of extra places rose by a mere 89, from 12,489 to 12,578.[46] The reason given by the Ministry of Education was that many authorities and their medical officers were reluctant to put a child on the waiting list unless there was a reasonable hope of placing them. Therefore, as demand for places appeared to be relatively constant, so was the supply. In reality, the majority of those awaiting a place in a special school remained in ordinary schools.

Another reason for the large number of children needing a place in a special ESN school was that, even if they had another more serious disability, schools for the PH, deaf etc. were often reluctant to take them. This was not a problem specific to the war years; the mixing of children with physical disabilities with those of low intelligence had long been a subject of debate, and postwar legislation did not address the problem. In 1953, at the Needwood Boarding School for partially deaf children, although there was sufficient accommodation, 24 children had been rejected for having other disabilities, including low intelligence.[47]

The problems associated with postwar provision for ESN children were, to some extent, a result of the new emphasis on national uniformity. For example, in her study of educational provision for mentally disabled children in Leicester during the interwar period, Emma Cliffe found that there was an intense interest in caring for the children, and that the individual development of a number of schools had benefited from the absence of a national policy.[48] Leicester has been described as a pioneering authority in the care and treatment of mentally disabled children prior to the 1944 act, but in the immediate postwar years its experimental work was sacrificed in order to conform to the national policy of placing children in special schools only if they could not possibly be educated in ordinary schools.

Epileptic children

Epileptic children had been seen as a distinct category in the 1921 act, and continued to be so after 1945. The number of special schools for epileptics, usually known as 'colonies', had remained static during the war; five were run by voluntary bodies and two by LEAs. The number of places was approximately six hundred but waiting lists were always long. However, with advances in the diagnosis and medical treatment of epilepsy, and an increasing awareness that the less severe cases were suitable for attendance in ordinary schools, demand for special education places declined.

Maladjusted children

The issue of maladjustment is perhaps the most relevant to the subject of the effects of war on children. Unlike most other categories of disability, for which provision had been evolving from the eighteenth and nineteenth centuries, the concept of the maladjusted child was relatively new. The conditions of war, and the evacuation in particular, presented psychologists and other professionals with an unprecedented opportunity to study the behaviour of children.

The category of 'maladjusted' was made official for the first time by the 1945 Regulations. The value of residential schools for certain maladjusted children was realised during the war, when many of them were accommodated in special hostels. In October 1944 Bosworth-Smith, head of the medical branch of the Ministry of Education, wrote:

> The problem of maladjusted children has been brought prominently to public attention as a result of the evacuation and other conditions arising out of the War. We at the Ministry of Education are very anxious to secure an increase in accommodation for these children at boarding schools since we feel that this is the best possible way to deal with a small minority of the children for whom nothing more than attendance and psychiatric treatment at a CGC is needed.[49]

Some hostels were taken over as residential special schools by the LEAs after the war, whilst others continued to function as hostels, with the children attending local schools.[50] For most, attendance and psychiatric treatment at a CGC was sufficient, but a small minority were thought to benefit away from their home environment.

It was widely believed, certainly at the Board of Education, that the largest single factor in the causation of delicate and social maladjustment in children was the unsatisfactory home.[51] In September 1944 'a correspondent' to the *TES* spoke of the condition of some children at the beginning of the war, warning that hostels would continue to be needed once the war was over. He believed that they would be particularly useful for first-offenders when residential care was first advised for what he termed 'pre-delinquents'.[52]

After the war maladjusted children whose home life was unsatisfactory could either be boarded with foster-parents and attend ordinary day school or be sent to a special boarding home similar to the wartime hostels for difficult children. The latter was usually preferred for children whose habits and conduct made them unsuitable for fostering. The success of hostels in meeting the needs of maladjusted evacuees during the war led to similar facilities being available for local (i.e. those already in reception areas) maladjusted children.

At the end of the war there were 79 CGCs; by the end of 1955 there were around three hundred. The LEAs provided around two hundred of these as well as maintaining 1,062 maladjusted children in 158 independent boarding schools. They also provided for seriously disturbed children in six children's departments in mental hospitals or other children's units, 45 approved 'boarding homes' (the new names for hostels for difficult children) with 1,100 places, and three day special schools with 168 places.[53]

In the first ten years at Brambling House (1939–49) maladjusted children formed between 25 per cent and 35 per cent of the total roll. However, in subsequent years they were by far the majority. When asked about this increase, which occurred over the county as a whole (and indeed, was a nationwide phenomenon), Dr Simpson of the Borough Education Committee replied:

> No reason has been found – but as physical illness decreases there appears to be an increase in mental disturbance. It seems to be part of the changing pattern of life, particularly of family life. Much of the disturbance can be traced to unsatisfactory home environment.[54]

Records show that this increase continued into the 1960s. At Brambling House there were 47 maladjusted and 91 delicate children in 1952. In 1963 the figures were 84 and 45 respectively. In 1964 the school was renamed the Frank Merifield School, after the first headmaster, recently deceased. In 1967 it was formerly listed as being for maladjusted children with some places for delicate and PH children. The school closed in 1989.

With the broader definitions of ESN children, and the introduction of the category of maladjustment, many more special schools were needed. In January 1946 this urgent need was addressed in the Ministry of Education Circular 79, which requested LEAs to make extra provision in boarding schools.[55] In keeping with the policy of acquiring country homes for use as special boarding schools, and as a direct consequence of Circular 79, the Liverpool County Borough Council decided to use the recently acquired Aymestry Court in Liverpool as a school for maladjusted boys. This was the first school to be maintained by an LEA for such children in the north-west.[56]

Although there was a growing interest in maladjustment before the war, it is evident that much was learned about the condition as a result of the evacuation. Perhaps surprisingly, the main causes of 'new' cases did not necessarily stem from the conditions of war but from an inadequate home life. For these children, residential care was advocated, but this raises the question of how they coped when returned home. Again, this is outside the scope of this study and, indeed, the long-term effects on the children would not be known for many years after the end of the war.

Physically handicapped children

At the end of the Second World War it was not known how many PH children would need special education in the near future. London and most large boroughs had already established one or more day schools. Twelve boarding schools existed for those who could not attend a day school, but these were provided by voluntary bodies and there was a long waiting list. It was not until 1950 that an inquiry was made into the number of places needed. This was instigated by a review of schools for disabled children made by the Ministry of Education Special Services Branch, in January 1949.

The department found that almost twenty-five per-cent of 'heart cases' could have been educated in ordinary schools. Staff shortages were partly blamed for the failure to detect this sooner and it was advised that regular examinations of the children must be carried out. Also, many 'orthopaedic cases' were kept unnecessarily in special schools. These were the slightly disabled children who would go to work straight from leaving school, and it was thought that subjecting them to a greater change of environment after leaving the relatively sheltered conditions of the special school would only serve to widen the gap between themselves and the able-bodied children.[57]

Special mention was made of such children in the report of Buckshaw House, which during the war had accommodated physically disabled evacuees from London, and had been retained as a special school after the war. Of the 33 children in residence at the time of the report, 30 required treatment because of home circumstances, and even the other three were not more seriously disabled than some day school pupils. The department proposed the provision of hostels for those with adverse home conditions, whilst attending day schools. This would reduce the cost, as residential education was much more expensive. However, it was recognised that practical difficulties would probably delay the proposal for some years.[58]

The results of the 1950 inquiry into the number of PH places suggested that day provision in England and Wales was reasonably adequate in all but a few areas, but that six to seven hundred additional boarding school places were needed. However, a detailed survey taken four years later showed a shortfall of 203 day school places, as well as approximately 525 boarding school places (the figure includes some children who were recommended for special school but whose parents refused to let them go).[59]

Some children required a boarding school place because there was no special day school within reach. The majority, however, were the more seriously disabled children, who were unable to walk or who needed special nursing care. The lack of provision for the severely physically disabled child was recognised both before and during the war. In July 1944, when reporting on the Potternewton School for PD Children in Leeds, HMI Lumsden noted the particular problems experienced in the north of England:

> The problem of the severe cripple who is not in need of hospital treatment has no solution in the north. A residential school for cripples unable to attend day special school, even though they could reach one, is needed. Some children need much attention but cannot come here because of the physical difficulties in dealing with them.[60]

With the decline in cases of TB of the joints and rheumatic fever, cerebral palsy became the most common physical disability suffered by children in special schools after the war (children with this disability were commonly known as 'spastics'). After the war the British Council for the Welfare of Spastics was formed, as was the National Spastics Society. Both were responsible for the foundation of a number of schools solely for children suffering from CP, the first of which was St Margaret's School in Croydon, a boarding school which opened in 1947. Although the schools were established by voluntary bodies they were all assisted financially by the Ministry of Education.[61]

The education of children with CP is one example of how, especially in these early years of the new act, the LEAs still relied very much on the co-operation and resources of voluntary societies. In the case of children with 'unusual' disabilities and/or combinations of disabilities, it was not unusual for LEAs to pay those voluntary societies to provide forms of special education it did not provide itself.[62]

It had long been believed that children with CP were practically ineducable. However, in the 1940s, practitioners in the USA had shown that in a high proportion of cases a considerable improvement in the mental and physical condition could be effected. Among these specialists was Dr Phelps of Baltimore, and in June 1945 the Ministry of Health in London agreed that treatment and training, on the lines advocated by Dr Phelps, should be undertaken at the CP unit at Queen Mary's Hospital, Carshalton.[63] In the same year the Minister's Advisory Committee on Disabled Children had recommended the setting up of 'a small but definite scheme for research into the medical and educational aspects of the problem of children suffering from cerebral palsy'.[64] The result of this was the publication in 1951 of *The Educability of Cerebral Palsied Children*.[65]

By the time of the report more schools had been provided specifically

for children with CP, by both voluntary bodies and LEAs. With extra places
available, children who before and during the war might have been regarded
as unsuitable for any school began to be admitted. However, when the specialised schools first opened, only those children whose intelligence appeared to
be roughly within the normal range were admitted.[66] Included in the 1944 act,
and the subsequent 1945 Regulations, was an attempt to address the problem
of the severely physically disabled child; the duty of all LEAs to provide education applied to all children regardless of whether or not they were able to
attend school premises.

It is perhaps in the education of severely physically disabled children
that the continuing but changing role of voluntary bodies is most apparent.
Although this has been touched upon in this section and will be again later, it
is a subject that is too broad and too complex to form a significant part of the
book as a whole. It is, however, an issue that warrants further research.

Children with speech defects

The official category of speech defect was new, although some provision was
already in place by the beginning of the war. In 1943 a committee from the
West End Hospital for Nervous Diseases approached the Board of Education
with a proposal to set up a school specifically for children with speech defects.
The initial response was to ask the LCC and LEAs to establish small boarding
schools, but this proved unsuccessful, mainly because of staffing difficulties. In
the same year, at a conference at the Ministry of Health, the well-known plastic
surgeon Sir Harold Gillies made a plea for a system of intensive treatment for
children who had been operated on for a cleft palate or hare lip. Again, nothing
could be done at the time but in 1945, one month before the end of the war,
plans to open the first special school specifically for children with speech defects
were approved.[67] In the same year the two separate bodies responsible for
existing provision amalgamated and founded the College of Speech Therapists.

In 1947 the Moor House Residential Special School for Speech Defects
was opened for children who required more highly specialised and concentrated treatment than the school speech therapists could provide.[68] The
school was established in association with the West End Hospital for Nervous
Diseases and incorporated the Speech Therapy Training School of that hospital. Dealing with severely aphasic children and those with severe speech
defects, including those with cleft palate or hare lip, the school had access
to a team of professionals, including a neurologist; plastic surgeons; an ear,
nose and throat surgeon; psychiatrist; psychologist; dental surgeon; speech
therapist and teachers.[69]

Speech therapy was regarded primarily as an educational service to be conducted in close association with the school authorities.[70] Therefore, after the introduction of the NHS in 1948, children requiring treatment continued to be provided for by the LEAs. The detection of speech defects was a major part of school inspection. With the improving standard of child health in the postwar period, there was a reduction in the proportion of children requiring treatment for physical defects, and this enabled the SMOs to devote an increasing amount of time to the development of speech therapy.[71] The number of children receiving such treatment through the School Health Service rose from around 16,000 in 1947 to 49,817 in 1957.[72]

There were, then, enormous changes brought by the 1944 Education Act, not least the increase in the number of categories. Another significant development concerned those children who could not, for a variety of reasons, attend school. Before the new act, many of these remained at home with little or no schooling. However, from 1944, these children, as with all 'educable' children, were entitled to an education regardless of where this was to take place.

'Otherwise than at school'

Of all the changes brought by the 1944 Education Act, with regards to physically disabled children it is perhaps the provision of education 'otherwise than at school' that had the most dramatic effect. For many of those in hospital prior to and during the war, the education authorities provided some form of education, but schooling for the more seriously physically disabled children, many of whom remained at home, had been largely determined by the actions of voluntary organisations. The new act legislated for the education of all (educable) disabled children:

> If a local education authority are satisfied that by reason of any extraordinary circumstances a child or young person is unable to attend a suitable school for the purpose of receiving primary or secondary education they shall have power with the approval of the Minister to make special arrangements for him to receive education otherwise than at school being primary or secondary education, as the case may require, or, if the authority are satisfied that it is impracticable for him to receive full-time education and the Minister approves, education similar in other respects but less than full-time.[73]

The 'extraordinary circumstances' are not specified in the act, but with regard to disabled children it was taken to include reasons of delicate health or a child awaiting a vacancy in a special school.[74] In such cases there were two possibilities by which the LEA could provide SET: home tuition or a hospital school.

In 1939 there had been 88 special schools in hospitals, accommodating 7,414 children. In 1955 the number of schools had increased to 120, but the number of children needing such provision had decreased to 6,476.[75] The fall in number was mainly due to fewer children requiring long-term hospital care. Medical advances, especially with regard to TB, meant that by 1955 there was a greater mix of short, medium and long-stay cases.

For children too seriously disabled to attend a special school, and who did not require a hospital stay, or were awaiting a vacancy in a convalescent hospital, their LEA had the power to provide tuition at home. In April 1947 the former head teacher and commandant Jessie Thomas, who had retired only a few months earlier, became one of the first home teachers provided by the LCC. She described the children who needed home tuition as including 'cases of severe incontinence, children with facial or bodily disfigurements which would be shocking to others, children who even with the help of transport could not leave wheelchair or bed'.[76]

Unfortunately, official figures for this category of SET are unavailable before 1949, but between 1949 and 1954 there was an increase from 780 children receiving either home tuition or individual tuition in hospital (separate from those attending special schools in hospital) to 3,708, of whom 1,425 were in hospital (but, again, not attending special school) and 2,283 at home or in small groups elsewhere.[77] 'Elsewhere' could mean the home of one child where others gathered, so that it was more convenient (and cost-effective) for the teacher, and so that the children could interact. If such a home was unavailable or unsuitable, a neighbour's sitting room might have been offered, or premises might have been hired nearby. Regardless of how the scheme worked, it expanded considerably in the postwar years, as did the special education system as a whole.

The expansion of special schools

With approximately 222,000 homes being destroyed in England and Wales by wartime bombing, the building or repairing of all types of schools was subject to limited resources and strict regulations were imposed on all types of building.[78] After the war a National Building Programme was established but in the first two years at least 60 per cent of new buildings had to have been in the form of housing, the remaining 40 per cent being shared between all other projects.[79] There was stiff competition for the limited amount of funding and materials (which could only be bought with the relevant purchase licence) that was available for all other types of building, which included hospitals, factories and schools.

Within the education services, special schools, which came under a separate Special Services Educational Building List, had to compete with the expansion of further education institutions, as well as the vast number of new primary and secondary schools that also needed building. As a result, temporary premises often had to be used, which were sometimes a little more long-term than was intended. In May 1945 the Ministry of Education issued Circular 48, which virtually confined all educational building to the erection of pre-fabricated huts, which could be put up quickly, using little skilled labour.[80]

An illustration of the extent to which these difficulties impacted on the building of special schools comes from Wythenshawe, to the south of Manchester. The district had a school population of 7,300, out of which 68 were classed as ESN. In January 1946 it was proposed to open a special day school for 100 such children, which would eventually serve a total school population of 15,000, including Wythenshawe and the surrounding area. In the meantime a local scout hut was approved. The 'hut' was 70 feet by 25 feet, timber-built, with a corrugated iron roof. It contained one large room with a platform, a kitchen, lavatory accommodation, electric heating and lighting. In the meantime the LEA submitted plans for a new school to the Ministry of Education. By 1950 the LEA had still not been given a date on which building could begin and, in June of that year the Ministry offered the following explanation:

> We are going faster in special school provision than at any time before the war. We have been expanding at the rate of something like 30 new schools a year – but owing to the tremendous pressure on the building programme for ordinary schools this progress has only been possible by using existing buildings with adaptations of moderate extent. In turn, this has meant in practice a programme of boarding rather than day schools, a priority which accords broadly with the advice of the Minister's Advisory Committee on Disabled Children, for it is in the case which can only be dealt with at a boarding school that the gravest problems lay.

The letter concluded:

> Through a long history of neglect, the general shortage of special school accommodation is so great that we have a very thankless task in deciding which proposals can be put in hand under the present economic conditions.[81]

The letter reveals the change in attitude towards the importance of special school provision. The official acknowledged the 'long history of neglect' and perhaps saw his department's role as remedying long standing inadequacies. However, he was obviously frustrated at the financial and other constraints imposed by the economic climate, a problem faced by many of those working towards postwar reconstruction.

Owing to the success of the residential schools that had been used to accommodate, and to educate, disabled evacuees during the war, the boarding

Table 1 Increase in number of special schools, 1945–55.

	Boarding	Day	Total
Blind and Partially Sighted	8	–	8
Deaf and Partially Deaf	12	–	12
ESN	83	59	142
Epileptic	2	–	2
PH and Delicate	46	11	57
Maladjusted	30	3	33
Speech Defects	1	–	1
Totals	182	73	255

school system was to be expanded. The 'Minister's Advisory Committee' alluded to in the letter was Circular 79, dated 1 January 1946, which called attention to the serious shortage of boarding school provision for ESN and maladjusted children. One possible solution that should be considered, advised the Minister, was the buying and adapting of large houses, a suggestion that was readily adopted. Despite the competition for such buildings (a number of enterprises were in need of such premises, for example industrial research laboratories), this method of provision played a large part in the postwar expansion of special schools.[82]

Between the end of the war and 31 December 1955, the number of special schools increased by 255 (182 boarding and 73 day). The types of extra schools (excluding hospital schools) are shown in Table 1.[83] However, during the same period 33 schools (21 day and 12 boarding) were closed, giving a net gain of 222 schools (52 day and 170 boarding). Of the new schools, 36 (boarding) were provided by voluntary bodies, the rest by LEAs.

The number of places in special schools had increased by 16,159 (excluding those in hospital schools). Of these, 10,221 were in boarding schools and 5,938 in day schools. The net figures, allowing for those which had been closed, were made up as shown in Table 2.[84] In addition to the day and boarding special schools, 68 new boarding homes were provided, from which 1,410 children attended ordinary schools in the neighbourhood (Table 3).[85] The vast majority of the boarding schools that opened after the war were in specially adapted houses which had been sold to the education authorities, sometimes for a considerable profit. One such case was Seacroft, a large house in Skegness, which had originally been used as a prepatory school for boys. Bought during the war as a speculation, it was then sold to the LEA after the war for use as an ESN school. As with many similar cases, there was a significant delay between the beginning of negotiations and subsequent purchase, and eventual use as a

Table 2 Increase/decrease in number of special school places, 1945–55.

	Boarding	Day	Total
Blind and Partially Sighted	419	−200	219
Deaf and Partially Deaf	992	221	1,213
ESN	5,393	5,593	10,986
Epileptic	216	–	216
PH and Delicate	2,146	156	2,302
Maladjusted	1,005	168	1,173
Speech Defects	50	–	50
Totals	10,221	5,938	16,159

Table 3 Number of new boarding homes and places, 1945–55.

	Homes	Places
Deaf and Partially Deaf	1	70
ESN	8	231
Maladjusted	53	955
Diabetic	6	154
Totals	68	1,410

special school. In the case of Seacroft, the period of delay was five years, and was due to agreeing costs and plans for adaptations. The school was eventually approved under the Education Act, 1944, in January 1950, for senior girls aged eleven to sixteen.[86]

Most delays to the use of these houses were due to the shortage of labour and materials; disagreements between LEAs and the owners of properties were usually solved by compulsory purchase orders and/or subsequent agreements between valuer and owner. Sometimes, though, a project was subjected to many different hurdles. One such case is Woodville in Preston, which eventually became a boarding school for ESN children. In September 1945 the owner of Woodville was asking for £6,000 for the property; the district valuer said it was worth £3,300. Six months later a compulsory purchase order was made by Blackburn Town Council and the valuer and owner agreed on the price of £4,250, which was paid by Blackburn LEA.[87] Adaptations to the property were to begin, under the Special Services Building Programme, in 1951, by which time the house had been unoccupied for six years and was in a serious state of disrepair, suffering from wood rot, dry rot, wet rot and furniture beetle. The cost of removing the rot and adapting the premises was £34,160, and a further £11,500 was spent on furniture.[88]

The policy of expanding the boarding school system was, to some extent, to the detriment of the special day schools (as can be seen in Table 1: 182 new boarding schools as opposed to 73 day schools). This discrepancy was noted by Bootle LEA in 1952, at a time when the supply of suitable houses for use as boarding schools was becoming exhausted, and when a new day school for ESN children was being proposed:

> At present the Authority has to rely on boarding schools for these disabled pupils and is anxious to provide facilities for *day* pupils in the area. Although a start has been made in a very limited way in providing special classes in ordinary schools, the limit of space and the pressure of numbers on existing accommodation will render progress in this direction very slow.[89]

Three months later the Ministry of Education gave the go-ahead for the new school to be included in the Special Services Educational Building List for 1953/54. However, the project was not included in this or the following year's list. Bootle's Director of Education said: 'As far as the building programme is concerned for the year 1954/55, we must concentrate, in the first instance, in the provision of primary and secondary schools in the area of the extended borough'.[90] This decision was in direct contrast to what was said by the Ministry of Education in 1950 when special education was seen as an important part of educational expansion. In Bootle at least, disabled children were seen as a lower priority, suggesting that, although attitudes had changed somewhat, there were still some who saw disabled children as being of lesser worth. However, the building of the school, called Orrell Lodge, was eventually approved in May 1955, at a cost of £46,441.

It was inevitable, perhaps, that the postwar reconstruction and expansion of special education would be a slow process. Competition from other educational projects, housing and the many other building initiatives at a time of severe shortages of labour, materials and finance meant that many of the objectives laid out in the 1944 Education Act could not be met, at least not for several years. The new administration blamed the old order for its 'history of neglect', yet in some areas special education was still not seen to be equally important to, say, primary or secondary education. Despite these problems, however, partly as a result of the purchase of large houses by LEAs, there was a considerable increase in special schools and boarding homes, as shown in Tables 1–3.

With the increase in children being ascertained as requiring SET, and the consequent expansion of special schools, it was inevitable that more teachers would be needed. Yet, of the many changes that occurred within education in the immediate postwar years, the training of teachers of disabled children was perhaps the area that failed the most.

Teaching

As discussed in Chapter 1, the only situation in which a special qualification was needed for prewar teachers of disabled children, apart from the general teaching certificate, was when teaching blind and deaf children. The situation after the war changed only in that special qualifications were required for 'the blind, the deaf, and the partially deaf'.[91] The requirement was not extended to teachers of other disabilities and the qualification gained for these three categories was still 'in-service', as opposed to full-time training courses. The exception to this was the one-year training course run by the Department of the Deaf at the University of Manchester. The course was established in 1919 and by 1956 could admit around 65 students per year.[92] In addition, following the establishment of the College of Speech Therapists in April 1945, a three-year course of training in speech therapy was created, although speech therapists were not classified as teachers but came under the category of 'auxiliary medical personnel'.[93] On the whole, there was a serious lack of postwar training courses for teachers of the disabled. Special education was still regarded as being outside the mainstream, and not many teachers wanted to restrict themselves to such a specialised area. Therefore, the cost of full-time training would have been regarded as a waste of funds if the teachers subsequently returned to teaching in an ordinary school.

The position of women teachers in the immediate postwar years was ambiguous. During the war the severe shortage of teachers meant that women were able to attain higher positions, including headships, but once the war was over many of these positions reverted to being male-oriented. At the Lord Mayor Treloar Cripples' College School, for example, a woman was in charge of the hospital school for PD boys during the war. However, in April 1946 the management declared that 'we are hoping to appoint a man to take sole charge, similar to pre-war days'.[94] In general though, the teaching of children requiring SET appears to have been regarded as a career particularly suited to women, especially with regards to ESN children. In 1946 the headmaster and author P. A Barons wrote: 'It is by virtue of those innate characteristics and acquired accomplishments of their sex that women, undoubtedly, are gifted to make outstanding contributions to the needs of the subnormal'.[95] From 1950 some non-compulsory one-year training courses were established for teachers who felt that they should equip themselves more fully. By 1955 there were two courses in London, one in Birmingham and one in Leeds, all of which were for teachers of ESN or maladjusted children. As was the case before and during the war, a number of short courses for teachers of all categories of disability were still being held by the Ministry of Education, LEAs and voluntary bodies.[96]

Despite the growing number of specialised courses, there was still a serious lack of teachers being drawn into the profession. It is likely that potential applicants were deterred by the conditions within special schools. Many of the teaching posts were in residential schools, which meant that a certain number of out-of-school hours had to be worked, which were not paid as salary but set against board and lodging. Also, whereas in a day school the teacher's role was mostly academic, in a residential school he or she was required to arrange and supervise a much wider range of activities. Another reason may have been the low status attributed to the profession; special education was seen as being quite low in the hierarchy of the education profession. There was also the issue of the stigma that still surrounded disabled children. As late as 1955 G.A.N. Lowndes found it necessary to explain the situation in special schools:

> It is fatally easy for anyone who has never been into close association with the nation's *schools for disabled children* to imagine that they must form a depressing no man's land peopled by unhappy children who feel themselves to be in some way different from their fellows in other schools, physically or socially outcasts, or pushed on to the side-lines where they are at best objects of compassion. Nothing in reality could be further from the truth. Compassion there is, of course, but it is a practical compassion sublimated into a determination, which has become second nature to the very fine and devoted body of teachers attracted to this service, that never by word or action, by loss of patience or by letting any child suspect the difficulty of their task, shall they allow a child to lose heart, still less hope.[97]

In reality, as highlighted several times throughout this book, not all special education teachers could live up to Lowndes's description of them. That said, there were several who did possess these qualities and saw their work with disabled children as a vocation. Jessie Thomas was, arguably, the epitome of the dedicated special school teacher.

Evidently, attitudes towards disabled people (and women) were extremely slow to change significantly, and special education was not regarded with the degree of importance that wartime reports, and the Education Act, 1944, had led people to believe. This is also apparent in the area of academic education. Despite the increased visibility of disabled children in the late 1940s and 1950s, and the expansion of educational provision, their future careers were still seen to be vocational and were aimed, wherever possible, at them leading independent lives. With certain exceptions, academic achievement remained a low priority.

Academic opportunities

As a result of the Education Act, 1944, the disabled children, like other (educable) children, could attend either secondary modern or grammar school.

However, one aspect of disabled children's lives that is apparent from this book is that, historically, the vast majority were perceived, by both the government and society as a whole, to be largely incapable of academic achievement. Consequently, as a result of the lack of academic encouragement and opportunities prior to the act, the vast majority were too far behind to qualify for grammar school, and so attended secondary moderns.

One of the exceptions to this concerns a deaf girl, who spent her war years at the Royal School for Deaf and Dumb Children in Margate, Kent. Towards the latter stages of the war the Board of Education expressed concern over the girl's educational prospects as she was 'above average intelligence'. The official explained to the school that it was difficult to organise secondary education on grammar school lines, because there were only a small number who might profit. However, there were plans to open a grammar school for the deaf.[98] Indeed, it is evident from the history of deaf children that they have long been at the forefront of educational provision for disabled children, and this was still the case in the immediate postwar period. In January 1946 the Mary Hare School for the Deaf in Sussex, previously a private school, was certified by the Ministry of Heath and became the country's first national grammar school for deaf children.

Similar schools were slow to materialise; by 1958 there were only six special schools maintained by LEAs designed to meet the needs of 'bright or intellectually gifted youngsters' who were unable to attend regular grammar schools. These were three schools for blind boys and girls, two for deaf boys and girls, and one for 'crippled' boys. In addition LEAs could meet the costs for sending such children to suitable private schools.[99] Not all disabled children who passed the entry requirements for grammar school education attended a 'special' grammar school, however. Ann Rattue (see Chapter 3) attended a 'normal' grammar school after several years attending hospital school and a special day school. Ann attributes her academic abilities not to the special education system but to the efforts and encouragement of family members.[100]

Owing to the lack of academic opportunities, for the vast majority of disabled school-leavers the only employment they would acquire was domestic or factory work. During the war obtaining such a position was relatively easy, but when the men returned to reclaim their jobs there was a danger that disabled people would once again become unemployable. In order to prevent this, and to provide employment for disabled war veterans, the other important disability-related legislation from 1944 was introduced.

Disabled Persons (Employment) Act, 1944

The key to this legislation was 'rehabilitation', a word that in 1941, according to Titmuss, became the most fashionable word in medicine.[101] Although there had been some interest in rehabilitating First World War veterans, it was not until 1941 that existing orthopaedic centres were supplemented by several hundred fracture departments and specialised clinics. The severe shortage of personnel had led to the need to (re)train disabled people for war work. In October 1941 the Ministry of Labour established an 'Interim Scheme for the Training and Settlement of Disabled Persons in Industry'. At the same time the Tomlinson Committee (for the Ministry of Labour and National Service) was reviewing the whole field of rehabilitation, and published its findings in November 1942.[102] The report recommended extending rehabilitation centres to all parts of the country, and to people with various types of disabilities and illnesses. A return to work for disabled people was emphasised and, in March 1944, the Disabled Persons (Employment) Act was passed.

This act was the first legislation to encompass all disabled people of working age regardless of their status as war veteran or civilian. In order to give an optimistic view of the future for disabled people, the government produced the film *Back to Normal*. In the film an engineer who had lost an arm in the war was seen carrying on his work using specially adapted tools.[103] As a consequence of the act, a disabled persons' register was set up and rehabilitation officers were appointed at employment exchanges. The act also introduced a quota system, whereby employers with twenty or more employees had to ensure that at least three per cent of their workforce were registered disabled persons. In practice this rule was hardly ever enforced and between 1944 and 1974 there were only three prosecutions for failure to comply.

Perhaps the most significant outcome of the act was the establishment of 'Remploy', a network of factories which employed disabled people. Founded in 1945, and originally called the Disabled Persons' Employment Corporation, the name Remploy, derived from 're-employ', was adopted in 1946. The organisation undoubtedly provided opportunities to many who would otherwise have struggled to find employment. On the negative side, the disabled were segregated once more, thereby creating a stigma similar to that of the special schools.

Under the act, the Ministries of Education and Labour were obliged to work together to provide disabled school-leavers with jobs. In order to do this, all schools were to provide details of each individual to the Ministry of Education. If immediate work was unavailable or unsuitable, he or she could be sent for instruction at one of the vocational training centres run by the

6 Cherry Tree House, postwar hostel for trainees at St Loyes College

Ministry of Labour. Training for school-leavers was in technical colleges, where they and the less severely disabled adults who required retraining could be trained for different occupations.[104] In order to secure a place on a vocational or industrial programme, the disabled person had to be registered. Therefore, in order to ensure that the child wasn't overlooked, parents were advised to register their children when leaving special school. The choice of career was then made at a meeting with the child, parent(s), head teacher, juvenile employment officer, school MO and social worker.[105] The more severely disabled school-leavers tended to be sent to one of the rehabilitation centres still being run by the voluntary sector, where extra hostels were established to house the trainees. The three main centres were Queen Elizabeth College, Leatherhead; St Loyes, Exeter; and the Sir John Priestman Hospital in Finchdale Abbey, Durham.

The scarcity of personnel during the war years led to the employment of those who at any other time would have been almost unemployable. However, the abatement of the labour shortage when the war ended meant that many disabled workers experienced the prejudices and discrimination of the prewar years. The increased 'visibility' of the disabled during the war led to a heightened awareness of their abilities and potential contribution to society. Yet, in an era of full employment, those 'less able' were once again at the back of the queue. The various initiatives introduced by the 1944 act undoubtedly aided the disabled in their search for work, but the focus on segregated workshops and manual labour (the designated employment scheme was restricted to lift operators and car park attendants) was retained.

Other legislation

The years between 1946 and 1948 saw a burst of legislation marking what has been described as the final abolition of the Poor Law and the achievement of social security.[106] The National Insurance (Industrial Injuries) Act of 1946 provided benefits and pensions for those injured or contracting prescribed kinds of diseases at work.[107] The National Assistance Act, 1948, provided for the welfare of persons substantially and permanently disabled by illness, injury or congenital deformity.[108] This welfare included residential accommodation for those who, by reason of age, illness, disability or any other circumstances, were in need of care and attention which was not otherwise available to them.[109] It was stipulated that all homes must be registered by the local authorities and be liable to inspection by both them and the Ministry of Health. Furthermore, the local authorities were empowered, and to some extent required, either by their own action or through voluntary organisations, to make schemes for promoting the welfare of the various categories of disabled persons. It was hoped that a more uniform standard would result and that the interests of such groups as deaf and crippled people (blind people were already provided for under the Blind Persons Act, 1920) would be more adequately catered for.[110]

Two other pieces of legislation also affected disabled people. Firstly, the Employment and Training Act, 1948, made special provisions for aid in training and obtaining employment for various groups of individuals including the disabled.[111] Secondly, the Children Act, 1948, made it the duty of the Children's Committee to receive into care any child under seventeen if it appeared 'that the intervention of the authority under this section is necessary in the interests of the welfare of the child'.[112] In particular this act would help those children who were likely to become emotionally disturbed owing to an unsatisfactory home life.

Undoubtedly, the legislation that affected the health of children the most after the war was the National Health Service (NHS) Act, 1946. From its implementation in 1948, citizens were entitled to the provision of medicine and hospital treatment, after-care, and the supply of surgical and other appliances, as a right not a privilege.[113] The aim of the NHS Act, as explained by its architect Aneurin Bevan to Parliament in 1946, was to 'universalise the best, that we shall promise every citizen in this country the same standard of service'.[114] It was assumed that distributing a 'national' service could be achieved only by means of central direction and planning. However, as Rudolf Klein points out, central control did not lead to the hoped-for measure of distributional equity.[115] A deeper discussion of this point is beyond the scope of this book except for the issue of the distribution of hospital resources, by far the most expensive part of the NHS.[116] This subject is best discussed in relation to the role of charities which, at least until the NHS Act, had been prominent in the supply of hospital services to disabled children.

The postwar role of charities

The implementation of the NHS act was the single most pivotal event to affect voluntary organisations in the immediate postwar period. The Ministry of Health took over the control of most of the hospitals and some of the convalescent homes, and Regional Hospital Boards, each convening a wide area, were made responsible.[117] The State took over financial responsibility for hospitals and other established areas of social care, and took on many responsibilities previously met by the various voluntary societies. Therefore, the role of charities changed, but in many ways they remained just as essential. Rather than concentrating on the basic care of disabled children as before, they expanded their services by working on new initiatives. Most importantly, perhaps, they were able to provide essential supplementary services and advice to the fledgling NHS.

Prominent charities, and the COS in particular, were influential in advising the government on the establishment of the new welfare state. In 1948 the social casework built up by COS, by now renamed the Family Welfare Association (FWA), was transferred to the State's new children's departments and, as with most voluntary organisations, its focus shifted to more specialised areas of care.[118] This left the FWA free to establish new territory. Partly funded by the State, it began to provide family therapy as well as training for student social workers.

The ICAA also had to revise its postwar function. In 1948, with medical care now being catered for by the statutory health services, the association was appointed as agent for the LCC, for the placement of physically disabled children needing holidays. Eventually, the scheme, named the Recuperative Holiday Scheme, developed into a major undertaking acting as agent and inspectorate for counties all over England.[119] Having many years' experience in dealing with severely disabled children who had spent long periods in hospital, the ICAA was able to advise the government on issues such as the importance of sending a child not too far from home so that the parents could visit, as well as stressing the benefits of small establishments which produced a more family atmosphere.[120]

As well as advice, the voluntary sector also provided 'extras' to disabled children in hospitals and other institutions. For example, amusements, toys and supplementary equipment were given to blind and PS children at St Vincent's School in Liverpool. In the school's annual report for 1949–50, acknowledgement was made of the 'comprehensive legislation for the welfare of the blind and the grants provided by the state', but added that 'it is becoming increasingly apparent that without voluntary assistance the work of maintaining and caring for the blind and PS cannot proceed satisfactorily'.[121]

The postwar period provided the opportunity to make changes that had been decided before or during the war, but had been put on hold. In 1946 the National Association for Mental Health (NAMH) was established by the merging of three major mental health organisations. These were the Central Association for Mental Welfare (established 1913), the national Council for Mental Hygiene (established 1922) and the Child Guidance Council (established 1927). The amalgamation had been recommended by the Feversham Committee on voluntary mental health associations, which had reported in 1939. Although the formal merger did not take place until after the war, the three organisations worked together during the war, through the Provisional Council for Mental Health. The government asked the Council to take on the task of providing a national after-care service for war veterans discharged on psychiatric grounds, and the service then extended to civilians.[122]

The immediate postwar period also saw new initiatives regarding physically disabled people. The British Council for the Welfare of Spastics and the National Spastics Society, both established after the war, were responsible for the foundation of a number of schools solely for children suffering from CP. The first one, as we have seen, opened in 1947. The following year the first school for children with multiple disabilities was opened.[123]

Throughout the Second World War voluntary organisations worked alongside government departments. After the war, responsibilities shifted but the voluntary sector retained a strong position in the care of disabled children. They continued to provide hospital beds, schools and equipment. They provided home tuition and teaching courses. Perhaps more importantly, they maintained their work as pioneers: endeavours that they had been undertaking since the nineteenth century and have continued into the twenty-first century. In the report of one blind school it was stated that their work could not continue without the assistance of voluntary organisations.[124] It is likely that this was true in all areas of caring for disabled children.

The long term

After the flurry of reports and legislation of the immediate postwar period, further initiatives in the care and welfare of disabled children were slow to materialise and there was nothing of real significance until the 1970s. Despite the emphasis on 'inclusion', children with severe learning difficulties continued to be regarded as ineducable and were denied a place in special education until the 1970 Education Act. Upon its enactment the following year, some 24,000 children from junior training centres and special care units across England, along with 8,000 in 100 hospitals, became entitled to education.[125] For the first time in England's history, all school-age children were now entitled to an education.

The other significant event, of the same decade, was the publication in 1978 of the Warnock Report on special education in England, Scotland and Wales.[126] This report was the biggest ever investigation into special education in these countries and put the issue of integration of disabled children in ordinary schools on to a national agenda for the first time. The integrative, or inclusive, approach was based on common educational goals for all children regardless of their abilities or disabilities. It was expected that more children would be taught in mainstream rather than special schools because provision for their needs would now be better, and would become part of the recognised mainstream provision. The report also laid the foundation for the introduction of 'statements' of special educational needs (SEN), which detailed the individual child's special needs and the specific help which should be provided to meet those needs. Both recommendations formed part of the 1981 Education Act and, as a result, there was a considerable decline in the number of children in special schools during the 1980s and 1990s as well as a gradual increase in the proportion of children both identified as having special educational needs and receiving statements.

With no additional funding for the new initiatives, both the Warnock Report and the 1981 Education Act remained controversial. In 1992 the Audit Commission and Her Majesty's Inspectorate issued a joint report on special needs provision and found 'serious deficiencies in the way in which children with special needs are identified and provided for'. In particular, assessments and statements took much too long to complete and were far too vague, thus devaluing the process; specific levels of provision for pupils could not be guaranteed by LEAs or schools; there was no clear accountability by schools and LEAs of progress made by pupils and when LEAs moved pupils from special to ordinary school, resources did not follow the child (an estimated £53 million was wrongly held back by special schools in 1991).[127] In 1996 the 1981 Education Act was repealed.

The 1996 Education Act provided for the publication of a SEN Code of Practice, giving education providers practical guidance on how to identify and assess children with SEN. All publicly funded pre-schools and nurseries, State schools and local authorities were required to take account of this code, as were health and social services when helping local authorities. The Code set out guidance on policies and procedures aimed at enabling pupils with SEN to reach their full potential, to be included fully in their school communities and make a successful transition to adulthood. For the vast majority of children with SEN, a mainstream setting was expected to meet all their needs, although some children would require additional help from SEN services or other agencies external to the school. It was thought that a very small minority of children would have SEN of a severity or complexity that required the local authorities to determine and arrange the special educational provision their learning difficulties called for. A revised SEN Code of Practice was introduced in line with the 2001 Special Educational Needs and Disability Act which itself amended the 1995 Disability Discrimination Act.

By looking briefly at the legislation enacted on behalf of disabled children in the second part of the twentieth century, and the early years of the twenty-first century, it is evident that inclusion was paramount. The 1998 publication 'Meeting Special Educational Needs – A Programme of Action', in conjunction with the 1999 Disability Rights Task Force Report 'From Exclusion to Inclusion', reinforced the rights of all pupils to be educated in mainstream schools, and Part 1 of the 2001 Act served to strengthen these rights. However, mainstream schools are not suitable for all disabled children and, as with the prewar and immediate postwar eras, the subject of separation versus integration remains the single most debated issue regarding disabled children.

Special boarding or residential schools were, and continue to be, used primarily by two main groups: the seriously physically disabled and/or children with multiple disabilities, and those with emotional and/or learning difficulties. In 1993 the chartered psychologist and Professor of Education Paul Cooper conducted a study of residential special schools for boys with emotional and behavioural difficulties. The main finding was that the overwhelming majority of the boys found their time in residential school rewarding and personally enriching. Many of the boys reported improvements in their self-esteem and their sense of control over their lives. These outcomes were considered to be due to the respite from distressing situations at their homes and previous schools; the high quality of relationships students had with residential school staff; and the opportunities provided by the special schools for enhancing self-esteem, being valued as individuals, participating in a community and experiencing personal achievement.[128]

In 2009 the Children's Rights Director for England carried out a much larger survey involving 338 students with a variety of disabilities, from 40 residential special schools. Again the results were mainly positive, with 'activities' and 'trips out' coming out top. The staff also came out well. Unsurprisingly, the worst aspect was listed as homesickness, with bullying being a problem for 12 per cent of the students. When questioned about the school premises, the students often spoke about being in old, listed buildings. Although some students found the buildings interesting, many were worried about the risks of fire. Problems with the heating, water pressure and noisy pipes were also mentioned and some questioned the fact that special mobility aids (for example, fixed ceiling hoists) could not be used, which created problems for students and staff alike.[129]

Without an extensive and independent survey of children's experiences it is impossible to assess the true benefits, and the more negative aspects, of the schools. Some advocates of full mainstream inclusion, such as the special school teacher and educational psychologist John T. Hall, regard special schools per se as useful only in a transitional role in supporting the mainstream until eventually there should be a complete closure of all segregated schools and separate classes.[130] Hall equates special schools with social devaluation, whilst Joe Whittaker goes as far as comparing them to twenty-first-century gulags, where: 'the collective fears of children is reconstructed as "special education" in a "safe" environment'.[131] Others, such as Suzanne Saunders, former head of an independent school for children with physical and learning difficulties, argue that, although inclusion is a goal which should be aimed for, attendance in a residential special school for some children in some circumstances represents a positive option.[132] Evidently, the debate over integration versus segregation continues but it is safe to say that residential special schools, in one form or another, are still going strong, at least for the time being.

Conclusion

It is inevitable that any discussion on children during the immediate postwar period will focus largely on the legislation that came into force during the years 1944 to 1948. This chapter has discussed those acts that directly concerned disabled children with regards to their health, education and prospective employment opportunities. Much of the discussion has concentrated on the reforms of the Education Act, 1944, and the subsequent Regulations for Disabled Children, 1945, and the difficulties in implementing the changes due to the conditions of war.

Much of the reorganisation concerning disabled children stemmed from

the recommendations of prewar reports. For example, the abolition of certification and an extension in the number of categories of disability had been
proposed long before the outbreak of war. The separating, for educational
purposes, of blind from partially sighted children, and deaf from partially deaf
children, had also been on the agenda before the war but as with any expansion
of the school system after the war, this was slow to emerge owing to the lack of
accommodation.

Although there was an overall increase in the number of children quali-
fying for special school places, there was a decline in some categories of
disability, for various reasons. Some PS and epileptic children, for example,
were provided for in ordinary schools. The latter group, in particular, benefited from advances in diagnosis techniques and treatment and, from the
1950s, there was a general decline in the number of delicate children owing
to an improvement in their general health. All children benefited from the
establishment of the NHS and, in particular, from the increased availability
of general practitioners, which meant that disabilities were often diagnosed
at an earlier age.

For maladjusted children, whose condition was often caused by inadequate
home conditions, the war had highlighted the benefits of residential accommodation, and the postwar years saw a significant rise in boarding schools.
Some of these were attached to CGCs, where mental health specialists were
able to expand their knowledge of the condition. The need for residential
places for seriously physically disabled children was also highlighted during
the war but, although the government did extend the home tuition scheme, the
expansion of special schools in this area was very slow, and new schools were
usually provided by voluntary organisations.

The continuing importance of the voluntary sector after the war is evident;
the various charitable organisations continued to provide all types of services.
They also continued to provide establishments which offered vocational
training. Postwar government legislation served to enhance the possibilities for disabled children, helping them to gain employment and to become
self-supporting adults. Initially aimed at war veterans, disabled 'civilians' also
benefited.

Although focusing primarily on postwar events, this chapter has highlighted the ways in which change came about for disabled children not only
in practical matters but also in regards to people's attitudes towards them.
Wartime conditions brought a new awareness of the capabilities of disabled
people, and in some ways their lives improved. However, real positive change
was, and is, extremely slow. Although advances have been made, it may be
many more years before disabled children, and adults, gain true acceptance.

Notes

1 LMA, LCC/EO/SS/1/68, LCC, 'Closure of Residential Special Schools in Evacuated (Reception) Areas', 1945.

2 TNA, ED32/1378, HMI reports of the Bethesda Home for Crippled Children in Cheetham Hill, Manchester, and the Tanllwyfan Convalescent Home in Colwyn Bay, Wales (1945–51).

3 TNA, ED32/2271, R.A. Butler to Colonel Sir Joseph Nall, MP, 5 May 1945; and ED32/2299, HMI reports of Oakfield Special ESN School, Liverpool, 1945–51.

4 J. Anderson, 'British Women, Disability and the Second World War', *Contemporary British History*, 20:1 (2006), 37–53.

5 Humphries and Gordon, *Out of Sight*, pp. 134–5, includes images.

6 TNA, ED32/764, Old Members Association Annual Report, 1941, of the Queen Elizabeth's Training College for the Disabled, Leatherhead.

7 L. Inskip (ed.), *National Cripples Journal (Leicester)*, 51 (1941).

8 B. Woods and N. Watson, 'In Pursuit of Standardisation: The Ministry of Health's Model 8F Wheelchair, 1948–1962', *Technology and Culture*, 45:3 (2004), 540–68.

9 This continued throughout the war and into the 1950s. The Mass Observation Archive is housed at Sussex University: www.massobs.org.uk.

10 S. Garfield, *Our Hidden Lives: The Remarkable Diaries of Post-war Britain* (London: Ebury, 2004), p. 313.

11 Garfield, *Our Hidden Lives*, p. 107.

12 W. Goodman, 'Review of "Thursday's Children"', *New York Times*, 7 October 1987.

13 S. J. Curtis, *History of Education in Great Britain* (London: University Tutorial Press, 7th edition, 1968), p. 383.

14 Stakes and Hornby, *Change in Special Education*, p. 25.

15 Board of Education, *Report of the Consultative Committee on the Education of the Adolescent* (Hadow Report) (London: HMSO, 1926).

16 G. A. N. Lowndes, *The Silent Social Revolution*, (London: Oxford University Press, 1969), p. 114.

17 Board of Education, *Report of the Consultative Committee on Secondary Education with Special Reference to Grammar Schools and Technical High Schools* (Spens Report) (HMSO: London, 1938).

18 R. Lowe, *Education in the Post-war Years: A Social History* (London and New York: Routledge, 1988), p. 6.

19 Gosden, *Education in the Second World War*, p. 237.

20 Board of Education, *Education after the War*, Foreword.

21 Board of Education, *Education after the War*, p. 36.

22 Gosden gives an extensive account of both documents in *Education in the Second World War*, chapters 11–13.

23 This brief summary of changes brought about by the act is sufficient for this study. For an in-depth examination of the act and its perceived failures/successes see

Lowndes, *The Silent Social Revolution*; G. McCulloch, *Educational Reconstruction*; and Lowe, *Education in the Post-war Years*.

24 Education Act 1921, Part V: Blind, Deaf, Defective and Epileptic Children.

25 Ministry of Education, *The Handicapped Pupils and School Health Service Regulations*, 1945, part II, s.3.

26 In 1929, 1934 and 1938 respectively.

27 Ministry of Education, *The Handicapped Pupils and School Health Service Regulations*, 1945, S.34 (5).

28 Ministry of Education, *Pamphlet No. 5: Special Educational Treatment* (London: HMSO, 1945).

29 Hansard 14 ii 44, Chuter Ede: Column 1139 (1944), as stated in Stakes and Hornby, *Change in Special Education*, p. 25.

30 Ministry of Education, *The Handicapped Pupils and School Health Service Regulations*, 1945, S.33 (2).

31 *Ibid.*, s.4 (1).

32 *Ibid.*, s.5.

33 *Ibid.*

34 *Ibid.*, s.27. Under the 1944 act, a maximum class size was also prescribed for ordinary schools, this being 40 for junior and infant classes and 30 for seniors.

35 Board of Education, *Report of the Board of Education on Partially Sighted Children* (London: HMSO, 1934).

36 Ministry of Education, *List 42: Recognised Special Schools* (London: HMSO, 1949).

37 In the mid- to late 1950s there would be an increase in the need for blind schools because of the increase in blind babies being born with retrolental fibroplasias at the beginning of the decade. This was as a result of an excessive use of oxygen on premature babies. Once the cause was discovered, the level of blind babies being born dropped again.

38 Pritchard, *Education and the Handicapped*, p. 212.

39 Ministry of Education, *List 42: Recognised Special Schools*, 1949.

40 TNA, ED32/2129, Lumsden's report on Thomasson Memorial School, 12 July 1946.

41 TNA, ED32/1927, HMI reports on Needwood Boarding School for Partially Deaf Children, Burton on Trent, Staffordshire, 1952–55.

42 Ministry of Education, *Pamphlet 30: Education of the Handicapped Pupil 1945–55* (London: HMSO, 1956), p. 21.

43 Ministry of Education, *Handicapped Pupils and School Health Service Regulations* (London: HMSO, 1953).

44 J. Read and J. Walmsley discuss the postwar development of occupation centres for the ineducable (including unofficial schooling) in 'Historical Perspectives on Special Education 1890–1970', *Disability and Society*, 21:5 (2006), 455–69.

45 Ministry of Education, *Pamphlet 5: Special Educational Treatment*, p. 20.

46 Ministry of Education, *Pamphlet 30: Education of the Handicapped Pupil*, p. 13.

47 TNA, ED32/1928, Notes of a meeting between the Ministry of Education and the Staffordshire LEA, 30 November 1953.

48 E. Cliffe, 'A Study of the Educational Provision for Mentally Handicapped Children in Leicester during the Inter-War Years', unpublished BA dissertation, University of Leicester, 2008. See also Leff and Leff, *The School Health Service*, p. 262.

49 TNA, ED32/247, Bosworth-Smith to Sir Robert Myer, 10 October 1944.

50 Pritchard, *Education and the Handicapped*, p. 213.

51 TNA, ED10/216, Notes of an informal discussion between several officers of the Board of Education, 17 June 1943.

52 *TES*, 2 September 1944.

53 Ministry of Education, *Pamphlet 30: Education of the Handicapped Pupil*, p. 15.

54 TNA, ED195/196, Dr Simpson, 1963.

55 Ministry of Education, *Circular 79: Disabled and Maladjusted Children* (London: HMSO, 1946).

56 TNA, ED32/2290, Aymestry Court Boarding Special School for Maladjusted Boys, Woolton, Liverpool, 1945–55.

57 LMA, LCC/EO/SS/1/118, Ministry of Education, Special Services Branch, 13 January 1949.

58 *Ibid.*

59 Ministry of Education, *Pamphlet 30: Education of the Handicapped Pupil*, pp. 16–17.

60 TNA, ED32/1302, Lumsden's report on Potternewton School for PD Children in Leeds, July 1944. The school was evacuated at the outbreak of war but re-opened the following year and remained open throughout the rest of the war.

61 Pritchard, *Education and the Handicapped*, p. 219.

62 J. Lumsden, 'Special Education for the Disabled', *Teacher of the Blind* (1968).

63 TNA, ED32/2179, Notes on Ministry of Health conference, June 1945.

64 Ministry of Education, *Pamphlet 30: Education of the Handicapped Pupil*, p. 18.

65 M. I. Dunsdon, *Report of a Survey on the Educability of Cerebral Palsied Children* (National Foundation for Educational Research in England and Wales, 1951).

66 Ministry of Education, *Pamphlet 30: Education of the Handicapped Pupil*, p. 22.

67 TNA, ED32/1948, Moor House Residential Special School for Speech Defects, Oxted, Surrey, 1945–47.

68 Pritchard, *Education and the Handicapped*, p. 213.

69 Ministry of Education, *Pamphlet No. 30: Education of the Handicapped Pupil 1945–55*, pp. 19–20.

70 Harris, *The Health of the Schoolchild*, p. 178.

71 *Ibid.*, p. 176.

72 *Ibid.*, p. 189.

73 Education Act 1944, s.56.

74 *Ibid.*, s.56 (b).

75 Ministry of Education, *Pamphlet 30: Education of the Handicapped Pupil*, p. 22.

76 Thomas, *Hope for the Handicapped*, p. 165.

77 Ministry of Education, *Pamphlet 30: Education of the Handicapped Pupil*, p. 24.

78 Lowndes, *Margaret McMillan: The Children's Champion*, p. 93.

79 For an in-depth view of postwar building see N. Bullock, *Building the Post-war World: Modern Architecture and Reconstruction in Britain* (London and New York: Routledge, 2002).

80 N. Middleton, *When Family Failed: The Treatment of Children in the Care of the Community during the First Half of the Twentieth Century* (London: Gollancz, 1976), p. 317.

81 TNA, ED32/2331, Morris at Ministry of Education to Fisher at Manchester Education Office, 14 June 1950.

82 Ministry of Education, *Pamphlet 30: Education of the Handicapped Pupil*, p. 5.

83 *Ibid.*, p. 3.

84 *Ibid.*, p. 4.

85 *Ibid.*

86 TNA, ED32/1642, Seacroft Boarding School for ESN Children, Skegness, 1945–52.

87 TNA, ED32/1620, Woodville Boarding Special ESN School, Longridge, Preston, 1945–51.

88 'Blackburn Children's School at £1,500 a Place: House with a Fearsome List of Defects', *Manchester Guardian*, 24 November 1951.

89 TNA, ED32/2130, Orrell Lodge Proposed Day Special ESN School, Bootle, Lancashire, Memorandum of Bootle LEA, 24 and 30 June 1952.

90 TNA, ED32/2130, Bootle LEA, September 1952.

91 Ministry of Education, *The Handicapped Pupils and School Health Service Regulations, 1945*, s.30(2).

92 Ministry of Education, *Pamphlet 30: Education of the Handicapped Pupil 1945–55* (1956).

93 Taylor and Taylor, *Special Education of Physically Handicapped Children in Western Europe*, p. 168.

94 TNA, ED32/1091, Lord Mayor Treloar Cripples College School, 1944–46.

95 'Teaching Mentally Defective, Dull and Backward Children', in *Careers and Vocational Training: A Complete Guide to Women's Professions* (London: The Women's Employment Publishing Company, 1946), p. 505. The text also includes sections on teaching blind and deaf and dumb children.

96 Ministry of Education, *Pamphlet 30: Education of the Handicapped Pupil*, p. 8.

97 Lowndes, *The English Educational System*, p. 117. It should be remembered that Lowndes was a government official.

98 TNA, ED32/1558, Bosworth-Smith at the Board of Education to the Royal School for Deaf and Dumb Children in Margate, Kent. The date of the letter is unknown but is likely to be c.1944.

99 Taylor and Taylor, *Special Education of Physically Handicapped Children in Western Europe*, p. 158.

100 As told by Ann Rattue to the author, 21 March 2006.

101 Titmuss, *Problems of Social Policy*, p. 478.

102 Ministry of Labour and National Service, *Report on the Inter-departmental Committee on the Rehabilitaion and Resettlement of Handicapped Persons* (London: HMSO, 1941).

103 Humphries and Gordon, *Out of Sight*, pp. 134–6, includes image.

104 Other disabled adults could attend residential rehabilitation units or receive industrial training on work premises.

105 J. Anderson, 'The Soul of a Nation: a Social History of Disabled People, Physical Therapy, Rehabilitation and Sport in Britain 1918–1970' (De Montfort University: unpublished PhD Thesis, 2002).

106 R. Chambers, 'The National Assistance Act 1948', *The Modern Law Review*, 12:1 (1949), 69–72.

107 Taylor and Taylor, *Special Education of Physically Handicapped Children in Western Europe*, p. 169.

108 *Ibid.*

109 History of mental health at www.mind.org.uk.

110 Chambers, 'The National Assistance Act', pp. 70–1.

111 Taylor and Taylor, *Special Education of Physically Handicapped Children in Western Europe*, p. 169.

112 Children Act, 1948, s.1 (1).

113 Taylor and Taylor, *Special Education of Physically Handicapped Children in Western Europe*, p. 169.

114 Hansard, 1946a.

115 R. Klein, 'Control, Participation, and the British National Health Service', *Health and Society*, 57:1 (1979), 70–94.

116 An extensive examination of voluntary organisations during this period can be found in F. Prochaska, *Philanthropy and the Hospitals of London* (Oxford: University Press, 1992); and M. Rooff, *Voluntary Societies and Social Policy* (London: Routledge & Kegan Paul, 1957).

117 Rooff, *Voluntary Societies and Social Policy*, pp. 69–70.

118 Family Welfare Association at: www.fwa.org.uk.

119 ICAA, now renamed ICAN: www.ican.org.uk/home/about.

120 LMA, 4248/D/01/006, ICAA Annual report for 1945.

121 TNA, ED32/2291, St Vincent's School for the Blind and Partially Sighted, Liverpool. Annual Report 1949–50.

122 Further information can be found at: www.mind.org.uk.

123 Rooff, *Voluntary Societies and Social Policy*, p. 247.

124 TNA, ED32/2291, St Vincent's School for the Blind and Partially Sighted, Liverpool, Annual Report, 1949–50.

125 M. Vaughan, 'Milestones on the Road to Inclusion, 1970–2002', http://inclusion.uwe.ac.uk/inclusionweek/articles/milestones.htm, accessed 20 December 2011. The article was one of several written to mark the twentieth

anniversary of the Centre for Studies in Inclusive Education (www.csie.org. uk/).

126 M. Warnock, *Special Educational Needs: Report of the Committee of Enquiry into the Education of Handicapped Children and Young People* (London: HMSO, 1978).

127 Audit Commission / Her Majesty's Inspectorate, *Getting in on the Act – Provision for Children with Special Educational Needs: The National Picture* (London: HMSO, 1992).

128 P. Cooper, *Effective Schools for Disaffected Pupils: Integration and Segregation* (London: Routledge, 1993).

129 Ofsted, *Life in Residential Special Schools: A Report of Children's Experience* (London: HMSO, 2009).

130 J. T. Hall, *Social Devaluation and Special Education: the Right to Full Mainstream Inclusion and an Honest Statement*, (London: Jessica Kingsley, 1997), p. 13.

131 J. Whittaker, 'Segregated Schools Must Close', *Coalition* (2001), 12–16. Joe Whittaker is a lecturer at the University of Bolton.

132 S. Saunders, 'The Residential School: A Valid Choice', *British Journal of Special Education*, 21:2 (1994), 64–6.

CONCLUSION

This book has been written with the aim of both highlighting the experiences of disabled children during the Second World War and analysing the debates and actions surrounding post-war change. It is hoped that these issues have been addressed adequately in Chapters 1–5. All that is left now is to highlight some of the more prominent issues that stand out from the study and that made a particular difference to the children's lives. Some aspects that came to light during the war, such as the level of poverty in which certain children were living and which was often the cause of poor general health, affected all children whether disabled or able-bodied, and have been discussed more than adequately in other studies. Disruption to the provision of education also affected both groups, although in different ways, as has been made clear. For disabled children, problems associated with physical access, medical treatment requirements and the continuing stigma surrounding certain types of mental health problems meant that the children's education and even safety often depended on their particular 'category' of disability.

During the war one of the most vulnerable groups of children was the severely physically disabled. Virtually abandoned by the evacuation authorities, these children more than most relied on their parent(s) and on the assistance of various charitable societies. The many and varied fund-raising programmes of the war years served to both raise awareness of these children's needs and to provide much-needed financial help. Thanks to the continuing generosity of the general public at home and abroad, and of individual philanthropists, the more prominent organisations were able to continue their operations, thereby helping children who were bedridden and/or unable to leave their home. After the war these same children, as well as those with multiple disabilities, continued to rely on charitable bodies, albeit in different ways and with financial assistance provided as part of the new welfare state. The role of the voluntary sector during the war, and since, should not be underestimated.

The majority of disabled children were provided for under the official evacuation scheme and, in the absence of more personal testimony and with certain exceptions, it would appear that the 'lucky' ones were those children accommodated within the residential special schools. The tangible benefits of these wartime schools are clear; the alternative was to remain in evacuating areas where the children would face not only greater danger from air attacks but also fewer education opportunities. Those who remained in the schools for the duration of the war suffered less upheaval, and being together with their classmates and regular teachers meant less isolation for them than for those not evacuated or, indeed, many of the able-bodied children. The more subtle advantages of the schools, and one of the main reasons for their success and expansion after the war, were the social aspects. Many children benefited from a level of social training that was simply not possible in special day schools. Those who came from an unsatisfactory home life and those with poor general health (malnutrition, asthma, and so on) benefited even more. The schools also raised awareness of children with disabilities among the general public who had previously been unused to seeing large groups of disabled children. This new awareness and understanding, especially in regard to children with mental health problems, was perhaps why those government officials and property owners who questioned whether they should have been evacuated at all were overruled, and the vast majority of children remained safe.

On a more negative note, homesickness was for some children a problem that just could not be overcome, and the more severe cases returned home quite soon, as did many able-bodied children who could not settle in their billets. During the war many children remained in their residential special schools or billets continually and, with petrol rationing and other problems associated with the conditions of war, parents often found it difficult to visit. Unsurprisingly, homesickness continues to be the main concern of children in residential special schools. What is surprising, however, is that the problems associated with old buildings remain a large concern of some residents. Fortunately, advances in medical treatment, a better health care system and a welfare programme that was unavailable during the war have led to fewer children needing residential care. However, although they are somewhat controversial in that the act of segregating children is vehemently opposed by those who advocate full mainstream inclusion, the schools continue to benefit the most vulnerable children.

After the war various pieces of legislation intended for the betterment of all children's health and education concerns were introduced. This was partly as a result of prewar debates and activities and partly due to issues raised during the war. One of the most significant aspects of the 1944 Education Act, for example, was the introduction of 'maladjustment' as an official category of disability which meant that, for the first time, the State was legally responsible for providing adequate education provision. Although it was recognised as a legitimate condition before the war, and despite the development of the Child Guidance Council in 1927, it was the evacuation that brought it to the national consciousness and highlighted the fact that not all sufferers displayed 'bad' behaviour. Emotional disturbance continues to be the subject of scholarly and professional investigation.

Much of the benefit felt by disabled children in the postwar era was the result of a knock-on effect of that intended primarily for children in general. In 1944 the Education Act and the Disability (Employment) Act promised much, and there were definite advances in education provision, but the fact was that in some respects, such as obtaining a grammar school place or non-vocational employment, disabled people were already starting from a disadvantageous position. Regardless of the reasons for the inadequacies in education and training, the result was that many children did not get the education they were intended to receive. Provision was patchy and, as in wartime, it was a matter of luck as to whether a child had a committed and motivated teacher. On the whole, teachers still tended to see special education as the 'poor relation'. The lack of specialised courses available to them highlights a continuation of the poor esteem in which the profession had so long been held. Apart from the associated stigma, the lack of opportunities was also a deterrent. Special education was still seen largely as a female profession and, despite women's advancements during the war, once it was over headships tended to revert to the prewar days and the preserve of male teachers. Added problems of a lack of finance, labour and materials meant that for some it was many years before the benefits of the new legislation were felt, if at all.

The period of the Second World War was clearly a turning point in the lives of disabled children. The Government Evacuation Scheme, with its successes and failures, brought awareness of the complex nature of disabilities and of the children themselves. In turn, many of the children were exposed to new experiences and, after the war, new opportunities presented themselves. This book has attempted to tell the story of these children although through necessity this has been done largely by a 'top-down' approach. Despite the generous participation of a handful of former evacuees there is still a serious shortage of personal testimony by those who were disabled during the war years. Similarly, although there has been a growing interest in disability studies and despite the fact that studies of the evacuation of the Second World War continues to attract scholars, the two disciplines are rarely connected. It is hoped that this book will serve both to provide an interesting subject for the general reader and to encourage further research within the academic community.

References

Primary Sources

The National Archives

Board of Education

ED10/216	Records relating to the Caldecott Community, 1942–44
ED10/252	Report on the Home Tuition Scheme, 1939
ED32/642	Correspondence with and regarding Colonel ffennell, 1941
ED32/666	Correspondence regarding the National Camp's Corporation camp at Sheephatch, during 1942–44
ED32/1039	Correspondence with, and documents relating to, the Shaftesbury Society, 1942–43
ED33/157	Springhill Private School for Deaf Boys, Northampton, 1940–44
ED50/11	Rules for Boarding Schools for Blind or Deaf Children, 1895–99
ED50/173	Mentally defective children in approved schools
ED50/188	HMI James Lumsden's Reports
ED50/258	Wartime Problems in Special Schools, 1939–41
ED50/262	Reorganisation of Schools for the Blind, 1938–45
ED50/266	Special Educational Treatment of the Feeble-Minded, 1935–45
ED50/268	Validity of Certification under the MD Act 1913, 1939–43
ED50/271	Provision of Special Schools for Epileptics, 1937–43
ED50/273	Special Educational Treatment for Maladjusted Children, 1936–39
ED50/274	Special Educational Treatment for Maladjusted Children, 1940–45
ED50/284	Reorganisation of schools for the Deaf, 1943–45
ED62/99	Chalfont St Peter Epileptic Colony, 1936–46
ED62/100	St Loyes Training College for Cripples, 1936–42
ED62/140A	School for Stitchery and Lace for Crippled Girls, Gt Bookham, 1936–42
ED62/140B	School for Stitchery and Lace for Crippled Girls, Gt Bookham, 1938–45

ED122/21	Little Beckett's Farm School for Difficult Boys, Safron Waldon, Essex, 1943–46
ED133/8	Unemployment Assistance Board, 1937
ED137/23	Brambling House, 1945
ED138 series	Sophia Weitzman's papers
ED195/196	Brambling House, Chesterfield, 1963

Individual special schools

ED32/235	Chalfont St Peter Colony for Epileptics, 1932–44
ED32/244	Sandlebridge, Mary Dendy Home, 1932–42
ED32/247	Chaigeley School for Maladjusted Children, 1944
ED32/254	Brambling House Open-Air School, 1936–40
ED32/264	Royal West of England School for the Deaf, Exeter, 1937–43
ED32/334	Ledbury Park Evacuated School for the Deaf, Bristol, 1942–44
ED32/347	Eastcourt House Residential School for MD Children, 1942–44
ED32/352	Lord Mayor Treloar's Cripples College, 1934–44
ED32/384	East Redhill School, 1935–44
ED32/391	Caldecott Community School for Maladjusted Children, 1941–44
ED32/646	Bowleaze Cove School for Evacuated PD Children, 1941–44
ED32/663	Banstead School for Evacuated Deaf and Partially Deaf Children, 1941–44
ED32/696	Dallington Home for Maladjusted Girls, 1930–40
ED32/764	Queen Elizabeth's Training College for the Disabled, Leatherhead, 1938–44
ED32/827	Besford Court RC School for MD Boys, 1934–44
ED32/829	Dudley deaf School, 1931–44
ED32/871	One Oak Parish Residential School for MD Children, 1941–44
ED32/909	Delamere Fresh-Air Home and School for Jewish Children, 1929–41
ED32/950	Allerton Priory Residential RC School for MD Children, 1934-43
ED32/954	Maghull Home for Epileptics, 1934–43
ED32/958	Pontville RC School for MD Children, Ormskirk, 1943
ED32/1006	Hollingdean Temporary MD School, Brighton, 1932–44
ED32/1015	Monghull Colony MD School, Birmingham, 1931–44

ED32/1020	Yorkshire Residential School for the Blind, York, 1930–44
ED32/1041	Alexandra Hospital School, Luton (formerly Swanley), 1934–45
ED32/1052	Liverpool Open-Air Hospital School, 1934–45
ED32/1054	Royal Cornwall Infirmary Orthopaedic Hospital School, 1936–45
ED32/1057	Brambling House Open-Air School, 1940–45
ED32/1091	Lord Mayor Treloar Cripples College School, 1944–46
ED32/1092	Lord Mayor Treloar Cripples Hospital School, 1932–45
ED32/1121	Embden St MD School, Manchester, 1939–44
ED32/1124	Chaucer St MD School, Oldham, 1932–41
ED32/1189	Horsley Green Camp School for PD and Delicate Children, 1940–45
ED32/1302	Potternewton PD School, Leeds, 1934–45
ED32/1378	Bethseda Home for Crippled Children, Manchester, 1945–51
ED32/1558	Royal School for Deaf and Dumb Children, Margate, 1945–51
ED32/1602	Pontville RC School for ESN Children, Ormskirk, 1945–51
ED32/1620	Woodville Boarding School for ESN Children, Preston, 1945–51
ED32/1642	Seacroft Boarding School for ESN Children, Skegness, 1945–52
ED32/1927	Needwood Boarding School for Partially Deaf Children, Burton on Trent, 1947–51
ED32/1928	Needwood Boarding school for Partially Deaf Children, Burton on Trent, 1952–55
ED32/1948	Moor House Residential School for Children with Speech Defects, 1945–47
ED32/2129	Thomasson Memorial School for Deaf and Partially Deaf Children, Bolton, 1945–55
ED32/2130	Orrell Lodge Proposed Day School for ESN Children, Bootle, 1945–51
ED32/2187	Royal School for the Deaf, Derby, 1944
ED32/2179	St Margaret's School for Spastic Children, Croydon, 1945–48
ED32/2271	White Heather Home School for Evacuated ESN Children, 1945–46

ED32/2290   Aymestry Court Boarding School for Maladjusted Boys, Liverpool, 1945–55
ED32/2291   St Vincent's School for the Blind and Partially Sighted, Liverpool, 1945–55
ED32/2299   Oakfield ESN School, Liverpool, 1945–51
ED32/2331   Wythenshawe Proposed ESN School, 1945–50

Ministry of Health
MH79/291   Sterilization of MD Boys at Gateshead Poor Law Institute, 1930
MH79/485   Evacuation of Mental Institutions, Colchester, 1941
MH95/39   Meanwood Park Mental Institution, Leeds, 1933–48

Miscellaneous
CAB102/786   Notes on the Invalid Children's Aid Association
CH/M/8/5   After-Care Association (PD Children), 1934–44
LAB18/460   St Loyes Training College and the Interim Disabled Training Scheme, 1941-50
LAB19/59   Grants for the After-Care Association, for PD Children, 1929–39

The London Metropolitan Archives

London County Council
LCC/EO/WAR/1/1   Housing Committee Papers
LCC/EO/WAR/2/21   Education Office Papers, 1939
LCC/EO/WAR/2/63   Accommodation for special parties, 1940
LCC/EO/WAR/2/28   Education Office Papers, 1941
LCC/EO/WAR/1/238   Education Office Reports, 1941
LCC/EO/SS/1/68   Records on the closure of residential special schools
LCC/EO/SS/8/7   Children reported on under MD Acts 1913–27: individual cases
LCC/EO/STA/2/36   The fluidity of movement of staff between authorities, 1931–38
LCC/EO/TRA/3/20   The teaching of backward children, 1936
LCC/EO/TRA/1/11   Training of Blind Teachers
LCC/PH/WAR/1/14   Evacuation of school children and wartime organisation of treatment centres
LCC/EO/SS/1/118   Ministry of Education, Special Services Branch, 1949

Invalid Children's Aid Association
4248   Notes on the wartime history of the Association
4248/D/01/006   Annual Reports

Miscellaneous

AST7/283   Documents relating to the Assistance Board and their co-operation with the Central Council for the Care of Cripples, 1936–42

SC/PPS/093   St Vincent's Orthopaedic Hospital Report, 1944

4305/3/31   Records of the John Groom Crippleage

Other archives

Modern Records Centre

MSS.378/APSW/P/20/5/7   Association of Psychiatric Social Workers

MSS.378/APSW/P/20/5/19   Child Guidance Council

MSS.16C/5/0/60   Institute for Juvenile Research

Birmingham Archdiocesan Archives (St Chad's Cathedral)

BCS/M4   Sterilization and Mental Defect Evidence of Monsignor Newsome, 1933

BCCCS2   Miscellaneous Papers, 1930–89

Nottingham Archives

SL159/2/1   Nottingham Road School logbook

Derbyshire Archives

D384/2   Reginald Street School logbook

Official publications (HMSO publications unless stated otherwise)

Board of Education

Report of the Royal Commission on the Blind, the Deaf and Dumb and Others of the United Kingdom, 1889 (Cmd. 5781)

Report of the Consultative Committee on the Education of the Adolescent (Hadow Report), 1926

Report of the Committee of Inquiry into Problems Relating to Partially Sighted Children, 1934

Report of the Consultative Committee on Secondary Education with Special Reference to Grammar Schools and Technical High Schools (Spens Report), 1938

Report of the Committee of Inquiry into Problems Relating to Children with Defective Hearing, 1938

Suggestions on Health Education: for the Consideration of Teachers and Others Concerned in the Health and Education of School Children, 1939

Education after the War (The Green Book), 1941

Educational Reconstruction (The White Paper), 1943

Report on a Five Year Experiment in the Combination of Open-Air Medical and Psycho-Therapeutic Treatment in a Midland Town, 1945

Board of Education and Board of Control
Report of the Joint Departmental Committee on Mental Deficiency (Wood Report), 1929

Board of Control
Report of the Royal Commission on the Care and Control of the Feeble-Minded, 1908

Ministry of Labour and National Service
Report on the Inter-Departmental Committee on the Rehabilitation and Resettlement of Disabled Persons, 1941

Ministry of Health
Air Raid Precautions: Evacuation, 1939
Memorandum EV4: Government Evacuation Scheme: Special Parties, 1939
Memorandum EV8: Government Evacuation Scheme, 1940
A Survey of Experience under the Evacuation Scheme: Hostels for Difficult Children, 1944

Ministry of Education
The Handicapped Pupils and School Health Service Regulations, 1945
Pamphlet 5: Special Educational Treatment (SET), 1946
Circular 79: Handicapped and Maladjusted Children: provision of boarding schools, 1946
List 42: Recognised Special Schools, 1949
The Handicapped Pupils and School Health Service Regulations, 1953
Pamphlet 30: Education of the Handicapped Pupil 1945–55, 1956

Home Office
Circular 701262/8, March 1938

Audit Commission / Her Majesty's Inspectorate
Getting in on the Act – Provision for Children with Special Educational Needs: The National Picture, 1992

Ofsted
Life in Residential Special Schools: A Report of Children's Experience, 2009

Other publications

Charity Organisation Society, *Report of the Committee for Considering the Best Means of Making a Satisfactory Provision for Idiots, Imbeciles and Harmless Lunatics*, 1877
London County Council, *The Special Services of Education in London* (London: Hodder & Stoughton, 1929)

M. I. Dunsdon for the National Foundation for Educational Research in England and Wales, *Report of a Survey on the Education of Cerebral Palsied Children*, 1951

Baroness Warnock, *Special Educational Needs: Report of the Committee of Enquiry into the Education of Handicapped Children and Young People*, 1978

Legislation

Mental Deficiency Act 1913

Education Act 1914

Education Act 1921

Mental Deficiency (Amendment) Act 1927

Camps Act 1939

Education Act 1944

Disability (Employment) Act 1944

National Health Service Act 1946

Children Act 1948

Book and articles

Bowlby, J., 'Phychological Aspects', in R. Padley and M. Cole (eds), *Evacuation Survey: A Report to the Fabian Society* (London: Routledge, 1940), pp. 186–96.

Bowlby, J., 'Forty-four Juvenile Thieves: Their Characters and Home Life', *International Journal of Psycho-Analysis*, 25 (1944), 207–28.

Burlingham, D., and Freud, A., *Children in War-time* (London: Methuen, 1940).

Chambers, R., 'The National Assistance Act 1948', *The Modern Law Review*, 12:1 (1949), 69–72.

Inskip, L. (ed.), *National Cripples Journal (Leicester)*, 51 (1941).

Isaacs, S. (ed.), *Cambridge Evacuation Survey: A Wartime Study in Social Welfare and Education* (London: Methuen, 1941).

Padley, R. and Cole, M. (eds), *Evacuation Survey: A Report to the Fabian Society* (London: Routledge, 1940).

Traill, P. M., 'An Account of Lowenfeld Technique in a Child Guidance Clinic, with a Survey of Therapeutic Play Technique in Great Britain and USA', *Journal of Mental Science*, XCI:382 (1945), 43–78.

Journals and newspapers

Catholic Herald

Daily Telegraph

Education Journal

Evening News

Journal of Mental Science

Manchester Evening Chronicle

Manchester Guardian

The Medical Officer

The Whitchurch Herald
National Cripples Journal
Special Schools Journal
Teachers World
The Times
Times Educational Supplement

Personal testimonies
Unpublished memoirs
Personal Memoirs of Mrs R. Balister, 1986, Imperial War Museum, IWM 92/9/1
G. R. Bevan, 'An active life, against the odds', www.bbc.co.uk/wales/southeast/sites/
   streetsofcardiff/pages/story_grahambevan.shtml
'World War Two and Me', Personal Memoirs of Dennis Ford, 26 June 1996, Imperial
   War Museum, IWM 96/55/1
K. A. J. Giles, 'Small World: My Memories of World War Two', 2001 (in the author's
   possession)

Letters to author
Jessica Axford (née Young)
Ken Giles
Ernie Jones
Sheila Meredith

Published memoirs
Cole, S., 'We Slept on Trestle Beds on a Concrete Floor', in A. Jones (ed.), *Farewell to
   Manchester: The Story of the 1939 Evacuation* (Didsbury: Didsbury Press, 1989), pp.
   85–6.
Park, N., *School Days at Chatsworth: A Personal Memoir of the War Years* (A. Quick &
   Co., 1986)
Smith, S., *Still Unique after All These Years: A History of Blanche Nevile School, formerly
   Tottenham School for the Deaf 1895–1995* (London: The School, 1995).
Thomas, J. E., *Hope for the Handicapped: A Teacher's Testament* (London: Bodley Head,
   1967).
Young, J., *I Lived in a Castle* (privately printed, 1990).

Oral testimony
Interview with Ann Rattue, 21 March 2006

Private documents
Courtesy of Sheila Meredith
Minutes of Old Scholars meetings – Lancasterian Special School
Video – 'visit to Cloverley Hall'

Courtesy of Ernie Jones

Memorandum concerning the evacuation of Lancasterian school to Cloverley Hall, 1939

'Evacuation Experiences', unpublished testimony of Frank Gee

Christmas card of Lancasterian special school at Cloverley Hall

Miscellaneous publication

Careers and Vocational Training: A Complete Guide to Women's Professions, London: The Women's Employment Publishing Company, 1946

Film review

Walter Goodman, 'Review of "Thursday's Children"', *New York Times*, 7 October 1987

Newsletter

The Evacuee: The Newsletter of the Evacuees Reunion Association

Websites

Mass Observation Archive	www.massobs.org.uk
MIND	www.mind.org.uk
Family Welfare Association	www.fwa.org.uk
Invalid children's Aid Nationwide	www.ican.org.uk
Eugenics-Watch	www.eugenics-watch.com
Centre for Studies in Inclusive Education	www.csie.org.uk
Evacuee's Reunion Association	www.evacuees.org.co.uk
Personal war stories	www.bbc.co.uk

TV documentaries

Doctors in the Third Reich (aired in UK, 2005, Channel Four): Programme 1: 'Racial Fanaticism'. Programme 2: 'Deadly Reforms'.

Reference

Samways, R. (ed.), *We Think You Ought to Go* (London: Greater London Record Office, 1995)

Secondary sources

Books and articles

Anderson, J., 'Turned into Taxpayers: Paraplegia, Rehabilitation and Sport at Stoke Mandeville, 1944–56', *Journal of Contemporary History*, 38:3 (2003), 461–75.

Anderson, J., 'British Women, Disability and the Second World War', *Contemporary British History*, 20:1 (2006), 37–53.

Atkinson, D., Jackson, M., and Walmsley, J. (eds), *Forgotten Lives: Exploring the History of Learning Disability* (Kidderminster: British Institute of Learning Disability, 1997).

Avery, G., *The Best Type of Girl: A History of Girls' Independent Schools* (London: Deutsch, 1991).

Bacharach, S., 'In the Name of Public Health: Nazi Racial Hygeine', *New England Journal of Medicine*, 29 July 2004, 417–20.

Barber, M., *The Making of the 1944 Education Act* (London and New York: Cassell, 1994).

Borsay, A., *Disability and Social Policy in Britain since 1750: A History of Exclusion* (Basingstoke and New York: Palgrave, 2005).

Boud, Roy C., *The Great Exodus: The Evacuation of Leeds Schoolchildren 1939–45* (Leeds: Thoresby Society, 2000).

Brown, Mike, *Evacuees: Evacuation in wartime Britain, 1939–1945* (Stroud: Sutton, 2000).

Bullock, N., *Building the Post-war World: Modern Architecture and Reconstruction in Britain* (London and New York: Routledge, 2002).

Cavannaugh-O'Keefe, J., *The Roots of Racism and Abortion: An Exploration of Eugenics* (Princeton: Princeton University Press 2000).

Compton, T., *The Brief History of Disability (or, The World Has Always Had Cripples)* (privately printed, 1992).

Cooper, P., *Effective Schools for Disaffected Pupils: Integration and Segregation* (London: Routledge, 1993).

Crosby, T. L., *The Impact of Civilian Evacuation in the Second World War* (London: Croom Helm, 1986).

Curtis, S. J., *History of Education in Great Britain* (London: University Tutorial Press, 7th edition, 1968).

Davidoff, R., 'Foreword', in P. Longmore, *Why I Burned My Book, and Other Essays on Disability* (Philadelphia: Temple University Press, 2003), p. viii.

Dent, H. C., *Education in Transition: A Sociological Study of the Impact of War on English Education 1939–1943* (London: Kegan Paul, Trench, Trubner and Co., 1944).

Department of Education and Science, *The School Health Service 1908–74* (London: HMSO, 1975).

Devereux, H. M., *Housecraft in the Education of Handicapped Children* (London: Mills & Boon Ltd, 1965).

Doulton, A. J. F., *Highgate School 1938–1944: The Story of a Wartime Evacuation* (privately printed, 1975).

Galton, F., *Hereditary Genius* (London: Macmillan, 1869).

Gardiner, J., *The Children's War through the Eyes of the Children of Britain* (London: Portrait, 2005).

Garfield, S., *Our Hidden Lives: The Remarkable Diaries of Post-war Britain* (London: Ebury, 2004).

Goddard, H. H., *The Kallikak Family: A Study in the Heredity of Feeble Mindedness* (New York: Macmillan, 1912).

Goodman, J., 'Reflections on Researching an Archive of Disability: Sandlebridge, 1902–1935', *Educational Review*, 55:1 (2003), 47–54.

Gosden, P. H. J. H., *Education in the Second World War: A Study in Policy and Administration* (London: Methuen, 1976).

Hall, J. T., *Social Devaluation and Special Education: The Right to Full Mainstream Inclusion and an Honest Statement* (London: Jessica Kingsley, 1997).

Harris, B., *The Health of the Schoolchild: A History of the School Medical Service in England and Wales* (Buckingham: Open University Press, 1995).

Hendrick, A., 'Children and Childhood', *ReFresh*, 15 (Autumn 1992), 1–4.

Humphries, S., and Gordon, P., *Out of Sight: The Experience of Disability 1900–1950* (Plymouth: Northcote, 1992).

Hurt, J. S., *Outside the Mainstream: A History of Special Education* (London: Batsford, 1988).

Kanter, J., 'Residential Care with Evacuated Children: Lessons from Clare Winnicott', Cyc-online, Issue 80, September 2005, www.cyc-net.org/cyc-online/cycol-0905-kanter.html.

Kevles, D. J., *In the Name of Eugenics: Genetics and the Uses of Human Heredity* (London: Penguin, 1986).

Klein, R., 'Control, Participation, and the British National Health Service', *Health and Society*, 57:1 (1979), 70–94.

Leff, S., and Leff, V., *The School Health Service* (London: Lewis, 1959).

Longmore, P. K., and Umansky, L. (eds), *The New Disability History: American Perspectives* (New York: New York University Press, 2001).

Lowe, R., *Education in the Post-war Years: A Social History* (London and New York. Routledge, 1988).

Lowe, R., 'The Second World War, Consensus, and the Foundation of the Welfare State', *Twentieth Century British History*, 1:2 (1990), 152–82.

Lowndes, G. A. N., *The English Educational System* (London: Hutchinson, 1960) (first published as *The British Educational System*, in 1955).

Lowndes, G. A. N., *Margaret McMillan: The Children's Champion* (London: Museum Press, 1960).

Lowndes, G. A. N., *The Silent Social Revolution* (London: Oxford University Press, 1969).

Maclure, S., *A History of Education in London, 1870–1990* (London: Penguin, 1990).

Macnicol, J., 'The Evacuation of Schoolchildren', in H. L. Smith (ed.), *War and Social Change: British Society in the Second World War* (Manchester: Manchester University Press, 1996), pp. 3–31.

Mann, J., *Out of Harm's Way: The Wartime Evacuation of Children from Britain* (London: Headline, 2005).

McCulloch, G., *Educational Reconstruction: The 1944 Education Act and the Twenty-first Century* (Ilford and Portland: Woburn, 1994).

Mess, H. A., *Voluntary Social Services since 1918* (London: Paul, Trencher & Trubner, 1947).

Middleton, N., *When Family Failed: The Treatment of Children in the Care of the Community during the First Half of the Twentieth Century* (London: Gollancz, 1976).

Middleton, N., and Weitzman, S., *A Place for Everyone: A History of State Education from the Eighteenth Century to the 1970s* (London: Gollancz, 1976).

Parsons, M., *Britain at War: Evacuation* (London: Hodder and Wayland, 1999).

Ponting, C., 'Churchill's Plans for Racial Purity', *Guardian*, 20 June 1992.

Potts, M., and Fido, R., *A Fit Person to Be Removed: Personal Accounts of Life in a Mental Deficiency Institution* (Plymouth: Northcote, 1991).

Pritchard, D. G., *Education and the Handicapped, 1760–1960* (London and New York: Routledge & Kegan Paul, 1963).

Prochaska, F., *Philanthropy and the Hospitals of London* (Oxford: Oxford University Press, 1992).

Read, J., and Walmsley, J., 'Historical Perspectives on Special Education 1890–1970', *Disability and Society*, 21:5 (2006), 455–69.

Rooff, M., *Voluntary Societies and Social Policy* (London: Routledge & Kegan Paul, 1957).

Rosner, D., 'Racial Hygiene: Medicine under the Nazis', *Politics, Policy and Law*, 16 (1991), 419–22.

Sampson, O. C., *Child Guidance: Its History, Provenance and Future* (London: British Psychological Society, 1980).

Saunders, S., 'The Residential School: A Valid Choice', *British Journal of Special Education*, 21:2 (1994), 64–6.

Segal, S. S., *No Child Is Ineducable: Special Education – Provision and Trends*, 2nd ed. (Oxford: Pergamon, 1974) (1st ed. 1967).

Solity, J., *Special Education* (London: Cassell, 1992).

Stakes, R., and Hornby, G., *Change in Special Education: What Brings It About?* (London: Cassell, 1997).

Starkey, P., 'The Medical Officer of Health, the Social Worker, and the Problem Family, 1943 to 1968: The Case of Family Service Units', *Social History of Medicine*, 11:3 (1998), 421–41.

Stephens, M., *Evacuation* (Hove: Wayland, 1998).

Stewart, J., 'Psychiatric Social work in Inter-War Britain: Child Guidance, American Ideas, American Philanthropy', *Michael*, 3 (2006), 78–91.

Stewart, J., 'I Thought You Would Want to Come and See His Home: Child Guidance and Psychiatric Social Work in Inter-War Britain', in M. Jackson (ed.), *Health and the Modern Home* (London: Routledge, 2007).

Stewart, J. 'The Scientific Claims of British Child Guidance, 1918–45', *British Society for the History of Science*, 42:3 (2009), 407–32.

Stewart, R., *Evacuation* (London: Evans, 2002).

Sutherland, G., *Ability, Merit & Measurement: Mental Testing and English Education, 1880–1940* (Oxford: Clarendon, 1984).

Swann, W. (ed.), *The Practice of Special Education* (Oxford: Open University Press, 1983).

Taylor, W. W., and Taylor, I. W., *Special Education of Physical Handicapped in Western Europe* (New York: International Society for the Welfare of Cripples, 1960).

Thom, D., 'Wishes, Anxieties, Play and Gestures: Child Guidance in Inter-war England', in R. Cooter (ed.), *In the Name of the Child: Health and Welfare 1880–1940* (London: Routledge, 1992), pp. 200–19.

Titmuss, R. M., *Problems of Social Policy* (London: Longman, Green & Co., 1950).

Wallis, J., *A Welcome in the Hillsides? – The Merseyside and North Wales Experience of Evacuation 1939–45* (Holywell: Avid, 2000).

Webster, C., 'Eugenic Sterilisation: Europe's Shame' *Health Matters* (Autumn 1997).

Welshman, J., 'In Search of the "Problem Family": Public Health and Social Work in England and Wales 1940-1970', *Social History of Medicine*, 9:3 (1996), 447–65.

Welshman, J., 'Evacuation and Social Policy during the Second World War: Myth and Reality', *Twentieth Century British History*, 9:1 (1998), 28–53.

Welshman, J., *Churchill's Children: The Evacuee Experience in Wartime Britain* (Oxford: Oxford University Press, 2010).

Wheatcroft, S., 'Children's Experiences of War: Handicapped Children in England during the Second World War', *Twentieth Century British History*, 19:4 (2008), 480–501.

Whittaker, J., 'Segregated Schools Must Close', *Coalition* (2001), 12–16.

Wicks, B., *No Time to Wave Goodbye* (London: Bloomsbury, 1988).

Woods, B., and Watson, N., 'In Pursuit of Standardisation: The Ministry of Health's Model 8F Wheelchair, 1948–1962', *Technology and Culture*, 45:3 (2004), 540–68.

Unpublished manuscripts and school projects

Anderson, J., 'The Soul of a Nation: A Social History of Disabled People, Physical Therapy, Rehabilitation and Sport in Britain 1918–1970' (De Montfort University: PhD Thesis, 2002).

Black, M., 'The History of the Lancasterian School, Manchester' (History of Education essay, 1929).

Cliffe, E., 'A Study of the Educational Provision for Mentally Handicapped Children in Leicester during the Inter-War Years' (Leicester University: BA Dissertation, 2008).

Dale, P., 'The Mental Deficiency Acts 1913–48: Medical Care, Control and Eugenics' (Exeter University: PhD Thesis, 2001).

Daynes, E., 'The Education of Mentally Handicapped Children in London in the Last One Hundred Years' (Leicester University: MEd Thesis, 1969).

Edwards, S., 'The History of the Lancasterian School, 1908–1969' (CSE History Project, Lancasterian School, 1980).

Index

Note: page numbers for illustrations are in italics